Cargoes of Despair and Hope

Cargoes of Despair and Hope

Scottish Emigration to North America 1603 – 1803

IAN ADAMS

and

MEREDYTH SOMERVILLE

JOHN DONALD PUBLISHERS LTD
EDINBURGH

ISBN 0 85976 367 6

British Libary Cataloguing in Publication Data
A catalogue record for this book is
available from the British Library.

Phototypset by D.S.R.U., The University of Edinburgh
Printed and bound in Great Britain by
Hartnolls Limited, Bodmin, Cornwall

ACKNOWLEDGEMENTS

We would like to thank the staffs of the Scottish Record Office, the National Library of Scotland, the University of Edinburgh Library, the Public Record Office, London, the British Library, the Halifax Memorial Library, the Public Archives of Nova Scotia, Dalhousie University Library, Halifax and the Hector centre in Pictou for all their endless care afforded us in pursuit of our reaserch.

We wish to thank Carolyn Smyth and Annebeth Mackie for their help and particularly Charles Somerville for his meticulous reading of the manuscript. The text was set and the maps and diagrams drawn by Nicola Exley, with some additions by Morag Gillespie and Elizabeth Clark, cartographic illustrators, Department of Geography, University of Edinburgh. The frontispiece is reproduced by kind permission of the Director of the National Maritime Museum, Greenwich.

We thank the Canadian Government and the staff of the High Commission in London for the award of a research grant to pursue research in Canada.

An English Snow, by C. Brooking, c. 1750

Contents

Contents

Illustrations

Abbreviations

APC	Acts of the Privy Council
CM	Caledonian Mercury
CHOP	Calendar of Home Office Papers
DCB	Dictionary of Canadian Biography
EA	Edinburgh Advertiser
EEC	Edinburgh Evening Courant
FM	Farmers Magazine
GJ	Glasgow Journal
NLS	National Library of Scotland
OSA	Statistical Account of Scotland
PRO	Public Record Office
SCA	Scottish Catholic Archives
SM	Scots Magazine
SRO	Scottish Record Office
VG	Virginia Gazette

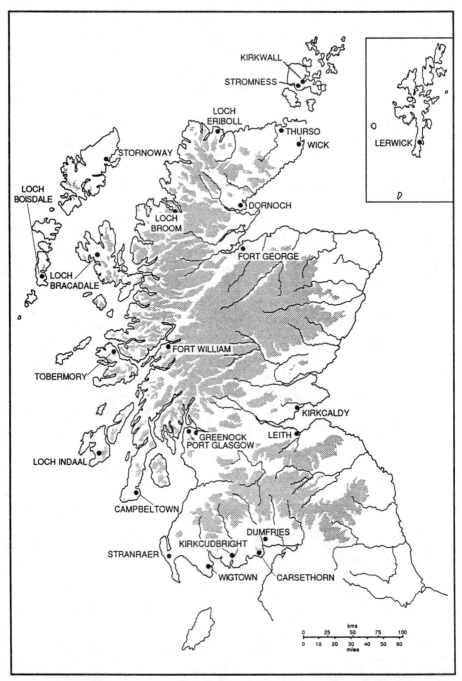

Fig. Intro.1 The limits of cultivation in Scotland. The stippled area shows land over 800ft.
Ports and harbours from which emigrants set sail in the eighteenth century.

Introduction

From the beginning of human history men, women and children, driven by hunger, oppression or pressure of population, have been forced from their homes to seek new lands from which to wrest a living. Evidence of these movements is to be found in artefacts, legends and history. The causes are varied and one can rarely point to a single factor as being the reason for a particular migration. Political and religious struggles have led to the departure, both voluntary and involuntary, of numbers of people to other areas and other countries. Changing climatic and weather patterns over longer or shorter periods may have resulted in a series of cold wet years or hot dry seasons with the loss of the grain harvest and the death of stock. Conversely, improved conditions resulting in bumper harvests may have produced population pressure and a forced exodus. Only in the past 150 years has the pattern been changing and the movements have been only too often from a degraded agricultural environment to a degrading life in an over-crowded city.

Professor Meinig has suggested that there were at least three stages in the colonisation of North and South America by Europeans- sea-faring, conquering and planting. Although his thesis encompasses Western Europe it encapsulates the Scottish experiences of colonisation. He suggested that the early European colonial nations were all sea powers and all had fishing fleets which were attached to the societies from which they came by their need for shipbuilders and chandlers, for clothiers to clothe them and for farmers to grow their food. The fishermen were skilled mariners and craftsmen who, either through a spirit of adventure or perhaps through some misadventure such as being blown off course in a storm, reached other lands. Some of these adventurers settled there. Stories were sent back to Europe with visions of great wealth in new lands still to be conquered. More elaborate plans and greater resources were needed for these new voyages; arms and trading goods were required for subduing and/ or befriending the natives. Many natives moved into the interior of their country if they were not ravaged by diseases brought by the invaders. It soon became necessary for a local population to serve the conquerors; if the local natives could not be coerced into being a labour force, then indented or free immigrants from Europe or slaves from Africa had to be imported. It was the failure to realise this need for a local self-sufficient base, combined with the choice of a poor site, that led, for example, to the failure of the Darien scheme.[1]

The period of this study is from 1603 to 1803, from the Union of the Crowns to the second phase of the French wars. The seventeenth century is dealt with briefly, as little emigration took place. Emigrations in the eighteenth century were still relatively small and local and mainly from the Highland areas, but were nevertheless significant in the history of both Scotland and North America. In these years Scotland was changed fundamentally from a feudal tribal society ruled largely by patriarchal chieftains to a modern unified state. By the end of the eighteenth century substantial progress had been made in agricultural reform and industrialisation and the country's intellectual leaders were making important contributions to European and American thought in many fields.

Although living conditions, particularly in the Lowlands, improved somewhat during the seventeenth century, Scotland was still a poor and backward country and was subject to periodic famines which caused the deaths of many people who lived, at least in the more remote areas, on the edge of starvation. James Somerville returning from France in 1617 reported:

> As he journied from Seatoune to Edinburgh, he beheld multitudes of poor people that wer gathering myles lam, latuce, and other potable herbes, from amongst the growing corne, there being a great dearth ... that year in Scotland because of the excessive raines that had fallen the preceding harvest, which rotted and spoiled the best part of the victuall. This sight even then inclyned him to return from whence he was come as having never seen such penurie and want, notwithstanding of the waistes and devastations made by the numerous armies in France.[2]

Sir John Sinclair estimated the total population of Scotland to be 1,048,000 in 1707. Slowly the numbers began to increase as a result both of a rise in the birth rate and a decline in the death rate. There were various reasons for this increase, ranging from the spread of the potato and other vegetables which provided some sustenance in years when the grain harvest was poor, to the introduction of inoculation against smallpox (before the development of vaccination). The kelp industry produced small increases in local incomes in the Islands and western coastal areas although the landlords pocketed huge profits.   An official census taken in 1801 showed a rise in the total population of Scotland from Webster's figure of 1,265,000 in 1775 to 1,608,000, a considerable increase despite the ravages of war and emigration.[3]

The relatively peaceful years of the reign of James VI and I allowed considerable economic development in the Lowlands. In the hope of extending law and order and of transplanting some of the Lowlands' surge of vitality, a scheme was developed to settle Lowlanders in new towns in the north and west, but this policy had only marginal success. The Ulster plantation, a major emigration starting in 1609-10 was a far more significant movement of people, the dramatic consequences of which are felt to the present day.

The rest of the century was dominated by religious conflicts. Transportation was the savage punishment not only for breaking the law, but also for holding the wrong opinions or being on the wrong side.   Such emigration as there was was mainly involuntary! Two abortive attempts at organised emigration were made - to Nova Scotia in the 1620s and to Darien in the 1690s- the latter was an attempt to establish a national Scottish colony and was met with implacable opposition from English commercial interests backed by protectionist legislation. The English had accepted a Scottish king, but they had not yet any intention of offering the Scots a share of their place in the sun. Towards the end of the century commercial relations between the two countries did improve and after the Union of the Parliaments in 1707 the open opposition to Scottish emigration came to an end.

In the eighteenth century, events in Scotland were shaped by a number of powerful elements. The failure of the Jacobite rebellions of 1715 and 1745 was followed by the collapse of the traditional Highland culture. In particular the status and authority of the clan chiefs were destroyed. The ringleaders of the rebellions lost their lives, others forfeited their estates to the Crown. Many of the remaining chiefs rapidly changed their role from patriarch to grasping landlord.

Because of the difficult geographical conditions of northern Scotland, the largest number of emigrants went from areas remote from the Lowlands where the industrial revolution was beginning to offer alternative opportunities of employment. There had been for many years some seasonal migration of Highlanders seeking work in the harvest fields of the south. This seasonal employment continued to be substantial well into the nineteenth century. Men, women and children had also begun to find work part-time in the linen industries in the new villages being built along the edge of the Highlands. As the demand for labour increased in the burgeoning industries, particularly coal, iron and cotton, so some of the part-time labourers stayed on and were joined by others. But the competition from Irish immigrants, who came initially to replace those removed from the farms of the south-west, increased towards the end of the century. Both as agricultural and as industrial workers they were willing to accept lower wages and it was easier for them to make the short sea passage than for people from the remoter parts of the Highlands and the Islands to journey to the industrial areas.

In the Lowlands agricultural reforms had been instituted in a few places during the late seventeenth century but the pace quickened with the formation in 1724 of the Honourable Society of Improvers in the Knowledge of Agriculture in Scotland, which within three years boasted a national membership of 300. By the end of the century enclosures, draining, new buildings and roads had changed the face of the landscape although early improvements were often bitterly opposed. However on the whole the dispossessed persons of Southern and Central Scotland were better placed than the Highlanders to move to the developing industries and to the areas being opened up for the new farms and market gardens which were producing food for the growing towns. There was less need for emigration except during years of industrial recession.

The rapid increase in demand for a large and reasonably educated labour force, both for agriculture and industry, quickly produced an important alternative to emigration. Working conditions in industry were in many cases deplorable despite some social experiments such as those of David Dale and Robert Owen. However the violent fluctuations of the economy, assisted by some reckless speculative banking, made the demand for labour erratic and at the low point in the business cycle left large numbers of the new industrial proleteriat without employment and destitute. The bank failures of 1772 led to an economic depression throughout the country, and caused acute problems particularly in the linen industry. This led to the largest Lowland emigration, when 500 "manufacturers" from Paisley left, because they "could not find employment at home".

Lastly, by the second half of the century the extraordinary phenomenon of the Scottish Enlightenment turned Edinburgh in particular into "a hotbed of genius" whose leading figures in many fields were able to complement theoretical principles with practical applications, in both industry and agriculture. Smout has summarised the influences that made this flowering possible:

> The golden age of Scottish culture was achieved largely by the Lowland middle class with the approval and patronage (but not the initiative) of the landed classes, against a complex background of historical change - of economic change enabling Scotland better to afford her culture, of educational change in her universities and schools, and of psychological change in

the attitude of society towards its own aspirations.[4]

A number of these men crossed the Atlantic and played important roles, especiaily in the development of education, in North America. Clergymen of all persuasions responded to specific invitations. Commercial links, particularly in the tobacco trade, resulted in a significant number of men settling in the States. Yet the popular image of emigration to North America well into the eighteenth century was that it was an irrevocable decision for a desperate person. It was neither respectable nor sensible:

> the majority of the population never thought about America at all; to them it was the dumping ground for thieves, bankrupts and prostitutes, for which we received tobacco in return.[5]

Indeed, it has been suggested that in the first half of the century nearly half the white settlers in the New World went involuntarily. In addition to prisoners many were forced to indent. Those with little or no money signed indentures with the ship's captain or his agent, who sold the indenture which normally lasted for five or seven years on arrival in America. Men and women were then set to work side by side with black slaves. The black slaves were considered to be property for life and were therefore generally better treated than the white slaves who had been indented for only a few years.[6] In the eyes of the English, Scots were little more than "white negroes". However Nicholas Cresswell, an Englishman living in Virginia in the 1770s testified that

> I was taught to look upon them [the Scots] as a set of men divested of common humanity, ungenerous and unprincipled. I have always found them the reverse of all this, and I most heartily condemn this pernicious system of education by which we are taught to look upon the inhabitants of a different nation, language or complexion, as a set of beings far inferior to our own.[7]

During the second half of the century, the Scots image of America began to change to that of a land of opportunity where a reasonable standard of life might be achieved, where the new demand for better education might be satisfied and where liberty from the puritanical control of the Established Church over both personal and commercial life might be obtained. The Roman Catholic population, in particular, was still subjected to intolerance and persecution.

The fluctuating scale and timing of emigrations were affected by events on both sides of the Atlantic. Not only reports of the availablity of cheap land but also encouragement by some major political figures lured the Scot overseas. The disbandment of many soldiers in America at the end of the Seven Years' War led to the arrival of further parties of immigrants. They were later joined by the soldiers and their families drafted across the Atlantic during the War of American Independence, although emigration as such stopped during the war.(Figs Intro. 1.& 2)

When peace came again in 1783, in the grip of famine and without the alternative of army service, many desperate Highlanders saw salvation in the lands that their adventurous forbears were beginning to tame. From the end of the war in 1783 until 1803, most of the emigrants sailed to Canada; nearly 12,000 in contrast to about 2,000 who went to America. Their reasons for going still stemmed from the economic conditions in the home country: the inability to survive the dearths of 1782-4 and 1793 and the continuing displacement of the numerous sub-tenants, who were ever more rapidly replaced by sheep farmers from the south. There were now three possibilities for

the dispossessed - emigration, migration to the industrial towns or moving ᵢ
settlements, mainly on the coast. These last were villages planned by lar
Government bodies with motives varying from paternalistic concern for the people, to
the desire to get rid of now useless encumbrances.

When the French Revolution broke out in 1789 waves of anti-landlord sentiment
surged through Britain and produced much radical unrest, but the excesses of the
Jacobins soon changed public opinion. At the same time the surplus male population
began to be absorbed into the army and navy, this time to fight Frenchmen rather than
their own kith and kin in America.

Although one may see cause and effect spanning a number of years, the decision to
emigrate was often triggered by events measured in days. An advertisement such as the
following, coupled with the hopelessness of finding the next meal or a night's shelter
was often the last straw which started the emigrant on the long journey to the New World.

To all Lovers of Improvement in Agriculture and Fisheries

Any person inclining to make their fortune and live happily in the island of St John's
Newfoundland where the soil is excellent and a good healthy climate, great plenty of stone and
timber and lime within a few leagues water carriage, the sea and rivers full of fish. Any man
who chuses to go there, may have from 20 to 30 acres at one shilling per acre of yearly rent, and
if a married man, and takes his wife and family with him, may have from 30 to 40 acres. For
particulars apply to Andrew Halyburton WS at Edinburgh or James Stewart writer at Glasgow.
(Glasgow Journal, August 29th 1771).

Such a picture of the new world gave a misleading impression of the conditions that
would be encountered even to the literate emigrant who was often ignorant of the
geographical realities of his intended new home. The humid summers and bitter winters
of eastern North America contrasted very unfavourably with the equable climate of
Western Scotland. For the Gael from a remote area and speaking only his own language,
embarking on a miserable merchantman hastily converted to carry too many passengers
beneath battened hatches, the New World was not perceived as a land flowing with milk
and honey. The minds of these poor people were already full of the terrors of the vast
forests inhabited by fierce Indians. Up to embarkation their contacts with the outside
world had been minimal and even locally there was little communication between
neighbouring communities. The geographical separation of the island and mainland
communities was reflected in the various local dialects of Gaelic. Their arrival in
America often left the emigrants isolated by language, culture, and agricultural skills in
an alien environment. A song written about 1770 and reputed to be the first Gaelic song
composed in North America sums up many of the feelings of a lonely person:

Tha sinne 'n ar n:Innseannaich cinnteach gu leoir;
Fo dhubhar nan craobh cha bhidh aon againn beo,
Madaidh-allaidh us beisdean ag eibheach 's gach froig.
Gu'm bheil sinne 'n ar n-eiginn bho'n threig sinn Righ
Deors.
(We've turned into Indians right enough; in the gloom of the forest none of us will be left alive,
with wolves and beasts howling in every cranny. We're ruined since we left King George).[8]

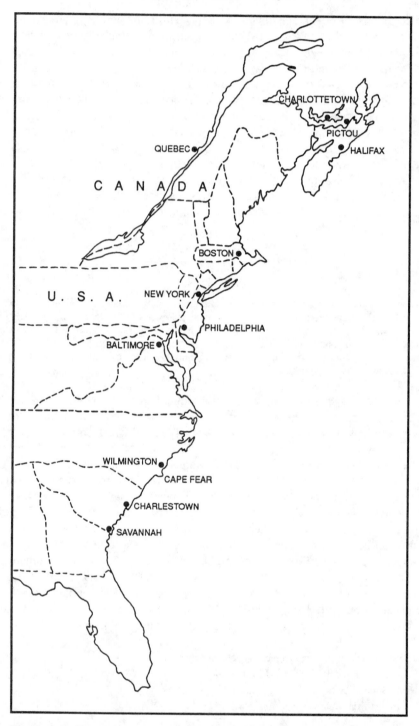

Fig. Intro.2 Ports of entry in North America for Scottish emigrants.

A New York correspondent described the reception of the survivors of the notorious *Nancy*, which sailed in the year 1773, as being in a

> wretched situation and must have died in the street had not the people of this town supported them. I hope this will be the last ship with Scots emigrants that will arrive at this port, for from a variety of reasons the Highlanders are most improper emigrants to this country, many of them being sold when they arrive here for their passage or debts, and in general they are not accustomed to labour.[9]

Whatever is made of these comments, this book is basically about such ordinary people; those who abandoned a life of struggle and abject misery with little expectation of a better future; those who resolved not to be defeated by oppression or intolerable conditions, and left Scotland determined to succeed in a new place; those who in ignorance or despair sold themselves into virtual slavery; the countless people, especially children whose deaths in dreadful conditions are so casually reported. But it is also concerned with many individuals, some who through their greed, ignorance or ambition created the conditions which made emigration inevitable, some who helped to organise it. They had various motives - from those who set about the creative building of new communities to the ships' agents and owners who were only out for profit. There were plenty of folk who appear to have enjoyed talking about its causes and desirability without doing much about it - the eighteenth century was a great era for the chattering classes. But on the other hand a number of decent men did their best to help people, whether *in extremis* or after disaster had struck. And there were a few who conscientiously and intelligently led emigrations and went on to take part in the establishment of successful settlements.

1

"Encouragement to Colonists"

For more than 400 years Scotsmen in search of adventure or in flight from troubles at home, whether religious, political or domestic, or simply to earn a living, had travelled abroad. Professor Donaldson has stated that for many years

> there was a quite substantial ... migration to England where Scots of all ranks had been finding employment even before the Union of the Crowns brought the common nationality ... Many Scots were settled in coastal towns round the Baltic and the number in Poland was put- by a wild guess- at 30,000.

During the sixteenth century licences were granted to raise men in Scotland for military service in Denmark, Sweden and the Low Countries, a traffic which increased in the seventeenth century. During the Thirty Years' War, 1618-1648, for instance, Donald Mackay, 1st Lord Reay, raised 3,000 men for Christian IV of Denmark and Gustavus Adolphus of Sweden who is said to have had 10,000 Scots in his army. Later about 9000 Scots served the Kings of France.[1]

The adventures of one young Scot, James Somerville, who decided to see the world and finance himself by service in any suitable Continental army, demonstrate how easy it was to obtain military employment. In 1614, he left Leith for Dieppe. "The day after he came to Paris he finds out Sir John Seatoune..." who promises "to list him a gentleman of his oune company within a few days ... wherein he continued three years," serving Louis XIII. At the end of that period, after a very short visit to his family, he returned to France where he decided to walk from Paris to Florence with two companions, one Scots, one French. The Scots enjoyed their stay in Italy, but finding their money running short, and after considering offering their services to the Spanish Crown which at the time ruled Naples, finally settled to go "directly for Venice, knowing weill that when ther money failled they might take on with that republict, many of their contrymen being in service of that state in the qualitie of officers..."[2]

Lowland colonists

The reduction of the power of the great magnates and the strengthening of the authority of central government were central to James VI's domestic policies. In particular he hoped to bring law and order to the Borders, where he was largely successful and to the Highlands and Islands, where the results were more mixed. The "forty years of unprecedented tranquility" of his reign allowed the Lowlands to become more prosperous and the king hoped firstly to bring some of that prosperity to the Highlands and Western

Isles by founding some vigorous settlements of Lowlanders in strategic places. His second motive in which both Scotland and England had an interest was to establish a wedge of Protestant Lowlanders between the Scottish Celts and the Irish. With both ends in view Parliament resolved in 1597 "that there be erected and builded three burghs and burgh towns in the most convenient and commodious parts meet for the same, to wit: one in Kintyre, another in Lochaber and the third in Lewis".

The Macleod clan held sway and defied royal authority in Lewis. In 1598 the Adventurers of Fife were given a contract to go and settle on the island, said to be rich in corn and fish. Their reception was hostile and the ill-prepared Adventurers were soon short of food and thoroughly discouraged. They left, but returned again in 1605 for a few years and a third time in 1610. However they sold their charter rights to Kenneth Mackenzie of Kintail who was given a special commission of justiciary to deal with the lawless Macleods. The Earl of Seaforth, the island's proprietor, had meantime been granted the privilege of the erection of a burgh of barony at Stornoway with the intention of attracting Dutch fishermen to settle and develop the fisheries. The Convention of Royal Burghs was so strongly opposed to the idea of foreigners monopolising the fishing which would so "destroy all trade and the haill shipping of the kingdom" that the king withdrew the charter; however some Dutch fishermen did settle and by 1630 the Convention of Royal Burghs was willing to allow Englishmen to establish themselves in the island providing they did not fish in the reserved waters. The Convention eventually moved, in 1898, that Stornoway's original charter be reinstated.[3]

The project for Lochaber and district was not started until a fort was built in 1654 for purely military purposes. It continued to be garrisoned until some years after the '45 rising and over the years a small settlement grew up around it. The settlement took its original name, Gordonsburgh, from the fact that it was built on the Duke of Gordon's land. Then it became known as Maryburgh after Queen Mary and finally Fort William after the fort which had been named after King William III.[4]

There was already a small settlement at Lochhead at the southern end of Kintyre when Archibald, 7th Earl of Argyll received a charter to the lands in 1607, to "plant a burgh to be inhabited by lowland men and trafficking burgesses". The Earl built a castle and probably introduced the first Lowlanders into the new burgh of Campbeltown, as it became known, in 1618. Thirty householders were named in a rental of 1636, of whom fewer than half were Lowland or non-Kintyre names. Other, Presbyterian, families from Ayrshire and Renfrewshire fled to Kintyre during the periods of Episcopalian domination in the second half of the seventeenth century. Inter-clan warfare continued as the MacDonalds tried to regain possession of the peninsula from the Campbells. When General David Leslie marched through Kintyre searching for MacDonald rebels in 1647 it is thought that about 800 men escaped to Ulster.[5] The task of transforming Kintyre from a lawless to a peaceful territory fell to the house of Argyll.

The Ulster Plantation

The lives of the peoples of south west Scotland and of north east Ireland have been inexorably intertwined throughout recorded history and their fates linked with imperialism. The north eastern corner of Ireland is clearly visible on many days of the year from parts of southern and western Scotland; the sea crossing between the two lands is short though at times dangerous and can be achieved in a small boat. Indeed it was easier for men from Ulster to sail to Scotland than to travel to the south of Ireland and similarly it was easier for Scots from the West Coast or the Islands to sail to Ireland than to reach the central belt of Scotland. The latter statement remained true well into the 19th century and the coming of steam.

Through the centuries there has been a steady trickle of Scots to Ireland and of Irish to Scotland. The first recorded invasion of Scotland by the Irish may have taken place c. 500 AD when the ruler of the independent kingdom of Dal Riata (on the north coast of Co. Antrim) conquered Kintyre and these two non-contiguous areas became known as the kingdom of Dal Riata, or Dalriada. The earliest connections between the two regions were cemented by the bringing of Celtic Christianity to western Scotland by St Columba in 563. Irish Gaelic was introduced into Scotland and the literature could be understood by the Gaels in the Islands.

In the 14th century, after King Robert Bruce had united the kingdom of Scotland he hoped to be recognised as king of Ireland also. His brother Edward Bruce's campaign in Ireland was at first successful and stirred up revolts against the English overlords throughout the country, but he was ultimately defeated in 1318. King Robert landed in Antrim again in 1327 and was soon able to enforce an humiliating truce on the Ulster chieftains.

About 1400 the Scots moved to Ulster in greater numbers when some of the MacDonells of Dunivaig and the Glens emigrated to Antrim where they acquired land as a result of a marriage contract. They were much disliked by government for they provided a further base for the galloglas- heavily armed hereditary mercenaries from the Highlands and Islands of Scotland. The Scots, particularly MacDonalds, continued to cross over and settle in Ulster. The complicated political situation between the three countries resulted in an army of 7-8000 Scots being sent to Ireland to fight the English in 1532 and when, later in the century, Agnes Campbell married an Irish chieftain she took with her about 1000 retainers- many of whose families settled there.

With the Union of the Crowns under James a new era dawned in the history of the three countries. By this time the English had effectively conquered the whole of Ireland. Their attempts to colonise parts of it included the unsuccessful plantation of Antrim in the 1570s.

Ireland was regarded as a suitable area for colonisation for strategic reasons but also because the soil was known to be fertile and the rivers and seas fruitful. Much of the country, particularly Ulster, had been depopulated by warfare, famine, pestilence and emigration. In 1603 King James granted over 300,000 acres of "waste" land (i.e. land devastated by war) in County Antrim to Sir Randall MacDonell and another huge area in County Down to Hugh Montgomery from Ayrshire. The planters had permission to carry all commodities from Scotland and England that would be necessary to establish a settlement and to sell surplus produce of the estates in Scotland or England. It was intended that in Antrim there should be a number of relatively small independent and therefore powerless Irish freeholders interspersed amongst British gentry who would live in fortified dwellings and become a stabilising influence. In County Down the Scots were to be concentrated in one area and not to live in fortified houses; they were to form a sort of Scottish Pale. In 1606 some of Montgomery's settlers arrived, including a number of his relatives to whom he gave freehold estates of up to 1000 acres; artisans and "wealthy able men" became landholders of two to four acres. In 1606 King James wrote of Ireland that the universal peace continued

> by reason of the neereness of our kingdome of Scotland to the most doubtful parts of it, whereby we shall have better commoditie at all tymes to transport men or victuals into those quarters.

These groups of settlers were the forerunners of the main plantation of Ulster which was organised in 1609 and 1610. Nine chief "undertakers", all of them Lowlanders, were chosen; they undertook to settle English or Scots on their newly acquired lands. Of the fifty ordinary undertakers who were chosen many had connections with the king or the court or with the chief undertakers. Between three and eight ordinary undertakers were assigned to each possession. Four types of men were taken to the new possessions - freeholders who were gentry "of [a] sorte", leaseholders and cottagers "the common sorte", artisans and servants, some ministers, some women and some families. Sir James Hamilton wrote of the plantation:

> The lands in the north certainlie in tyme will doe well, but they will drowne for the present the man that undertakes and is not well furnished and stocked to performe what the land may requyre, to advance the goodness of it.

Between 1606 and 1609, 81,000 acres were distributed among 59 undertakers and by the middle of the century Cromwell was able to tell Parliament: "You have a company of Scots in the North of Ireland, 40 or 50,000 of them settled there, that, I hope, are honest men".[6]

These Scots were not Gaelic Roman Catholics but Protestant Lowlanders who therefore brought a new element into the life of Ulster. So many Scotsmen seem to have gone over that their landlords back home were complaining that many of their holdings were being left empty and by 1636 it was ordained that no tenant or labourer could take passage for Ireland without a certificate from his landlord or a justice of the peace.[7]

It was these new Scots Irish settlers who gave refuge to their Covenanting brethren fleeing from Scotland and who themselves went back to Scotland to escape similar harassment. Among the signatories of the National Covenant in 1638 were some Ulster Scots who in due course took copies back to Ulster for further signatures there. A further outbreak of insurrection in Ulster against the English in October 1641 sent more refugees to Scotland so that special provision had to be made for them by the Scots parliament. It was agreed with the English government that 10,000 Scots troops should be sent to Ulster where they continued for some years. The chaplains of the occupying army instituted Sessions which were constituted into a Presbytery in June 1642. Thus the establishment of Scots Prebyterianism led to a two way traffic of ministers and other settlers as tension in Scotland and Ireland waxed and waned. The Scots emigrated to Ulster in greater numbers during the 1660s when the religious conflict once more became acute. Charles II called for military help from the Irish government in 1675 and 1676 though no troops were actually sent. Scots emigrated again in the 1680s and 90s. Such was their influence that they helped to swell the numbers of Presbyterians in Ireland to approximately 400,000 or half the Irish Protestants by the end of the century. Of that number about 100,000 were said to be Scots immigrants.

With the accession of William and Mary in 1689 the ecclesiastical problems in all three countries became quiescent and no further land grants were made. Thereafter intending emigrants from Scotland looked not to Ulster for a new home but across the Atlantic- a policy which for England had been suggested to Queen Elizabeth a hundred years earlier by Sir Walter Raleigh and Humphrey Gilbert who were then serving in Ireland. They had argued that future English settlers should be sent to a safer area across the Atlantic.[8]

Early colonisation

The first Scottish attempts at the colonisation of North America took place in Newfoundland and Nova Scotia. Captain John Mason petitioned the King in 1620 to develop a more settled plantation in Newfoundland for establishing good order and preventing "enormities" among the fishermen and for securing the plantation and the fishermen from pirates. Captain Mason produced four reasons for the furtherance of his colony at Couper's Cove (now Mosquito Cove) rather than the colony in Virginia. Firstly, Newfoundland was nearer to Scotland; secondly, there had been trade with the area for more than 60 years; thirdly, new planters could easily be transported to Newfoundland at the rate of 10s per man and 20s for his victuals against £5 per man and £3 the tunne to go to Virginia; fourthly, there was good security against domestic and foreign enemies.

On his return to England the following year Mason met King James's Master of Requests, Sir William Alexander of Menstrie, later the Earl of Stirling. Sir William became determined to develop a colony in Nova Scotia, inspired by the English in Virginia, the French in Port Royal and Quebec and the Dutch on the Hudson. His plan involved the creation of Nova Scotia baronets who would be expected, not to settle there, but to provide men and capital for the colony. The King did indeed create Nova Scotia baronets - each of them was "to set furth sex sufficient men, artificers or labourers sufficientlie armeit, apparelit, and victuallit for twa yeares" and also to give 1000 marks Scots money to reimburse Sir William for money laid out on his previous efforts. Few men came forward to receive this dubious honour, although certain recalcitrant lairds were ordered to apply for a baronetcy. To make the scheme more attractive the new baronets did not have to provide men, but only to pay Sir William 3000 marks each, nor did they have to cross the Atlantic to receive their titles, they only had to travel to Edinburgh Castle, where part of the ground now covered by the Esplanade was designated as Nova Scotian territory and there the new barons took sasine of their inheritance. Among the new baronets were Sir William himself, Sir Robert Gordon of Gordonston, Lord Cullen and Lord Ochiltree.

Sir William petitioned the King in 1621 for a plantation in Nova Scotia, it

> being ane fitt warrandable and convenient means to disburding this his Majestie's said Kingdome of all such younger brether and meane gentlemen, who otherwayes must be troublesome to the houses and friends from whence they are descendit (the common ruynes of most of the ancient families), or betak themselves to forren worke or baisser chifts.

Sir Robert Gordon of Lochinvar was also involved in this scheme. After he had acquired New Galloway, which was part of Sir William's grant of Cape Breton Island,

Sir Robert Gordon published a pamphlet entitled *Encouragements to New Galloway* in 1625 offering substantial assistance; nothing came of this project. It transpired that when Sir William sent a boat to Kirkcudbright to collect emigrants Sir Robert was not there to assist because the harvest had been very poor and provisions for the voyage scarce and expensive so that the intending emigrants were loathe to leave. Although a few people eventually settled at St John's Harbour, the colony did not survive.

Sir William was not to be defeated by this lack of success; he wrote an enthusiastic but rather vague *Encouragement to Colonists*. It took time to mount an expedition; the two boats that were prepared in 1627 were delayed by war between England and France. Difficulties were also encountered on the other side of the Atlantic, where English privateers were disputing and overcoming French claims to Port Royal, Nova Scotia. The result was the formation of the Anglo-Scottish Company in 1628-9 which completed the capture of Quebec. In the summer of 1629 Sir William's son carried colonists to Nova Scotia. In another venture some 60 colonists under Lord Ochiltree landed on the east coast of Cape Breton Island, near Louisbourg, while the rest of the party later landed at Port Royal. Both colonies were to be short-lived; Louisbourg was retaken by the French within a few months. Although the Port Royal colony was reinforced, Sir William was ordered by King Charles I to abandon the site in 1632 and for it to be returned to the French.[9]

Sir William, now Earl of Stirling, concluded that "Scotland by reason of her populousness being constrained to disburden herselfe (like the painfull Bees) did every yeare send forth swarmes". This was an allusion to the changing land tenure system in the Lowlands and Borders whereby the number of landless tenants was considerably increased.[10] He continued to take an interest in the colonial schemes by becoming, with his son, councillor and patentee of the New England Company which was granted Long Island. Although Sir William did not send out any more colonists, his deputy sold land to some of the earliest settlers on Long Island.

Lord Ochiltree, who had superintended the unsuccessful colony of Louisbourg, had meantime returned to Scotland and busied himself trying to find more colonists. In 1631 he became a Nova Scotia baronet and so was helped by the judges "in transporting thither such persons as shal be willing to be imployed in that plantation" and in granting facilities for the dispatch of "victuall, ordinance munition and other necessaries whatsoever fitt for their use". This venture also failed, for it lost its leader when Lord Ochiltree was himself imprisoned for 20 years for falsely accusing the Marquis of Hamilton of high treason.[11] This marked the end of seventeenth century colonial endeavours in what was to become Canada. The Earl of Stirling did not lose his enthusiasm for overseas settlements but he channelled his zeal into schemes much further south on the American coast. The city fathers of Edinburgh also devised a plan in 1647 for a Scottish plantation in Virginia but nothing came of it.

Individual enterprise

George Scot of Pitlochie, son of Sir John Scot of Scotstarvit who had been associated with Sir William Alexander, was fined and imprisoned several times for attending conventicles (the prohibited open air religious services of the Covenanters), and eventually decided to take his family to East New Jersey. In 1676 New Jersey was divided into East and West New Jersey. East New Jersey was sold in 1682 to twenty-four proprietors, of whom five were Scots - the Earl of Perth and his brother James Drummond (later Earl of Melfort), Robert Barclay of Urie and his brother David, and Robert Gordon of Cluny. Pitlochie had written a *Model of Government* to inspire his fellow countrymen to go to New Jersey where they would find rich lands, a healthy climate, accessibility, a free democratic constitution and freedom of religion. Pitlochie chartered the *Henry and Francis* which sailed from Leith in September 1685 with about 100 prisoners on board as well as others who had contracted to go. The voyage was disastrous for more than 60 people, including Pitlochie and his wife, died of fever. It was said that:

> much of the flesh which the captain of the ship had provided for the prisoners began to stink before they sailed out of Leith Road, and in a few days it was not eatable...And so Pitlochie enjoyed nothing of the produce of near an hundred prisoners gifted him by the Council.

Pitlochie's son-in-law, John Johnston, was committed to looking after the remaining prisoners who refused to make "a voluntary declaration" that they would become indentured servants for four years after landing. The New Jersey law courts upheld their decision because "they had not of their own accord come to that ship, nor bargained with Pitlochie for money or services, and therefore they were assoiled" [acquitted, absolved].[12] Several hundred Scotsmen were settled on the grants of land during the next few years though many of them later moved to New England.

Lord Niall Campbell, brother of Archibald, 9th Earl of Argyll, was another refugee from persecution. He had been cited before the Privy Council in 1684, but although he had committed no offence he was confined to the environs of Edinburgh. He was soon released and allowed to transport abroad "any whom he could engadge ... providing these persons so to be transported be not declared traitors, rebels, or fugitives". Lord Niall was one of the early group of proprietors of land in East New Jersey and in due course augmented his estate to about 8000 acres. Most of the indented servants whom he took with him were young single men, though there were also some married men with families. Their indentures ran for four years and many expired in the early 1690s. Few of those who were able to, sought to acquire land of their own, they preferred to stay as free servants, often on their original master's estate.

Robert Barclay, a Quaker, had earlier suffered persecution and spent some time in prison for his beliefs. However in 1682 he also obtained an interest in a grant of land in East New Jersey, indeed he became governor of that colony although he never set foot there. In his broadsheet issued in 1684 Barclay appealed

> To all tradesmen, Servants and others who are willing to Transport themselves into the Province of New-East-Jersey in America, a great part of which belongs to Scotsmen, Proprietors thereof.

It is hardly surprising that he addressed a wide public, for, being one of the foremost improvers, he knew the conditions of the farm servants in Aberdeenshire, and his description of life of the poor is pitiful:

> There is nothing more strange than to see our Commons so besotted with the love of their own

misery, that rather than quit their Native Country, they will live in much toyl and penury so long as they have strength, being hardly able all their life to acquire so much Riches as can save themselves from begging or starving when they grow old: meantime their children (so soon as they are able to walk) are exposed to the Cruelties of Fortune and the charity of others, naked and hungry begging food and Rayment from those that either can not or will not help them: and yet can hardly be perswaded to go to a most profitable fertile and safe country, where they may have everything that is either necessary, profitable or pleasant for the life of man with very little pains and industry.[13]

A number of political/religious prisoners went to East New Jersey under Robert Barclay's scheme which was headed by his brother David. Ned C. Landsman has suggested that the relative failure of the Scots' attempts at colonisation in East Jersey was due to the proprietors' determination to replicate the social hierarchy that had developed in north-east Scotland. In Aberdeenshire at that time the landlords leased few farms to tenants, rather they kept the farms in their own hands and worked the land with paid servants. Thus they encouraged their servants rather than their tenants to cross the Atlantic, so that they could keep the reins of power within the confines of their own group.[14]

One disgruntled settler certainly did not appreciate the Quakers, for he wrote to the Chancellor of Scotland, the Earl of Perth, stating that he had been unable to obtain possession of land in New Jersey which had been sold to him by the Earl of Perth as "all the campine ground and river sids ar takine up allradie by Quakers, Independents, Presbiterians, Anabaptists, and in a word by all the off scourings of hell".[15]

The Darien Scheme

Slowly colonisation had become a matter for business consortia to discuss. A committee of Scottish merchants met with the Scotish Committee of Trade in 1681 to discuss ways of opening up new markets; they produced a *"Memorial Concerning the Scottish Plantation to be erected in some place in America"*. A decade later the Convention of Royal Burghs urged the establishment of a Scots colony; this led to the Committee of Trade of the Scottish Estates considering the matter in 1693. That year the Scots Parliament passed an Act for Encouraging of Foreign Trade: wide but vague privileges were to be granted to companies engaging in foreign trade. A copy of the Act was sent to some of the London merchants, including William Paterson, (who had founded the Bank of England). The English government had already become suspicious during the discussions leading up to the Act and had passed the Navigation Act of 1690, by which all public offices in the colonies were to be held by Englishmen. This meant that a number of Scotsmen were removed from their positions, including the Governor of East New Jersey.

The Company of Scotland trading to Africa and the Indies was founded by an Act of the Scottish Parliament in 1695 and was granted the exclusive trade between Scotland and America; the perpetual monopoly of trade with Africa and India; the power to arm and equip ships; and to plant colonies to be held in the name of the Crown; no customs or duties to be exacted in Scotland for 21 years. Any damage to the company was to be made good by public expense; 50% of the directors were to be London merchants, the others to be Scots merchants and men of affairs. Backed by "almost everyone who had money to spare", it has been estimated that 50% of the total capital available in Scotland was invested in the company, but the company never received the hoped for backing from London or continental interests, largely due to the destructive efforts of the English financial world.

William Paterson envisaged a free port on the Darien Isthmus [in Panama] because it would involve less time and expense sailing there than to the East;

> trade will increase trade, and money will beget money, and the trading world shall need no more to want work for their hands, but will rather want hands for their work.

Twelve hundred planters, many of whom had seen service abroad, set sail in July 1698 and arrived in Darien in October; they laid out the site of Fort St Andrews and the township of New Edinburgh. Little had been known about conditions in the area; it was proved to be unhealthy, there was no secondary provisioning of the expedition and when one of the ships returned from Jamaica after several months, not with the expected provisions but with the news that King William had issued a proclamation forbidding the giving of any help to the expedition, the planters decided to abandon their venture.

The Governor of New York, Lord Bellmont wrote of these returning planters: "I apprehend the Scotch that come in, from a starving condition they were in at their first coming, grew very insolent while they were at New York"; he ordered his agents "not to suffer the Scots to buy more provisions than would serve to carry them home to Scotland". The Scots settlers in East New Jersey had been put on oath not to help the members of the expedition. In fact one of the ships did go into port there and several of the crew settled in the colony.

Before the stragglers of the first expedition returned to Scotland the second expedition had already left the Clyde (in the autumn of 1699). Inadequate support was again the chief reason for the failure of this venture. The whole scheme had been doomed from the start, through lack of capital and the ill-chosen site. The English financial community had succeeded in obtaining the opposition of Parliament and of the King although the King had originally supported the project, it is said to divert attention from the Glencoe massacre. The English merchants had all too easily defeated their Scots rivals.[16] The Darien adventure proved to be the last desperate attempt to achieve an independent Scottish success, but should also be seen in the context of the struggle for sea power between England, France and the Netherlands during the War of the League of Augsburg (1688-1697). The war upset the established English commercial system and caused profound modifications in the working of the Navigation Acts. These depended on the existence of certain conditions favourable to English shipping and shipbuilding. During the war conditions had to be relaxed so that, for instance, foreign-built ships could be naturalised in order to carry essential naval stores. Again, the Navy was taking so many men into its service that the manning of merchant ships became difficult until the 1690 Navigation Act allowed a ship's company to be composed of 50% English and 50% foreign seamen.

Despite the failure to found a colony the merchants of Scotland continued to develop trade and commerce. They sent their employees across the Atlantic to the trading posts to organise the sending back of the produce and the importation of all those items necessary for living and trading in the American colonies in the 18th century. Many letters survive from men and young boys who had been sent as representatives of family or firm; the letters attest to the difficult conditions under which they lived, not least the loneliness and homesickness for their native land.

2

"A Sale Will Commence"

The accession of Charles I in 1625 marked the beginning of a period of religious turbulence, coming to a climax with the signing of the National Covenant in 1638 and culminating in the disastrous defeats of the Scottish army by Cromwell at Dunbar in 1650 and Worcester in 1651. Of the thousands of prisoners taken after the battle of Dunbar 1110 were sentenced to transportation to Virginia and 150 to New England, but few ever reached there. Another 1600 prisoners were sentenced to go to Virginia after the battle of Worcester though it is not known whether they actually went. 150 more were transported to Massachusetts in 1651 aboard the *Unity*. The *Sarah and John* sailed from London with 227 prisoners on 4th November 1651, arriving in Boston on the 24th February 1652, where they were indented.[1] In 1651 John Becx of London, a shareholder in the Saugus ironworks, outside Salem, Mass, the first to be established in the New World, purchased a number of Scots prisoners to work in the foundry. Of the 62 men in the original group, 35 were on the company's books in the autumn of 1653. Quarters were built in Hammersmith for some of them; the rest were farmed out to board with the English workmen employed by the company.[2]

The occupation of Scotland by Cromwell's army brought an end to current Scottish schemes for plantations. Up to this time Scottish shipbuilders had had a considerable reputation, but Cromwell destroyed the industry. At the time of Thomas Tucker's survey in 1656 there were only 80 ships in Scotland capable of carrying on overseas trade. The first Anglo-Dutch War created further chaos.[3] Recovery after the Restoration was very slow, mainly because Englishmen were still able to regard Scotland as a foreign country. The English Navigation Act of 1661 laid down that no goods could be shipped into America except in English ships or ships of the country of origin. Sugar and tobacco grown in the colonies could only be shipped to English ports. The response was the immediate passing of the Scottish Navigation Act which roughly copied the restrictions of the English Act, but it lacked any real authority because Scotland had no colonies and only a small merchant fleet. The English Act virtually excluded Scotland from the fertile field of colonial and foreign trade though sometimes the Scots did succeed in evading the English jurisdiction. Charles II had meantime authorized his Commissioner in Scotland to encourage plantations, thereby hoping to ease the tension between the two nations.

The bitter conflict between the King and the Covenanters continued until the Covenanters were finally routed by Monmouth at the battle of Bothwell Brig in 1679. According to Robert Chalmers two ministers were hanged, others were executed; 400 men were allowed to go home after swearing not to rise in arms again; 250 were dispatched to Barbados but their transport was sunk off Orkney with the death of 200

men who were battened below hatches.⁴ Sir George (Bluidy) Mackenzie wrote ,
Vindication of Charles II's Government:

> As to sending away to the plantations, none were sent away such as were taken at Bothwell
> Bridge, or in Argylle's rebellion; and the turning capital punishment into exile was an act of
> clemency not cruelty.⁵

A number of prominent men who were Covenanters were involved in colonial
activities. They included Sir John Cochran of Ochiltree, Sir George Campbell of
Cessnock, William Lawrie of Blackwood who was arrested for harbouring rebels after
Bothwell Brig, and William Dunlop, a Presbyterian minister who was tutor to Sir John
Cochran. In 1684 these men were involved in sending to America 35 prisoners and about
100 colonists under Lord Cardross. They sailed in the *Carolina Packet* to found Stuart's
Town, situated on Port Royal Sound in South Carolina. The settlement was soon
destroyed by the Spanish. That year two other ships left Montrose and Aberdeen with
160 and 130 passengers respectively. One emigrant wrote "we were all very well at sea,
only we had more stomachs than meat; to prevent which, if you or any other commorad
come this way, it will be prudence to fortifie themselves with good cheese, butter, cakes
and brandie".⁶

The Jacobite Transportations

In theory the Union of Parliaments in 1707 resolved the political and economic
confusion over the Scots' access to British North America. In practice the Scots were
still outsiders without the power to take an equal place in that land and it took another
fifty years to achieve this. This period was marked by the two great Jacobite rebellions.

After the '15 rebellion about 700 prisoners were taken at Preston. The prisoners
included all ranks from chiefs to their lowliest vassals. Some of the chiefs had their
estates forfeited to the Crown; most of the estates were eventually sold but 13 in the most
notorious Jacobite areas were annexed inalienably to the Crown. These annexed estates
were administered by Commissioners on behalf of the government until they were
returned to the heirs of the former owners in 1784. Many of the prisoners were sold as
slaves to West India merchants. Later, J.H. Burton wrote:

> It is painful to see on the lists the many Highland names, followed by 'Labourer'. Implicit
> obedience to their chiefs had been their crime, and in many instances they had been forced into
> the service for which they were punished, as absolutely as the French convict or the British
> pressed seaman.⁷

About 600 men were transported to South Carolina, Maryland and Virginia. One
batch of prisoners sailed on the *Scipio* in 1716.⁸ A certificate dated at Wellington, Ohio,
states that "Robert Stewart, one of the rebel prisoners taken at Preston, is to continue
servant to Captain Edward Traffod for seven years".⁹

The collapse of the '45 rebellion after the battle of Culloden led to the capture of over
3500 prisoners. As the government considered that the prisoners could not be tried in
Scotland because of possible partiality they were sent for trial in various English cities.
The legal proceedings after the '45 were well documented and have fortunately survived

so that we know the miserable fate of the men who were "out", though we do not know the fate of the many hundreds of women and children who were the necessary camp followers of those days.

The prisoners were sorted into different categories - those implicated to "an extraordinary degree of guilt"; the gentlemen or men of estates; those indicted for religious reasons; those willing to turn King's evidence. For the rest it was a lottery, for one in twenty was taken for trial. Once tried a prisoner could appeal for the King's Mercy, a dubious alternative of a lingering rather than a more rapid death. At least 866 men, women and children appealed and the mercy was extended under Letter Patent of 24th February 1747:

> George the Second, by the Grace of God, etc ... being moved with compassion of our especiall Grace, certain Knowledge, and meer motion, Have pardoned, Remitted, and released, and by these presents for our Heirs and Successors Do pardon, Remit, and Release (here follow 744 names).
>
> All Treasons, Misprisions of Treason, High Treason, Insurrections, rebellions, Murders, Homicides, Killings ... and Felonies ... perpetrated by themselves alone or with any other persons ... before the 23rd day of January 1746/7 by reason of their being concerned in the late Rebellion ...
>
> Provided nevertheless, and these our Letters Patent are and shall be under this express condition, that, if they ... upon request to be made to them for that purpose, shall not seal an Indenture to be made between them of the one part and Richard Gildart of Liverpool, Merchant, or Samuel Smith of London, Merchant, of the other part ...by which Indenture they shall bind and put themselves An Apprentice and Servant to the said Richard Gildart and Samuel Smith ... to serve them or their Assigns in our Colonies in America during the term of their natural lives ... together with a Covenant in such Indenture truly and faithfully to serve such their Masters or their Assigns in such our Colonies for and during the Term of their respective Lives according to the Laws and Customs thereof ...
>
> And if they ... shall not consent and submit themselves to be Transported by such Masters or their Assigns into our Islands or Colonies in America ... or shall not remain and continue in the said Islands or Colonies ... or shall, at any time after this our Pardon and before their Arrival in any of the said Islands or Colonies, be without some lawful cause at large in our Kingdom of Great Britain or Ireland or elsewhere.
>
> Then, this our pardon as to such of the persons ... who shall not perform or fulfill our Express Conditions shall be altogether void and of no force ...

There were different degrees of exile - 121 people were sentenced to banishment outside HM dominions; 37 were banished to America; 33 were sentenced to transportation without indenture and 866 were sentenced to the severest form, transportation with indenture. Government agreed to pay Mr Samuel Smith and Alderman Gildart £5 per head to transport prisoners. Those in the *Veteran* were comparatively lucky, for this ship with 150 men, women and children was captured by the French and taken to Martinique; the Governor refused to give them up and eventually freed them.

Another source suggests that of the 739 prisoners sentenced to transportation 610 went. It is known that 153 arrived in Maryland and that from another batch of 88 prisoners all but four were sold on arrival in America and immediately set free. Little is known of those who survived the journey. Already demoralised and ill-nourished, many must have suffered in the harsh circumstances in which they found themselves. Not all the prisoners were sent to America. Of the rest we know that 1195 were pardoned and so were eventually able to find their way home though knowing that there would be little prospect of employment when they got there; 92 men did as so many of their fellow countrymen had to do to keep from starving- they enlisted; at least 83 died miserably in gaol and 120 had their sufferings ended by execution; the fate of the remaining 684 is not known.[10]

Vagabonds and felons

The transportation of vagabonds, felons and other undesirable characters started in the seventeenth century. At the request of King James VI & I in 1617 the Star Chamber had considered plans for the suppression of disorder in the Middle Shires of the Borders, which would "send the most notorious leiveris of thame into Virginia or to sum remote parts, to serve in the wearris (wars) or in collonies". The Scots Privy Council at first refused any suggestion of similar treatment being meted out north of the Border. However the seed of an idea was sown and many convicts were later sent to the colonies.[11]

An unsuccessful attempt to transport vagabonds to New York had been made in 1669 by a group of men which included Sir William Bruce, the architect of Kinross House, (Sir) William Binning, James Standsfield of Newmilns, Robert Baird of Saughtonhall and James Currie. The Privy Council allowed John Kennaway, the town clerk of Culross who was brother to James Kennaway, chamberlain to Sir William Bruce, to collect vagabonds and other undesirable characters from fairs at Stirling, Dunfermline and the Laurence Fair at Old Rayne (Aberdeenshire). They were to be shipped in the *Hope* and *James* along with traders and planters to New York where the boats were to remain to trade and fish but to return to England to declare their goods to the English customs houses. This expedition ended in disaster with the wreck of the *Hope* off Fraserburgh in April 1673.[12]

The masters of such transport vessels gave a bond of 1000 marks for each prisoner to the effect that the prisoner would be duly transported and a certificate of landing produced. James Hamilton was one shipowner who received a warrant from the Privy Council to take a cargo of Scottish servants to the colonies. The Privy Council issued 26 such warrants between 1665 and 1685 for more than 800 men and women to be transported, while many others were sent to the West Indies. One Glasgow merchant, Walter Gibson, was prepared to transport "thieves and robbers sentenced by the Lords of Justiciary or other judges, to be banished thither, and all sorners, lusty beggars or gipsies" in 1683.[13]

The transporting of servants was not always an easy operation. Daniel Campbell of Shawfield was assured by his agents in Montrose, Thomas Coutts and Company, that they would not again undertake an assignment of that nature for three times the very moderate sum they charged. The agents had "much trouble in procuring and vexation in resisting the solicitations of gentlemen in demanding back ye serv^{ts} after on board". Nevertheless the *Lilee* of London sailed from Montrose in February 1696, bound for Pennsylvania, with 112 men, women and boys who were all fit although some had "from time to time" had to be put ashore on the way north because of ill-health. The agents' accounts included among the items:

for procuring boys and their maintenance,
for boys in ye Tolbooth and correction house procuring their consent
to goe to America,
to soldiers who brought the women to Leith and went to Montrose to
guard them,
for maintaining serv[ts] ashore and procuring serv[ts]";
to the various officials and for bedding, provisions and other
necessaries for the seamen and servants.[14]

The chief landowners or barons also had the power to transport criminals from their estates or baronies until the power of the barons was broken in 1747. Lord Lovat either transported his convicted lieges or forced them to enlist in regiments that his friends were raising. In 1739 Norman McLeod younger of Berneray admitted forging a document permitting his men "to search for and apprehend such persons that were convicted of theft before my courts" to be delivered to McLeod and shipped on the *William* of Donaghadee, "to be transported to any of H.M. plantations the said Norman pleased to go to America". McLeod went on board with over 100 men, women and children and landed at Donaghadee where the prisoners were shut up in two barns while the boat was fitted out for America. The prisoners managed to escape and the whole ghastly episode was uncovered. There are also letters incriminating McLeod of McLeod and his friend Sir Archibald MacDonald of Sleat in similar exploits.[15] By the Disarming Act of 1746 the government hoped to annihilate the clan tradition with its associated historic associations and to make the clansmen loyal and obedient citizens; tartan, the wearing of the kilt and the carrying of arms were proscribed. Heritable jusisdictions had become an anachronism and served only to debase the administration of justice. Long overdue reform was enacted by the Heritable Jurisdictions (Scotland) Act of 1747. Although the remaining legal powers of the barons have never been abolished they withered away as a result of the changing economic and social climate in Scotland.

The transportation of convicts to America continued up to the outbreak of the American War of Independence. More than 50 convicts were transported from Glasgow prison as late as March 1775.[16] Most of the convicts or indentured servants ended up in the plantations of Virginia, where the arduous conditions kept up the strong demand for labour. The indentured servant was but a "white negro"; his arrival was welcomed by an advertisement such as this in the *Virginia Gazette*:

Just arrived the *Neptune*, with 100 healthy servants, men, women and boys, among whom are many valuable tradesmen, viz tailors, weavers, barbers, blacksmiths, carpenters and joiners, shoemakers, a staymaker, cooper, cabinet-maker, bakers, silversmiths, a gold and silver refiner and many others. A sale will commence...[17]

James Baird and Patrick Colquhoun both contracted to carry convicts at a cost of £5 per convict. Colquhoun wrote to John Davidson, agent to the Crown, in 1770,

I did inform Mr Grant that I was willing to undertake the business of transporting all the felons that might occasionally be cast for transportation in Scotland ... I am not altogether prepared for an immediate transportation of the six or eight felons you mention, but they shall be sent by the first vessel offering to any of the Southern provinces. I propose at all times to transport them from the ports adjacent to Glasgow, tho' I would not wish to be confined to these alone ... If I engage in this business I must no doubt conform to the principal regulations in former contracts ... it would be agreeable to me to know as early as possible on what footing I stand and what particular duties and obligations are expected from me.[18]

An even more unsavoury trade was that of kidnapping young children for sale to owners of plantations. Aberdeen became the centre of the trade which arose from the food riots of 1740 and which lasted some 30 years. For some time earlier it had been common to send younger siblings of transportees in the shipments, but during the famine years parents, in the interests of their children's survival, handed over the youngsters to the shipmasters. Soon parents were selling children for one shilling to one shilling and sixpence. When the famine eased this source of cheap servants dried up so the merchants formed kidnapping companies and sent parties out from the city to steal children from the countryside. At £16 a head in the colonies this was even more lucrative than the African slave trade.

Some 500 boys were abducted from Aberdeen and district in the years 1740-5 with the connivance of the town clerk depute and some of the baillies. One of the few boys to return to his native city was Peter Williamson. He came home in 1758 and wrote an account of his adventures; it was seized by the Aberdeen magistrates and burned at the Mercat Cross by the hangman. Williamson himself was thrown into the Tolbooth but escaped to Edinburgh where he settled and became known as Indian Peter. He organised the city's first penny post and street directory. He eventually won damages and costs against the baillies who had kidnapped him.[19]

In 1774 Lord Seaforth maintained that as well as putting undue pressure on individuals to emigrate there were no fewer than seven different companies in Lewis kidnapping boys and locking them up in their ships so that their parents and masters could not see them again. He felt he could not really deal with these atrocious villains without military aid, though he did take a kind of protest against the commander of one vessel, the *Philadelphia*, and its owners. Lord Seaforth requested the Earl of Suffolk to send some militia, but the Earl feared that the effect of such a force would be thoroughly detrimental and would further emigrations, and anyway he could not send a force "on the suggestion of a private agent". In defence of the Lewis request Lord Justice Clerk Miller noted that there was no judge, magistrate or justice of the peace in the island, so that no person had any legal authority over the people except Lord Seaforth's bailiff and he could only levy rent and judge small cases and assaults. Although Lord Seaforth's steward had apparently accepted a commission of the peace "one justice of the peace has no powers by the law of Scotland to try any offence". Lord Miller argued for a measure to restrain the ship masters and owners from beating up for passengers in every creek and island; and to ensure that they clear out at known ports under the inspection of the proper officers who would have powers to refuse clearance where sufficient room and provisions were not provided. Such a measure would increase costs for the shipmasters and thereby increase the charge to passengers, thus giving them time to reflect as they travelled to a recognised port of embarkation.[20] Legislation was passed thirty years later.

These were difficult times as an Edinburgh baker testified in an advertisement for the detention of a carrier who not only owed him money but also absconded with his 17 year old son whom he had apprenticed to the baker. The advertisement continued:

It is a pity such practices were found in this nation; and more so from one whose conversation ever spoke the reverse. We hope that all shipmasters who should and who do abhor such practices and who are bound for America will be so good as not to indent or take away any of the above mentioned persons. Nor is it right, that any should open a passage for such persons, to impose upon strangers in a foreign land.[21]

Those who sailed the seas whether taking convicts or emigrants were in danger not only from the elements but also from the press-gangs. The *Matty* was wrecked on the voyage from Virginia to Clyde in 1770 because all the men except the master, first mate and apprentice were taken. The *Buchanan* suffered the same fate.[22]

The hazards of early emigration were considerable whether the emigrants were adventurers, fortune seekers or traders, but were even greater for the larger number of involuntary emigrants who were transported as punishment for religious, political or criminal acts. These wretched people were soon to be joined by a much larger number-the first wave of refugees from starvation, huge rent increases and the tyranny of certain landlords.

3

"Rid Scotland of Feudalism"

A major consequence of the collapse of the Jacobite rebellions was the destructon of the feudal authority of the old clan chiefs, who had combined naked power with paternalism. Those chiefs who remained rapidly transformed themselves into landords, often absentee landlords. Chiefs who had counted their rental in the number of their retainers, many of whom were idle while waiting for the call to arms or forced labour, became landlords interested in the emergent money economy and determined to "rid Scotland of feudalism". They were encouraged by those men empowered by government to oversee the estates that were forfeited to the government by the rebellious chiefs.(Fig. 3.1) In the Lowlands, while the social implications of agricultural improvement were profound, they did not involve the virtual destruction of an unique culture.

Concurrently, the golden years of the Enlightenment, a short period of about 60 years, produced men such as David Hume and Adam Smith and pioneers in the fields of medicine, chemistry, geology and sociology, a flowering of architecture and a number of notable academic teachers. They not only made a European reputation for the Scottish Universities but played a significant part in the development of higher education in America. The ideas and vitality of the Enlightenment spilled over into many practical aspects of Scotland's life, in particular into agriculture, banking and the beginning of the industrial revolution.

Improved farming

Agricultural reform had begun earlier and developed more quickly in the Lowlands and southern Scotland where there were more contacts with the improving farmers of England and where the climate and soil conditions were more favourable. A few landowners had started enclosing their farms as a result of the Divison of Commonties Act APS ix.462 (1695 cap.69) and the Act for Consolidation of Runrig Lands APS ix.421 (1695 cap.36). The process of enclosing was not always achieved easily especially in the south west which saw some of the earliest enclosures in connection with the cattle trade with Ireland and England. The Levellers, a body of between five and six hundred sub-tenants and cottars with a few tenants, continued the "demobilising of enclosures and gentlemen's parks" for about a year in spite of the soldiers who had been called in by the landowners. In May 1724 Rev Robert Woodrow wrote:

It's certain great depopulations have been made in the south, and multitudes of familys turned out of their tacks and sent a-wandering ... Some parishes, particularly that of Girton (in

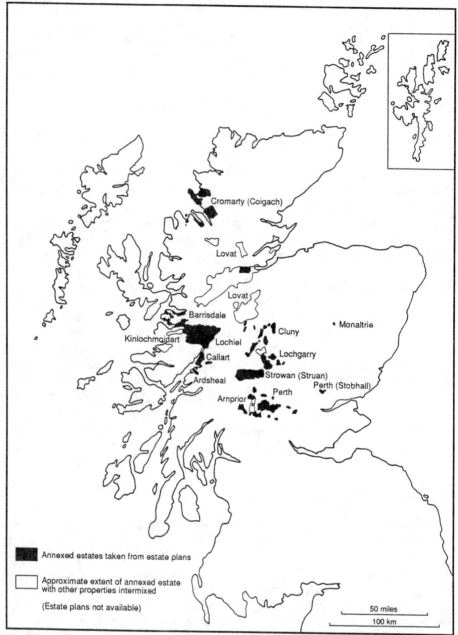

Fig. 3.1 The Annexed Estates. The areas of the Lovat Estate and parts of certain other estates, for which there are no plans, are approximate.

Kirkcudbrightshire) are almost whole enclosed and scarce six or seven familys left.[1]

Conditions for agriculture in the Highlands were often marginal and farming practices backward. The infield/outfield system which was still generally practised meant that a relatively small parcel of land near the houses was enclosed temporarily for cropping; the cattle were herded in common on the higher ground and brought back at night to leave their dung on the infield. It was difficult to improve the strain of cattle, which were generally of poor quality when herding was in common, or crops when there were few enclosures. Many areas were over-stocked, for cattle were the main form of currency and an important item in the rent.

Changes could not have been carried out without the work of the members of a new profession, land surveyors. These men spent many weeks in the field studying the soil and laying out new farms. They advised the landlords what crops to grow and what rents their tenants could pay. These surveyors were greatly respected and were able to pass on their knowledge as they moved from estate to estate.[2] Improvements involved the abandonment of the runrig system, the enclosure of fields (much of the field system laid out at that time still exists), drainage, the introduction of crop rotation, the improvement of stock and seed and the building of steadings, bridges and roads.[3] The almost total lack of roads meant that most goods were moved on horse back by land or, where possible, by boat on rivers or on the sea. The work of improvement required labour, but as steadings, bridges, drains and roads were completed the labour once absorbed by the estates became redundant.

The introduction of sheep-farming into northern Scotland as a commercial activity was a gradual, but uncoordinated, process beginning in Perthshire in 1762 and finally reaching parts of the Hebrides and Shetland only towards the end of the nineteenth century. In 1770 sheep farming was begun in Invernessshire, spreading to Ross and Cromarty in 1774. In 1792 Sir John Sinclair introduced black faced sheep into Caithness and in 1807 they first appeared in Sutherland. By the end of the eighteenth century it was estimated that of the three million sheep in Scotland one half were in the Highlands (including Perthshire and Argyll). The growth of sheep-farming was probably inevitable, although it has had such serious consequences both human and ecological. However the first movements of the population from the land preceded the introduction of sheep and had different causes. The major brutalities of the "Clearances" came later and are outwith the period of this book. Only one contemporary reference from the period of emigration 1768-1775 has been discovered attributing the need to remove from Scotland to the introduction of sheep.[4]

By the middle of the 18th century, many landowners were enjoying the fleshpots of London and returned to their estates determined to wring more income out of their unfortunate tenants in order to support their new life style. Under the feudal law of Scotland landowners held their land by heritable tenures as vassals of the king. As head of his clan the chief farmed the best land either himself or under the management of his chief tacksman or factor. He then rented the remaining farms to his relatives and clansmen, the more important men holding their farms by tack or lease. These tacksmen, in turn, sub-let their land, or parts of it, to sub-tenants who did virtually all the work on the estates; beyond them were the landless labourers and cottars who had only the right to graze their few beasts on the common land. Many sub-tenants held their land on very short lease or at the will of the landlord. Very little rent was paid in money as most of it was paid in services such as ploughing or carrying coals, or in kind such as a cow or a number of hens. Not until specie became more readily available was it possible to convert the rent into a money rent. The landowners recognised their diminished need for labour and gradually introduced clauses into the new long leases which specifically forbade sub-tenancy.

The obvious way to increase the income of the estates was by introducing new farming methods involving radical changes. An improving landlord would concentrate his efforts on the home farm and make a success of that before expecting his tenants to adopt his newfangled methods. But many landlords looked for immediate results and it was the tacksmen who bore the heaviest burdens since they were frequently expected to pay higher rents even before the effect of any improvements could be experienced.

Although some tacksmen had been good and innovative farmers, others had obtained their living simply by sub-letting their farms. Either way they siphoned off revenue from their landlord. Margaret Adam concluded that the emigrations between 1769 and 1775 were due to the obsolescence of the role of the tacksmen. The reforms of estate management had made their position untenable and an expensive anachronism.[5] While some could and did very successfully adjust to the new order, this period saw many of the tacksmen taking up an offensive position, deploying many of their vast army of sub-tenants against the landowners. By encouraging emigration they were effectively removing labour from the system and thus depressing the rental values.

From being the most loyal clansmen they became the promoters and leaders of emigrations. They had the skills and resources, for the necessary organisation was not a simple matter; to obtain a grant of land in America the prospective emigrant had to write to London, an activity that required literacy, a knowledge of institutions and of the English language. The sub-tenants and cottars who formed the bulk of the population turned to the tacksmen for leadership, for the only other source of authority- the factors, were ominous figures who represented not only the shadowy absentee landlord, but were also the agents of the changes which were losing them their land. The tacksman thus often remained in immediate and total authority. However they frequently went to considerable lengths to make sure that the sub-tenants had sufficient capital to pay for their passages by buying their stock and arranging for its sale. Not all emigrations were organised by tacksmen, merchants from the cities saw commercial opportunities in developing the trade, which some exploited unscrupulously. However organised, many persons who could not pay for their passage were indentured and the indenture sold to another person at the end of the voyage.

Some contemporary reports accuse the sub-tenants of preferring idleness and poverty to going to work as a day labourer when they might have earned a little by digging ditches or building dykes. But even that large part of the population, possibly up to 50%, who were landless labourers living on the fringes of the settlement found that with improved technology and organisation a good deal of their periodic labour was no longer needed. Enclosures made the herd redundant. The threshing machine removed one of the most important inputs of manual labour from the industry. The new light plough required only one operator instead of the team which drove the old Scots plough and its oxen.

Even if the countryman was not converted to a day labourer or evicted, those who remained in the old subsistence farming found their perquisites reduced. Minor, but not necessarily unimportant buttresses of country life were whittled away by landlords and their factors. Access by all to wood for fuel, for building and repairing houses and for making implements had been allowed as long as the tenants preserved the woods and plantings on the land. The taking of game and fish had been accepted as normal rights from time immemorial, but now the landlords began to view these rights as sporting, if not economic, assets to be preserved for themselves. In some areas fuel from peat banks became scarce as landlords drained ground. Similarly, the old custom of wintering, the keeping of cattle in woodlands, was forbidden as scientific forestry was adopted; the dyked landscape reduced the need for herding. In short, few areas of traditional country life were left undisturbed.

The building industry

The newly discovered use of lime in building farm houses, steadings and walls encouraged people to erect more permanent homes and gave a boost to the building industry during the second half of the century. In some cases the agricultural workers were sent to new planned villages nearby, or to the coast where they were expected to become fishermen and to live in the new villages. Roads and bridges were built to accommodate the increased traffic as markets were opened up for the goods that were coming out of the new factories.

Some landowners became involved in the construction of planned villages to house displaced countrymen and in various enterprises for their alternative employment; others were only concerned with increasing rents, or in increasing their own comfort, regardless of the human consequences. The Duchess of Gordon, for instance, disliked seeing the township of Fochabers close to the castle, so when the new town was to be built in 1776 the old houses were ruthlessly torn down.[6] Dr Porter who was employed by the British Fisheries Society wanted the government to grant certain immunities to the Society villages so as to encourage the Highlanders to collect themselves into towns in Britain rather than see them add strength to other nations by leaving the kingdom.[7] Mr James Grant of Grant planned to establish an industrial town to help reduce the poverty of his clansmen in an 'unimproved' area. Thus in 1766 tenants built their own stone houses on their plots; advertisements sought traders and manufacturers to come and settle in the new town. Mr Grant built advance factories in the shape of a bleachfield and a linen manufacturing house, he subsidised ongoing industries and lent capital when necessary. He also encouraged his industrial enterprises by granting markets and fairs and free customs; and by founding schools for the teaching of stocking knitting and the spinning and manufacture of wool. Although his vision was not entirely realised, in that the industrial activity did not last much more than twenty years, Grantown-on-Spey has continued to be an important local centre.[8]

Along with the building associated with the farms, the increased urban population required many more new houses; some of the old houses in the old town of Edinburgh which were left by those persons who moved to the new town were soon filled again by incomers from the countryside. The same was true of nearly all the towns of Scotland-industrial workers had to be housed but the sudden increase in demand led to jerry-building, the consequences of which created many social problems in the nineteenth century.

Few records survive recalling in detail the movement of people from the countryside
to the growing towns. Information about individual households was not required until
the 1841 census and the parish of birth was not included until the next decennial census,
by which time two generations of countrymen had drifted into towns. However this
migration was well established by the 1790s when, for example, it was reported from
Kilwinning in Ayrshire that

> Every farm had formerly one or two, or more families upon it. The cottages are now, in great
> measure, demolished; and this mumerous and industrious people has been under necessity of
> removing to Irvine, and to other towns in the neighbourhood.[9]

Greenock, on the banks of the River Clyde, received many incomers from the
Highlands. Of the 3387 families in the town in 1792, no fewer than 1825 heads of
families had been born in the Highlands:

> Most of the labourers, boatmen, sailors etc, in Greenock are from the Highlands, and they often
> settle there with large families to support which requires their utmost industry and application.
> This large import of Gaelic culture was met in various ways: by a voluntary subscription ... the
> wealthier part of the Highland inhabitants have lately erected a large, elegant and commodious
> Gaelic chapel ... One may at times walk from one end of the town to the other, passing many
> people without hearing a word of any language but Gaelic.[10]

Although the pace of change varied in different areas, the landscape and the lives of
the community were being changed fundamentally. A new pattern of fields and
buildings was emerging and the traditional small tenant farmer's links with the soil were
being slowly severed. In Ayrshire, Robert Burns's father, William, struggled with
excessive rents for sixteen years from 1765 to 1781 and died bankrupt. Burns himself
continued the battle for ten more years until he became an excise officer. He even, in
despair, booked his passage to emigrate to Jamaica but withdrew on the publication, in
1786, of the Killmarnock edition of his poems which he hoped would ease his financial
problems.[11]

In addition to the major economic trends specific events contributed to the decision
to emigrate. The bad winter of 1771 led to large price increases especially of oatmeal,
which was the staple of the tenantry. Emigrants in 1772 and 1773 mentioned this
particularly. It is strange to note that although high rents were cited time and again as
the main reason for going, there appears to have been little unrented land in Scotland
so some men must have been able to pay the higher rents. On the whole, the emigrants
represented that part of the rural population which was either not selected for or not
financially able to participate in the new, 'improved' agriculture. The landlords
required increased productivity and those people who could not respond became
redundant. Some, mainly the older and less able men and women neither received
tenancies nor were they able to emigrate; they were often left destitute without land or
employment.

A Banking Disaster

Development, whether for agricultural improvements, for the first phase of the industrial revolution, or for the burgeoning foreign trade, depended on short and long term capital. In the mood of optimism which existed great faith was placed in the prospects of the rapidly developing banking system. Sir William Forbes, in a caustic comment, wrote that the gentlemen who were endeavouring to live up to their new style of living in their new mansions had

> recourse to the ruinous mode of raising money by a chain of bills on London; and when the established banks declined to continue a system of which they began to be suspicious, the Bank of Douglas, Heron and Company, commonly known as the 'Ayr Bank' was erected.[12]

A far more sinister motive was attributed to these men by Robert Heron who wrote in 1792 that the aims were to form an

> engine by which the elections of parliamentary representatives for the West of Scotland might be subjected to the control of a certain interest; to give the country more of the advantage of the transactions of the landholders; and to make it easier for landed gentlemen to obtain money to improve their estates.

Whatever the original motive, Douglas, Heron and Company was launched on August 24th 1769 with the quite inadequate capital of £150,000.[13]

The Duke of Queensberry was appointed Governor with a board of 24 directors. The Earl of Dumfries, the Hon. Archibald Douglas of Douglas, Patrick Heron of Heron and many landowners and merchants in south west Scotland and a good number from farther afield were amongst the 141 men who invested in this new venture. Most of the men bought one £500 share, but a few invested £1000, the limit being not more than four shares to any one person:

> The promoters were, seemingly, men who thought that the old banks selfishly studied their own interest to an extent both unnecessary and injurious to the progress of the industries of the country; and that, at the same time, they were monopolising a lucrative trade, which could be comfortably competed for by men of larger views.

In the event many of the original subscribers failed to pay up when it came to fulfilling their subscription.[14]

Branches were opened in Edinburgh and Dumfries with, however, separate boards and independent powers; agencies were also opened in Glasgow, Inverness, Kelso, Montrose, Campbeltown and Inverary. From the start the bank seems to have been ill-managed, the directors being too eager for business, thus making too many advances of money beyond their funds. As early as January 1770 the Edinburgh and Dumfries branch managers wrote to the directors at Ayr protesting at this mismanagement. The directors were not deterred for they continued issuing paper notes and making loans.[15]

The signs of imminent disaster were evident by early 1771 when Dimsdale and Company, the London correspondents, refused further assistance. Undaunted, the directors of the Ayr Bank continued to mismanage affairs and even bought up two local banks - John MacAdam and Company in Ayr and Alexander Johnston, Hugh Lawson and Company in Dumfries, both of which were then barely solvent. At last, by May 1772 the directors began to realise the gravity of their situation.[16] Edinburgh banks refused to hold their paper and on June 12th news was brought from London that the banking house of Neale, James, Fordyce and Downe had failed and brought down other firms with it. At first the cashier managed to bluff his way out, but on the 25th the Ayr headquarters of the bank and five other private banks suspended payment. The directors attempted to get help from the Bank of England but the terms were thought to be too harsh. Some individuals and companies were able to assist so that the offices were re-opened on September 18th and the Bank struggled on until August 1773.

In December 1773 a meeting was held at which the proprietors present subscribed £200,000 for the relief of the company, of which the Duke of Buccleuch subscribed £20,000.[17] The proprietors of the Bank set up an inquiry. The report criticised almost all the directors' activities:

> It was unfortunate that a variety of enterprising companies engaged in different kinds of foreign and domestic trade had, about this time, been established in that place, under different firms indeed, but all of them closely connected and linked together, and that the members which composed these several companies became all of them partners in Douglas, Heron and Company. It was still more unfortunate that the cashier (James Hunter) and most of the directors at Air ... were concerned in one or more of these trading companies ... Most exorbitant and profuse credits were immediately given out, in various forms, to the individual members of these trading companies and to the companies themselves, under their respective firms. The same set of people became security for each other.[18]

Shareholders, however, continued to be burdened by debt to help to redeem the company during the next 60 years. A House of Commons Committee Report was critical of foreign competition, a suggestion that many merchants rejected saying that there was a general stagnation of credit and that indeed trade was already reviving. In a recent appraisal Henry Hamilton suggested that the failure was part of the economic pattern of that time, that although economic progress had started in the 1740s it had an uneven rise to a peak in 1771.[19]

Richard Sheridan has pointed out that this financial crisis started in London but quickly spread to Scotland, the continent and parts of the British Empire. The newer colonies had an insatiable demand for capital but abundant resources of land. This forced the colonists to offer a higher rate of return and as surpluses were hard to achieve the colonists were always in arrears on interest payment. There was a considerable expansion of domestic and foreign trade in Britain in manufacturing and in mining in the years 1770-2 while there was a big increase in the quantity and price of imports of rice, tobacco and wheat from America.[20]

The economic difficulties in Scotland were inevitably closely linked with affairs in America. In 1772 the Glasgow tobacco merchants, William Cunningham and Co, had to adopt a more frugal way of carrying on their business. They therefore limited the size of the drafts that their factors in Virginia could make on them, but also reduced the supplies of goods as they feared that orders would decline the following year. Indeed the company's shortage of cash quickly increased so that the factors' drafts were limited still further and for some time no bills were to be drawn on the parent house.[21]

Industrial progress

The growing and spinning of flax had been largely for domestic use until the experiments of Cockburn of Ormiston in the 1740s; slowly a linen industry developed with expertise introduced from Ireland and Holland. In 1746 the British Linen Company was established to provide the growing number of spinners and weavers with short-term credit and the industry continued to grow for the next 30 years. But the collapse of the Ayr Bank combined with the importation of better quality linens from the Continent and the resistance of the Americans to buying British goods decimated the industry in a few years.

Important developments were taking place in other industries, particularly in iron and steel manufacture. The most convenient date we can clearly identify as the onset of the Industrial Revolution is the firing of Carron Company's first blast furnace on January 1st 1760. As new technology was introduced into old and new industries, so men and women were drawn from the land to the towns. During the next 40 years the cumulative effects of the industrial, urban and social changes were to point the direction that Scotland's economy would take.

Although there had been a few other companies involved in iron smelting and refining in Scotland, Carron Company was the first major works and the one that survived. During 1759 William Cadell had started building a cupola furnace for experimental rather than commercial purposes and on November 11th that year articles of copartnery were signed and thus was formed the company of Roebucks, Garbett and Cadells. The company was reorganised and renamed Carron Company in 1771. The works were set up on the banks of the River Carron in Stirlingshire, situated near supplies of ironstone at Bo'ness, timber for charcoal from woods on nearby estates, coking coal from the local coal mines and good communications by water. None of these supplies was satisfactory for long: the ironstone was not as suitable as had been anticipated; timber, though plentiful, was not suitable, and the labour force was initially made up of inefficient colliers. Garbett determined to introduce six English foremen into the works. To increase the numbers of workers pauper children were recruited as apprentices; however their guardians in the workhouse insisted that they were not to be bound at the end of their seven-year apprenticeship.

By the end of August 1760 a total of 80 tons of ironstone a week was being smelted. Additional pig iron and bar iron had to be imported from America. The company made a variety of products which did not require great skill; but from the start it specialised in cast iron pipes, cylinders for pumping engines in collieries, domestic stoves and grates, many of which were shipped to America and carried ornate designs by the Adams family. Many of the agricultural utensils were designed for the emigrant market in America. As early as 1761 James Dunlop was able to report that Carron axles, bushes and plough plates were giving every satisfaction in Virginia. After the Seven Years' War, Carron Company was able to re-enter the American market with machinery for sugar mills.

Early attempts to produce guns were unsatisfactory, but the difficulties were over-come and many a merchant ship was armed with 'carronades' during the Seven Years' War. In order to facilitate the delivery of their goods to London and elsewhere the shipping company Samuel Garbett and Campany was formed. Francis Garbett and Company was also formed to build a new wharf and shipping facilities at Carronshore. Due partly to the personal problems of the directors and partly to the incredibly complicated financial arrangements of commerce and industry in the United Kingdom at that time the finances of the various companies associated with Charles Gascoigne and his partners were always in a state of crisis. So when the Ayr Bank failed in 1772 Carron Company nearly went down too; Francis Garbett and Company failed, five partners in Carron Company (including Gascoigne) went bankrupt and Samuel Garbett never fully recovered from the troubles. David Hume wrote to Adam Smith the "Carron Company is reeling, which is one of the greatest calamities of the whole; as they give employment to near 10,000 people". The situation gradually improved during 1774 and continued to do so until the company was in a sound financial position by 1786.[22]

Depression

The social consequences of the financial crisis of 1772 were immense; economic depression spread throughout Scotland; much land had to be sold, riots broke out in Perth, Fife and Angus, significantly the seat of the linen industry. Yet weavers from Paisley were the first non-agricultural emigrants to leave these shores:

> Many, many of the poor in this place and country, who formerly subsisted by their industry, cannot now find Employment; and those who are employed, from the reduction of wages in every stage of manufacture, cannot, by the hardest labour, obtain Bread: And I am convinced this has introduced a state of Despair among the People that has occasioned the late desperate and tumultuous riots we have had here. Meal, and other necessaries of life, are no dearer, nor no scarcer, than they have been for some time; but I do believe, the Poor cannot, from their labour, find money to obtain them as formerly.

Another person suggested that the riots were occasioned "not so much by the scarcity of victual in the country, as by many of the industrious Poor being idle, and rendered incapable to purchase the Necessaries of life".[23]

These words of the Roman Catholic bishop of Edinburgh and St Andrews, Bishop George Hay (George Daulis) describe some of the problems facing Scotland in 1772:

> money is not to be had at any rate, people are diminishing their servants, tradespeople giving up their workmen; no trade going on of any kind but everything at a stand, hence incredible numbers of poor everywhere and vast numbers of robbers in all parts of the country of Scotland and England whilst everything is at the most extravagant price, and in some places the greatest scarcity. Things here have really at present the most dismal appearance ... the landed men continue the most oppressive measures with their poor tenants, who are breaking every day and especially from the Highlands coming in shoals to this and other cities begging their bread with their families; here all our public and private buildings are at a stand partly by the season and much more for want of money to carry them on, by which numbers of families are starving.[24]

With agriculture shedding a significant part of its labour force, with the rapidly growing but wildly fluctuating industrial labour market and with only a few tentative social experiments which could offer alternative employment and habitation, the decision to emigrate was for many Hobson's choice.

4

"Land of Promise"

The Beginnings of Mass Emigration

In the years between the two Jacobite rebellions emigration began to take on the characteristics of a mass "voluntary" movement. The largest and most important settlements of Scots developed along the Cape Fear River, in what was to become Cumberland County, North Carolina. In 1729 Hector McNeill of Lossit in Kintyre established a colony of West Highlanders on Cape Fear River. Ten years later his brother Neil took another 550 people from Argyll to settle New Campbeltown (which became known as Lafayetteville after Independence). The *Thistle*,carrying 350 emigrants arrived in Brunswick in September. The following year, 1740, the State government encouraged immigrants by advancing £1000 to five men to distribute amongst emigrant families and exempted the families from taxes for ten years; the leaders, who were all related, were each granted from 300 to 640 acres of land.[1]

In 1735 General Oglethorpe, on behalf of the Trustees for Establishing the Colony of Georgia in America, sent Lieutenant Hugh Mackay, the second son of Baron Reay to recruit Highlanders, for immigrants were needed to fill up the land and defend the new colony. Mackay was at first unsure of finding suitable emigrants for Lord Sutherland and other gentlemen were "not so very favourable for fear of losing those poor creatures, who they look on to be their property as Much as their Cattle". Eventually, on October 18th the ship *Prince of Wales* of Dunbar sailed from Inverness carrying 130 Highlanders with 50 women and children. There were 12 paying passengers who each had a grant of 500 acres of land. Mackintosh of Borlum, who had been involved in the '15 Rising, and their minister, Rev John McLeod from Skye, led the party, who were mainly from Strathdearn. The ship reached Tynhie in December and the party then went by boats to Altamaha where they established the town of New Inverness. There is some indication that a second wave of 165 MacKintoshes left Invernessshire the same year.[2]

Scots were also interested in the northern frontier of America, in the colony of New York. In 1734 Governor Cosby of New York province offered 100,000 acres of land near Lake George to loyal Protestant families from Europe. Captain Lachlan Campbell, one of the tacksmen on Islay, was tempted and in 1738, 1739 and 1740 took a total of 423 people to New York, according to him, at his own expense; (in fact, the men paid their own passages or were indentured servants). Campbell saw land in Pennsylvania and Maryland which he considered too expensive, and although the land that had been advertised in New York had already been allocated he was promised some of it for his people. Years later some of his followers did receive some of this land while others procured some on their own initiative. Campbell's sons Donald, late of the 60th

Regiment, George and James and his daughters Rose, Margaret and Lily acquired 30,000 acres in New York state in 1764 and in 1766 100,000 acres near Albany for the family and a number of families "already sent over by his father".[3] The land was divided into 141 lots of between 250 and 600 acres. According to Professor George Pryde the whole affair could never have succeeded. Campbell "had conceived hopes of erecting a Lordship for himself in America", but his emigrants had no wish to become his tenants. He tangled with the Council, submitting excessive claims for land while asking for ridiculously low prices for the necessary survey charges; added to which were obvious discrepancies between various lists of settlers and their requirements. All in all the Council "were altogether at a loss how to make any tolerable construction of it in his favour".[4] A tradition involving the Campbell clan recounts that some settled in the Mohawk valley in the early 18th century but were so unpopular with their Dutch neighbours that they moved to Saratoga where they were later nearly all massacred by Indians.[5]

In 1738, John Lindesay promoted a Scottish community in Cherry Valley, Otsego County, New York. The Americans had never come to terms with the Indians on their western frontiers; they had annexed vast amounts of Indian territory so that when war started the Indians were willing to be encouraged by the British to raid American settlements. The Mohawk, Joseph Brant, formed an alliance with the notorious John Butler of Butler's Rangers. This force massacred forty or more families in Cherry Valley in 1778; a few refugees were able to return after the war to start reconstructing the settlement.[6]

Emigration was reduced to a trickle from about 1741 to 1763 though, as we have seen, many men were transported after the '45 rebellion. There appears to have been an abortive emigration from Jura to North Carolina in 1754; Captain Neill Campbell had failed to find passengers waiting for him in Jura but he thought he would nevertheless eventually find a full complement. Meantime the owners advertised the snow *Argyll* to be ready to sail between March and July 1755 and that a minister, Mr Neill McLeod, was ready to go with any intending emigrants.[7] No record of this sailing has been found.

Baronial empire

Then came a demand for more soldiers during the Seven Years' War between 1756 and 1763. Although much of the action took place on the continent of Europe the campaigns in India and in America were of paramount importance to Britain: French influence in these countries was greatly diminished and the foundations of the British Empire were laid. The ending of this war meant that the landed classes could turn their attention to more peaceful matters such as the development of the newly won territories in America. They hoped to create baronial holdings by encouraging their surplus tenants at home to go and work some of the empty lands that were being granted by the government. Scotsmen who received titles to land in Florida included Alexander Wedderburne, Lord Chancellor, Col. Robertson, barrack-master general, and Lord Adam Gordon. Those who did not take up their grants included the Duke of Buccleuch and the bankers James and Thomas Coutts. Grants in the other provinces - 82 acres in Nova Scotia, 65 acres in New York, 41 acres in West Florida and 11 acres in Quebec - came to over two million acres.[8]

The vast tracts of land in *America* which have been ceded to His Majesty by the late treaty of peace, contain such a variety of soil, as, with proper culture, would supply us with all the materials for our manufactures, that are produced in hot climates; and even with many of our most expensive luxuries. These materials are, at present, purchased in countries where we are constantly liable to have the price raised upon us by our rivals in trade. A large extensive dominion, without inhabitants, must be an expense, in lieu of an advantage, to the mother country; at the same time the utmost attention is necessary, not to nourish vipers in our bosom by bringing in an improper kind of inhabitants.

So wrote Archibald Menzies from Mergeny Castle in Perthshire on 23rd October 1763. He suggested that these lands in Florida should be cultivated by oppressed peoples brought from countries bordering the eastern Mediterranean Sea.[9] Indeed Dr Andrew Turnbull, a Scots physician in London accepted the challenge and took over 1000 people from that region although he settled them, not in Florida, but in New Smyrna, Georgia in 1770.[10]

In 1763 Lord Shelburn (President of the Board of Trade and Foreign Plantations) was concerned with the exorbitant grants of land in America in favour of individuals. The matter was discussed in a memorandum to him:

the settlement and population of the colonies has by this means [.i.e. huge grants] been retarded and every good end expected from such population frustrated and disappointed ... some grantees by companies and individuals were all right but many more ... entirely neglecting the lands so granted or by insisting upon terms which effectually prevented the settlement of them; and indeed many patentees rather desired their lands should remain uncultivated till the improvement of the adjacent country rendered them of greater value.

The memorialist suggested that there might be restrictions on acquiring too much land, for 1000 acres of good land were not equal to 5 or 10,000 acres of poor land. Perhaps the Governor should copy the rules laid down in Carolina where a single person acquired 100 acres but the head of a family 50 acres more for each member of the family - children, servants and slaves - on oath that no other land had been granted to them. The survey of the land should go to the Secretary's office to process a grant, not just a warrant of survey. The Governor should send annual returns to the Board of Trade and should have a proper map. The granting of land should lie in the Governor's hands not in England where ministers were too easily impressed by paper schemes.[11]

Florida

Florida was ceded to Great Britain by the Treaty of Paris in 1763 but reverted to Spain in 1783 and many of the British settlers then left. In the meantime, between 1764 and 1770 the Privy Council issued 227 Orders in Council for lands in East Florida, amounting to nearly three million acres. Only 121 of the 227 Orders were taken to the Council in St Augustine, which conveyed the titles for all but seven. The first Governor (1763-71) was James Grant of Ballindalloch, who had been involved in the Seven Years' War. He started a plantation and was said to have been very helpful to new settlers. Others who made settlements included Richard Oswald of Mount Oswald, John Tucker and Sir William Duncan. It was reported that several people destined for East Florida reached Charleston in December 1767; and in January 1772, 60 people from

Skye, part of a group of 300 who had landed in N. Carolina, reached the area under their leader, John Bethune, a minister from Prebost in Skye. Bethune became a chaplain to the Loyalists during the War of American Independence and was taken prisoner. After the war he eventually settled in Glengarry County, Canada, on land he had been granted by the British government.[12]

In 1767 Lord Adam Gordon and other gentlemen took out grants for land in Florida,

> at five years end to pay quit rent for half our quantity and at the expiry of ten years to commence quit rent for the whole, some 10 some 20 thousand acres, some 5, I find in general however Gentlemen who are accustomed to these country lands, prefer taking up their land, on the spot, by Family right, from the Governor, rather than by Grant from Home. I have some in both ways.[13]

The Earl of Cassilis was another member of the aristocracy in Scotland who was involved in the purchase of lands, called the Mount Royal plantation, in East Florida. In 1767 William Stork wrote from London to the Earl that he intended going to Florida in a few days' time to "begin some frugal plan, and to place at first five white men servants, consisting of three carpenters, one cooper and an overseer together with ten negroes upon your estate". Scots white servnts were preferred to Englishmen on account of their industry and sobriety; they were covenanted for eight years; at the end of which time each would receive £20 and 50 acres of land "with some encouragement to settle upon your Lordship's barony". It cost £10 per head to engage these servants, fit them out for the voyage and transport them. In comparison, the negroes from Carolina or Georgia would cost between £36 and £40 per head because of the demand for them in East Florida, for "they had to be used to the different cultivations". Other expenses for this enterprise would be about £70 for tools and implements, £100 for a survey and locating the lands and the remaining £500 for the purchase of negroes and a stock of cattle. William Stork intended starting his labours in Florida by clearing and fencing "a due proportion of ground and compleating houses for the people". As soon as he was raising sufficient vegetables and other grains for sustenance, Stork hoped to start cultivating cotton and indigo or whatever seemed most suitable.

The Mount Royal plantation did not have a happy start. Because of their starving condition four of the negroes had to be transferred to James Grant's plantation until the Earl could decide what to do with them. Two of the three carpenters had been discharged "in order to get rid of their claim for £20 a piece when their time was elapsed". In the light of this fiasco James Grant advised the Earl of Cassilis, who had apparently acquired a further grant of land, to send

> an intelligent good farmer from the country who is well known to you and who you can certainly depend upon. He will soon become an American planter and will easily acquire the proper method of managing your slaves.

Grant further advised that some seasoned negroes should head the team so as to help the new overseer and that it would be more economical to start with 30 rather than 20 negroes.[14]

One of Scotland's leading agricultural improvers, Sir Archibald Grant of Monymusk, was caught up in the post-war speculative fever. In 1764 he set out his thoughts on the advantages of acquiring land in North America, a country which would become "the grand seat of empire and all it's concomitants". He favoured, on the whole, an area on either side of the Bay of Fundy especially near St John's River and opposite Halifax, or in the South near Pensicola, Mobile or on the Mississippi River. He thought new land could be settled "without injury to private estate or mother country because all countries and estates ... have some people ambitious, avaricious or somehow uneasy or whimsical which will make them ramble to army or somewhere abroad", not to mention "some whose absence is the best improvement as they corrupt others while they remain". He himself was too old to think of going abroad but he was willing to advance £5,000 or £6,000 and would "find in Scotland at least 100 families of sufficient substance to move and settle themselves, each of whom would carry some underlings with them to manage sub-grants or leases". He could even find Protestants from Ireland, or elsewhere, willing to go.[15]

Sir Archibald sent out two men in 1767 with detailed instructions as to the sort of land they should look for, how to set about looking for it and what to do while negotiations were proceeding. Before they went the men were to provide themselves with notebooks and pencils for writing "in the field, or when in company" when it would be difficult to use pen and ink; they were to jot down anything that occurred so that as soon as they had leisure, for instance on the journey home, they could each make a fair copy, but without collusion so that nothing would be forgotten. The men were to travel via London so while waiting for a ship they were to fill their time by "enquiring at Dyers and Druggists what drugs come from that or similar countries and if possible get small specimens from them and Prices". They were also to learn about the trees and herbs they would find.

Once in America the men were to consider possible lands with regard to such things as their soil and water potential; if it was possible to grow rice; the position with regard to navigable rivers and seas.

> If you meet with any Indians whether you have an interpreter or not make all possible signs of friendship and confidence by bowing and putting hands to mouth yet take care not to give them or but very little liquor if you have it.

The men were to look for indications of wet or dry climate from the types of natural vegetation; the possibilities of the lumber trade and "the prices and kinds of negroes how fed, clothed and managed; likewise the price and sort of all bestial, male and female and all sorts of poultrie and how fed all the year and management of them for work or any uses". There was no possibility of the men having any leisure for

> When location is finished or fixed upon, not to lose time whilst it is going threw the forms choose a proper place for a small garden, I mean by small one or two or more acres as circumstances determine and try to clear as much of that as you can. When trees are cut down roll them in heaps in lines to gain spaces between and dig or scratch the ground as you can or are advised and sow even betwixt the roots of the trees such seeds as you get out with you or can produce in that countrie for present use or for tryal or accommodation some that may be sent. Especially some of different turnips, peas, veaches, clovers, lucern, potatoes, some sorts of kail especially sea kail, asparagus, lavender, flowers, saffron, rhubarb, etc. also some stones of European fruits and seeds or plants of pimento, cotton, coffee, Indian and Guinea corn or what else is advised. What are of importance and take time to grow and can be planted as a nursery to be transported afterwards at proper distances. Dig and sow first as it is supposed nothing will instantly disturb the seeds and inclosing will be easy by splitting wood for stakes

and rails at least stakes upright one end in the ground and rails on top to bind all by nails or auger and holes, by which some acres may be soon inclosed. If necessary the stakes may be so close and strong and high as may be a fence against any animal and you can if needful place your hut within it ... Be sure to try the different strata in different parts and in all three locations as deep as you can, and if time allows build as advised one or more huts to be ready for others that may be sent, also to inclose and cultivate with grasses etc, more land for a person and food for bestial, poultry etc. Try if you could confine swine that could live and breed in them of your absence.

Presumably their report favoured development in the South for Sir Archibald received a charter for a grant of 20,000 acres of land in East Florida in 1771 on condition that he settled the land "with foreign Protestants or persons that shall be brought out from other colonies in N. America within ten years ... in the proportion of one person for every 100 acres". If one third of the land was not settled within three years the whole was to be forfeited and that part not settled within ten years to revert to the Crown. The charter was given under the great seal by James Grant Esq Governor and Commander in Chief. The outbreak of war probably put an end to Sir Archibald's plans for he did not send any settlers to his new lands.[16]

New York state

Early groups of Scots had settled near Albany in New York State; they were soon to be joined by others of their countrymen after the Seven Years' War. A key figure in the colonising of upper New York State was Sir William Johnson. Sir William was born in Ireland in 1715 and had emigrated before 1738 to New York where he prospered in the fur trade. His dealings with the Indians were regarded as fair and reasonable by both Indians and government. He bartered huge chunks of Indian land in exchange for peace and for many years was the Manager for Indian Affairs. At one time he was Governor of New York State. Having been granted 100,000 acres of land in the Mohawk Valley for services in the French War, Sir William built up his own empire which was supposed to be one of the largest estates in the Colonies.

I am the only person in these parts who (far from preventing) takes measures for settling the lands which I purchase by the encouragement of industrious people to whom I grant lotts on the most reasonable terms.[17]

Hence he was more than willing to accept any potential settlers and encouraged Scottish landowners to take up grants of land to perpetuate a Scottish feudal landowning system in America. Sir William had been responsible for helping to found Hebron (Washington County) by grants to discharged men of Montgomery's Highlanders. In 1764 Captain John Campbell, late of the 42nd regiment, had applied for a tract of land; and in the following year Lieutenant James Macdonald had been granted 10,000 acres.[18]

The government had accepted Pitt's advice in 1757 and adopted a policy of conciliation towards the Highland Jacobite families. Letters of service had therefore been granted to the Hon. Simon Fraser (son of Lord Lovat who had been forfeited and executed for his share in the '45) to raise a Highland regiment (the 78th) from his family's territories which were vested in the Crown. Such was the influence of the Chief of Clan Fraser that, though possessing neither money nor land, he had managed to recruit upwards of 600 men within a few weeks. The gentlemen of the country and the officers of the regiment had raised a further 700 men, so that a battalion was soon formed. The regiment saw service mainly in Canada and Nova Scotia and at the end of the war a number of the officers and men took their discharge locally and received a grant of land.[19] One of the officers was Hugh Fraser who hoped for 100 acres for each of the people he had brought out in 1764 "and something more for himself, in which case he says he will use his endeavours to bring over more of his countrymen from the encouragement he may receive". Sir William Johnson supported Fraser's request and petitioned Sir Cadwallader Colden, Governor of New York State, on his behalf. Fraser settled in Albany and engaged in the linen industry.[20]

Lord Adam Gordon also became involved in a land transaction in New York state. In 1767 he and the Duke of Atholl wished Sir William to find them 10,000 acres near the Mohawk River and to tell them the price

and what cultivation you would most recommend to us, we are determined to set about settling it immediately, either by appointing an agent there, and granting it out to those who desire to be our tenants; or by sending out to it some people from Scotland, Ireland and Germany, as we can get them. But all will depend on a report from you. The Duke has entered much into the spirit of it and means it for an establishment for his second son, Lord James Murray, who comes into our line and is to be under your humble servant, next war, and an *American* of course. I should not have thought of such an acquisition but as you have been so kind as to think of me I am very thankful to you for it; and I hope to see it before I die. I would keep that is nearest you for myself to be called in the survey *New Huntly* and what is to be for Lord James Murray, *New Atholl*. It will be a good retreat when the sun is too much for me in East Florida.[21]

John Watts, Lord Adam's agent in New York wrote to Sir William later in the year that

As my Lord Adam's head is full of matrimony, he desires me to write to you, but for what purpose I don't see, as the Joshua and Caleb he has sent to view the Land of Promise will be able to tell you ten times more of their errand than I can. All that is wanted of any of us or all of us together, as I apprehend, is to aid them in getting to this land of promise, to give them such information as they desire and let them return, with their own story, as soon as may be, to prevent the accumulation of expenses, as his Lordship and his noble associates are to pay the bill of cost attending this experiment. It will have a happy effect if such people as these from conviction of their own eyes, set the example of colonising to their neighbours, and for that reason, I think they should have as favourable terms as can be afforded, otherwise their minds will be certainly poisoned with the ignominy, disgrace and disadvantage of being tenants in this wide country of freedom, where all want to be independent and masters in the highest sense, especially men of any property or substance.[22]

Rev. Thomas Bateman from Boston in Lincolnshire, England wrote to Sir William,

Lord Adam Gordon from the report the two persons made of the situation of his lands and their great distance from a navigable river, apprehended his making a settlement upon them as he proposed would be attended with too great an expense and therefore dropped the design notwithstanding the great number of persons who declared themselves ready to embark.

To which Sir William replied:

I am sorry to hear from you that Lord Adam Gordon has dropped his design of making a settlement to the westward of this place as the lands are good in general and the situation not so inconvenient as may be imagined from a cursory view at an improper season.

Lord Adam wrote to Sir William about his decision:

I am most particularly in your debt for the clear, candid and sensible state of the carrying place
and what might attend a settlement there in the present situation of things which are really so
confused and awkward, I confess I lose hope of seeing them mend in America and I therefore
drop all present intentions, of doing anything there, and sorry I am to say, we are just as bad at
home ... but the confusions in America and expenses of fitting out our colonists have *scared*
both the Duke of Atholl and me and we are determined to suspend for some time any plans or
intentions either of us had formed in that corner of the globe - at the same time I would wish
to continue in possession of the land you procured for me (near the German Flats in Oneida
County), if it can be held without any immediate very considerable outlay, otherways I will
dispose of it, to whom, and in what manner you shall like best.[23]

A patent for a grant of land was taken out in February 1769 and endorsed in February
1771; it consisted of 10,000 acres of land above Cosby's Manor, the patent fees were

25s per 1000 acres with the expense of survey and Indian purchase, etc comes to about £37 10s
New York money for every 1000 acres and is much cheaper than land purchased at that time
or than can ever be had again, for the Indians in proportion as their possessions decrease in
quantity raise the price of the rest, and discover much more of interest and cunning in these
matters than they did a few years since.[24]

Later that year Lord Adam wrote to Sir William that:

marriage put a stop to my American plans of improvement, and quickened those at home, for
I think two or three seasons more will compleat the plan of everything I possess in Britain, it
consists of about 750 acres and I am hopeful to bring it to a neat £1000 per annum, after which
I shall be more free and more able to do something in America.[25]

The Great Glen Emigration

If the Scottish nobility largely failed in their efforts at planting feudal colonies, Sir
William Johnson made a notable success. He encouraged one group of tacksmen and
their followers to transplant the Scottish way of life overseas. The Glengarry Highlanders, whose native home was in the vicinity of the Great Glen, were forced to flee an
incompetent landowner, to settle briefly on the frontier in New York state, to become
refugees from the Revolution and to serve the Crown in the army before settling and
eventually prospering in Glengarry, Canada. There, over the years, they were joined by
many more of their clansmen. James Willox at Polmally wrote in January 1773,

there is an association in Glenmoriston for America already (tho' the lands are low rented) and
begins to make a noise in this country ... Finlay Cameron in Lossit is to displenish at Whitsunday
and go for America, he has some friends there since last war and some of the gentlemen in the
country help him to correspond with them he being illiterate himself.[26]

We have a first-hand account from Dr Johnson of the innkeeper at Anoch who could
not carry on because his rent had been raised twice as high as he could afford. This man

was "by no means an ignorant or weak man; there were books in the cottage, among which were some volumes of Prideau's Connections; this man's conversation we were glad of while we staid". His proprietor

does not, with all his pressure upon his tenants, raise more than four hundred pounds a year for near one hundred square miles, or sixty thousand acres. He let us know that he had forty head of cattle, an hundred goats and an hundred sheep, upon a farm he remembered let at five pound a-year, but which he now paid twenty.[27]

This man was being forced to join the 70 men who had left Glenmoriston in 1772 as a result of

the general dissatisfaction which is now driving the Highlanders into the other hemisphere. When asked whether they would stay at home, if they were well treated, he answered with indignation that no man willingly left his native country.[28]

Duncan MacDonell of Glengarry had become the focus of the malaise in Glenmoriston. He had come of age in 1768 and for the first time for many years a chief had taken control of the estate. It was heavily in debt and to avoid the complete disposal of the lands, the chief tenants and wadsetters offered to surrender their tacks and wadsets and rent their farms for a higher rent. A wadset was a mortgage in which the landowner pledged some of his land in return for a loan but with the reserve power of recovering his land on repayment of the loan. A tenant thus became a wadsetter, a quasi landowner rising to the rank of gentleman. Surrendering the wadsets was therefore a gesture of the highest order of clanship, the abuse of which could not ever be contemplated. Yet after his marriage to Marjorie Grant in 1772 Glengarry (a gentleman was known by the name of his estate), decided that the land no longer belonged to all the clansmen and re-let the estate on commercial principles. The remaining wadsetters were given notice and offered tenancies on more stringent terms. To crown it all, the higher rents were spent on ostentatious living rather than on agricultural improvements.(Fig. 4.1.)

It was three of these wadsetters who led the emigration to America in 1773 - Alan Macdonell of Cullochy and his two brothers, John Macdonell of Leek and Alexander Macdonell of Aberchalder. They were accompanied by their brother-in-law Ronald Macdonell of Ardnabee and a first cousin, John Macdonell of Scotus. All had been "out" with Bonnie Prince Charlie in the '45 and all had taken tacks from MacDonell of Glengarry. Their connection with North America was through Leek's second son Archibald who had emigrated to New York some time earlier and had become a businessman and an acquaintance of Sir William Johnson. It was upon Archibald's advice that the Macdonell clan in Glengarry decided to emigrate.(Fig. 4.2) Bishop Hay was concerned about these and other Highland Catholics:

As everything has the most gloomy prospect with them they want nothing but a proper opportunity to go to America and save the little subsistence they have rather than it should be eaten away at home and fall a prey to their rapacious masters. This being the case then it naturally occurred that if they could get a colony of themselves in one place where they could have all freedom in religion it would be infinitely preferable, and the persecution in Uist arising at the same time has made many of the leading people among them enter more ardently into the scheme hoping that if the ire were once broken and the masters made sensible that their people could have an asylum elsewhere they would alter their measures with them.[29]

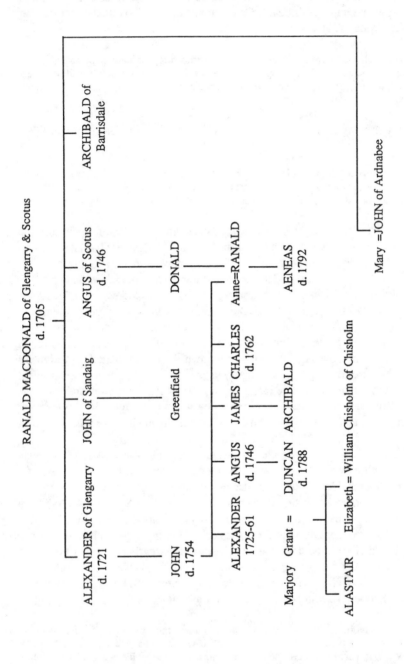

Fig. 4/1 The MacDonalds of Glengarry

Families began to assemble at Fort William from over a wide area - Glengarry, Glenmoriston, Glenurquhart and Strathglass - to await the arrival of the *Pearl* from Greenock.[30] Between 300 and 400 people embarked at Fort William on August 20th 1773.[31](Figs. 4.3 & 4.4) The MacDonells had a "charming" passage of six weeks' duration arriving at New York on October 18th.[32] The mayor and corporation of New York were so impressed by such a colourful and large body of Highlanders that they laid on a banquet. The hosts, however, considered it unbecoming to ask any mere merchant to dine with gentlemen and so Archibald, at whose suggestion they had come to America, was not summoned to the feast. The Highland gentlemen did not disappoint their hosts for they turned up in full Highland dress with belted plaid and armed with broadsword, dirk and pistols.

The families soon moved to Albany where they were to stay the winter. Alan Macdonell wrote to Sir William Johnson on 14th November about the possibility of acquiring lands, possibly adjoining Lord Adam Gordon's or near the Sesquehanna for four recent immigrants had spoken very favourably of that situation to his friends. They asked the "set of the fee simple" and the conditions for saw or grist mills, fish or fowl; but reminded Sir William that:

> customs and carriages was a nuisance in the Mother Country and the cause of removing thence many of its inhabitants and the latest of them do not incline to be the first introducers of it by compact in the New World.

Macdonell hoped that the people with him would stay and that others of his countrymen might follow:

> if Sir William gives the encouragement their sobriety and industry will merit. The principle of which is a year's maintenance to each family that will settle upon his estate: for which they would become bound to pay him. If their endeavours are found worthy of a cow and horse or the value it's hoped they will be indulged in it upon giving security for principal and interest ... Should any of us calling ourselves gentlemen incline to remove after a few years expense and toil in clearing lands etc it is hoped Sir William will agree to accept of their plantation at the appreciation or estimation of honest men mutually chosen.[34]

Sir William settled them at Kingsbury (later renamed Gloversville).

The families' spiritual needs were attended to by the Rev John McKenna, an Irish priest who had been born within ten miles of Sir William's birthplace, but had spent five years ministering in Lochaber and Badenoch. Under the aegis of Sir William, Father McKenna was safe from harm although an act of Governor Belamont's time still stood on the statute book forbidding priests to enter the Province. Isolated on the frontier, not only by culture and language, but also by religion, the settlers knew little of the politics that were engulfing the colonies at the time. They soon found themselves denounced as Tories, papists and friends of British tyranny by the older established colonists. Rightly so as it turned out for both priest and people

> did in good earnest appear for the Interests of the Mother Country, holding out with arms that part of the country for His Majesty in Anxious Hope of Support.

Congress complained that "The Roman Catholic Highlanders in and about Johnston have armed themselves to the number of one hundred and fifty, ready to aid in the

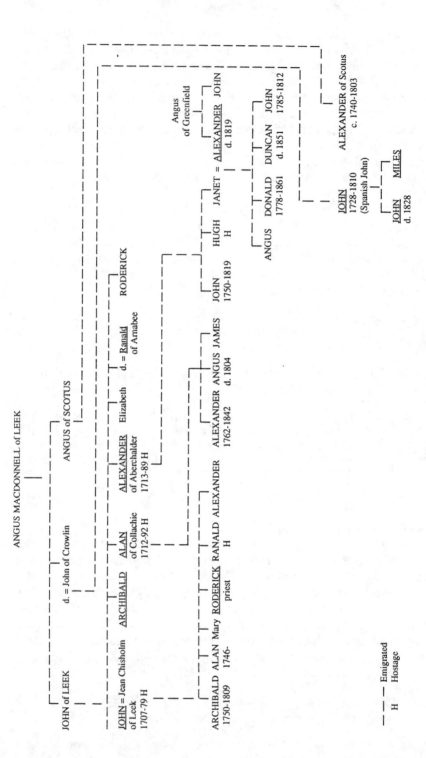

Fig. 4/2 Some of the Glengarry emigrants

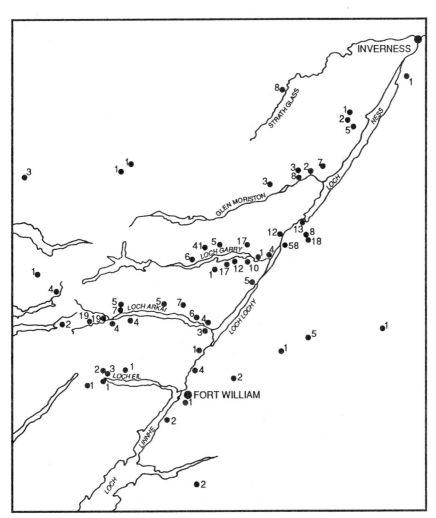

Fig. 4.3   The Glengarry emigrations of 1773 showing the settlements and the numbers of emigrants.

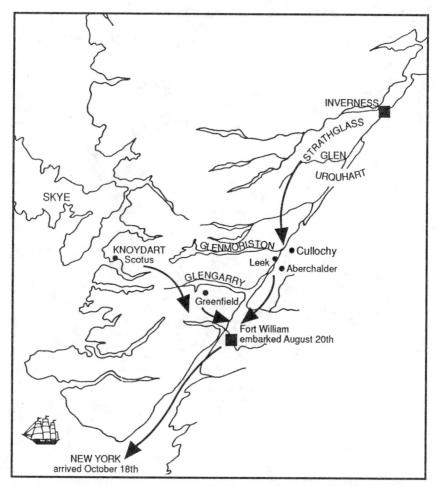

Fig. 4/4   The Great Glen emigration, showing the paths of the Glengarry emigrants who embarked at Fort William on August 20th, 1773 for New York.

suppression of any outbreak in favor of the growing cause of Liberty".[35]

In Edinburgh Bishop Hay saw this emigration in its wider perspective:

> The consequence of this will be that numbers more will go off next year who only waited accounts of their success to follow their example; and I don't wonder at it for it is incredible what misery and wretchedness is everywhere throughout I may say all this country especially in the Highlands. The oppressive measures are still pursued with unrelenting rigour and forcing numbers of families to run about the country to beg their bread to keep themselves from starving. This town is like a common refuge to which numbers have recourse in hope of finding help and relief but alas! they find themselves greatly disappointed; the amazing multitudes of poor and universal distress for want of money, making it impossible to get that help for them of which they stand in need.[36]

It was not just amongst the Catholic Highlanders that Sir William encouraged settlers. Vigorous recruiting was going on on his behalf in other quarters. Rev Harry Munro, a native of Dingwall, went to North America in 1757 as Episcopal chaplain to the 77th Regiment. At the end of the war he returned to Britain for a few years, then went back to America where he became rector of St Peter's Church, Albany. He introduced Daniel Urquhart who hoped to settle near his fellow countrymen. Munro admitted that he barely knew the man though he had seen a certificate of good character signed by the parish minister in Scotland. In 1773 Rev Harry Munro wrote to Sir William:

> The bearer hereof will inform you that there are 17 families just now arrived here. They are looking out for land and have applied to me as their countryman for advice. Much pains have been taken to keep them near Albany; but I have at last persuaded them to pay you a visit. You have land enough and these poor people may in time prove useful and good tenants, especially under so generous a landlord as Sir William Johnson. They have assured me, that they are under no particular engagements, and I flatter myself they will find your proposal agreeable.
>
> My only motive in this is purely friendship to your family and a grateful sense of the many civilities received from you.
>
> I am not personally acquainted with these people but have seen their credentials and testimonials, containing a fair unblemished character. By letters from Scotland it appears that the lower class of people are generally discontented and the spirit of emigration prevails greatly: and if these will like your proposals, I have reason to think some hundreds of families will soon follow. The 17 families make in all 70 souls including the women and children.[37]

These people from Rosshire had sailed from Dublin on the *Britannia* at the end of March 1773 and arrived in New York about the 15th May. Colonel Philip Skene, originally from Fife, had first gone to America as a soldier in 1756. After the war he acquired an estate on Connecticut River and was soon able to induce 30 families and some indentured servants to his land. Nearly 300 ex-soldiers decided to settle on his estate and it was to this land that the Rossshire party was first directed. However they preferred to settle on Sir William Johnson's estate near Albany.[38] The following year Sir William wrote to John Donnell

> that the Highland families who settled here last year are doing very well and so I hope will those who settled here lately. They are about 40 families in all, a very heavy burthen on me I assure you and full as much as I can bear, but should they prove industrious and get forward, it would heighten my happiness there being nothing on earth delights me more than to see the rude woods made cultivable and afford sustenance to the poor and distressed.[39]

Another party from the Great Glen left in 1774. It was reported that Lt. William Grant and his family and about 150 other people from Urquhart and Glenmoriston had boarded a ship in Fort William to sail to Mull where they would join the *Moore*, going to New York. Lt. Grant was said to have rented "a considerable farm", but an extravagant rent had obliged him to abandon it. Many of the steerage passengers were poor to the point of being indented.[40]

Despite the efforts of Sir William Johnson many of the Scottish settlements in New York state did not last, for most of the Highlanders remained loyal to the government amd in due course moved north to Canada. The attempts to establish baronial estates in America were inevitably doomed to failure and ended with the outbreak of war. The ties that bound clansmen to their chief had already been loosened if not destroyed by events in Scotland, and the circumstances of settlement and the whole social atmosphere in North America were profoundly opposed to feudalism. The harsh realities of land and climate, the sheer struggle for survival in the early years, the belief in their right to land of their own, were the dominating factors in the settlers' lives. By the time some stability had been achieved, old ways of thinking had gone forever and a different pattern of society was accepted.

5

"Got With Propierty"

Sir James Montgomery

European settlement in St John's Island (later renamed Prince Edward Island) began in 1720 when a French fishing company established a base there. The company soon left, but fear of British intrusion caused the French authorities to send troops in 1726, to maintain French sovereignty and to convince the settlers to stay. In spite of appeals to France no fort was built and the settlement was captured and burned by British colonial troops in 1745. Returned by treaty to France it was again surrendered to the British in 1758 and annexed to the government of Nova Scotia in 1763.

The forces under Lord Rollo which had helped in the defeat of the French at Quebec in 1759 had been sent to St John's Island to expel the French settlers (Acadians) and those refugees who had fled from Nova Scotia and Cape Breton Island during the war. A scheme of settlement put forward by Lord Egmont (First Lord of the Admiralty) in 1764 envisaged the whole of St John's Island being made over to him as his own private kingdom. The government rejected this fantasy and ordered a survey of the island to be made by the soldiers. They then helped to build the capital, Charlottetown, before the garrison was withdrawn in 1768. The island was granted a separate government the following year. Meantime some of the British settlers who had arrived from England and from New England were becoming restive by November 1766 and were threatening to return home "unless something speedy was done as to the distribution of lands there".[1]

As a result of the survey, the island was divided into 67 townships, each of 20,000 acres.(Fig. 5.1) and in 1767 the Board of Trade and Plantations undertook a lottery of the various townships. In this way many ex-army and navy officers received a grant upon very easy terms - a quit rent of six shillings per 100 acres reserved to His Majesty, his heirs and successors was levied on each of 26 lots; four shillings on 29 lots and two shillings on 11 lots. Some land in each township was to be set aside for public buildings, a church and a school. Government was to have the reservation of all mines of gold, silver and coals. It was ordained:

That the Grantees of each Township do settle the same within ten years from the date of the Grant, in the proportion of one person for every 200 acres; that if one-third of the land is not settled in the above proportion within four years from the date of the grant, the whole to be forfeited to His Majesty, his Heirs and Successors; That the settlers so to be introduced, be Protestants from such parts of Europe as are not within His Majesty's dominion, or such persons as have resided in His Majesty's dominions in America for two years antecedent to the date of the Grant.[2]

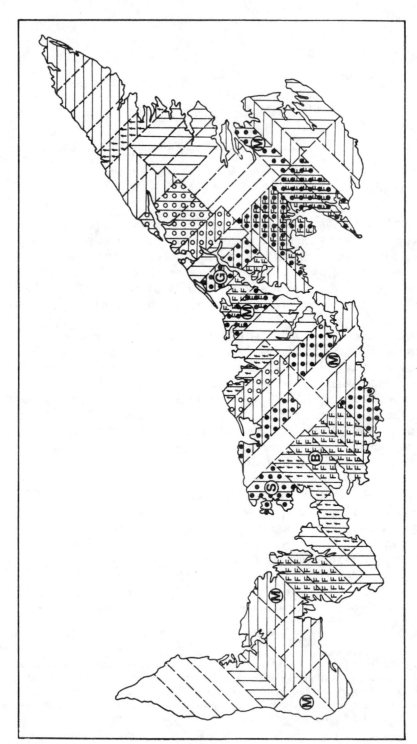

Fig. 5/1   The 67 lots of St. John's Island (Prince Edward Island) showing the progress of settlement in the eightenth century.

On the surface a lottery appeared a reasonably fair way of dealing with the problem, but beneath the procedure lay a murky world of wheeling and dealing. One of the most active in this twilight world was Sir James Montgomery, Lord Advocate of Scotland. He was an improving laird from Peeblesshire, a member of the Board of Trustees for Fisheries and Manufacturers and a Commissioner for the Forfeited Estates. On 3rd August 1767 he wrote to John Spottiswoode at the Inner Temple, London:

I was favoured with your letter some days ago giving me an account of my fate in the island of St John's being determined, but have been so much hurried of late as not to have time either to think or write about the American acquisition. However, I lay hold of the first spare minutes to return you my sincere and hearty thanks for your care and attention in this matter and to suggest what occurs to me upon the subject proper for your consideration and further attention.

I like your description of Mr Dickson's No.37 lott very much and it is probable that Mr Murray's No.30 is a tolerable good one. I have a letter from Mr Pringle who says that his No.51 which lies at the head of one of the three rivers is reported to be a good one tho' inland, so it is likely the worst of them has been drawn in my name. It was lucky you did not agree to the proposal of taking the lotts following if mine came up first and was to regulate, but if I had been present the conveniency of contiguity is so great that it would have determined me to have had two lotts thrown together by the method proposed and this leads me to beg that you will endeavour to acquire a lott contiguous to Mr Dickson's by exchange if you happen to know any gentlemen who have got lotts contiguous to it.

If one person is permitted to have in his name more lotts than one I would like to have as many in my name as can be got with propriety; at any rate I would wish to have Mr Dickson's lott in my name if it can be done, and mine put in his. And whatever authority is wanted either from Mr Murray or Mr Dickson for the grant of their lotts being made out in my name or for my exchanging with Mr Dickson; you have only to send me a copy of what is proper to be wrote, and I will get them to write whatever is thought necessary for the purpose. I am for allowing Mr Pringle's lott to remain in his own name at any rate because so many coming into my name might create suspicion which is to be avoided.

Upon looking at the map of the island you will easily determine the lotts that would suit most with Mr Dickson's and if a little money could be useful in bringing about an exchange, or if a contiguous lott could be purchased at a small price I would not grudge the money. But money will not operate with gentlemen who go upon such adventure unless the half pay officers have got lotts, many of whom cannot settle them.

I imagine Mr Murray's lott is not too different from Mr Dickson's and absolute contiguity is not necessary tho' eligible if it can be got. But when lotts are distant it renders the settling often more difficult and expensive.

Learn from the map if you can the quantity of cleared ground in each lott of mine and enquire into the nature and size of the trees if you happen to see any person who is acquainted with the island and lotts.

P.S. I presume the instruments and conditions are not yet settled as you say nothing of them. Enquire into the intentions of the Board of Trade as to the marking and marching the lotts upon the ground.[3]

Clearly, we have here a government minister doing his best behind a shield of nominees to accumulate a massive holding of some thousands of acres in St John's Island, quite at variance with government policy. In a letter of 16th [blank] 1767 Sir James again wrote to his man in London:

Enclosing this is an ostensible letter wrote with a view of its being shown or transmitted to Lord Clare if circumstances should lead you to judge such a step to be proper. I observe and think myself much obliged in your attention to this affair and I doubt not of its having the desired success. Major Maclean knows of my being a petitioner, but nothing of the other manoeuvre which I beg may be kept a secret from all. If you have mentioned anything of it to the Major let me know it. As Mr Pringle has not spoke with Lord Clare you may judge how far it may be prudent to avoid the appearance of taking any concern in that while under the consideration of the Board unless circumstances should render it necessary. I shall write to Mr Pringle by this post and recommend his endeavouring to get as large and good tracts as possible ...

P.S. When you see Major Maclean tell him I have received his letter and will attend to its contents.

P.S. Keep me advised of what is done and of what you can learn as to the Board of Trade's intentions as to [?the lottery].

P.S. Since writing this I have wrote the letter which will cover it and in my apprehension, if you should have no opportunity of communicating the contents to Lord Clare it would not be improper for you to transmit it to him, in a letter, at the time you think it can be of most use.[4]

Preparations for sending over emigrants took time. Sir James was a Commissioner of the Annexed Estates and was thus aware of problems created on the estates as a result of improvements. From 1756 some of the tenants were removing their sub-tenants; although some stayed as day labourers others were expected to find work elsewhere or to emigrate. But the new arrangements did not suit everyone and there was continued unrest on the Athole estate in Perthshire. Complaints of oppression reached the Commissioners in 1767.[5] Sir James engaged David Lawson, a tenant in the mill of Callander, Perthshire, on 20th June 1769. He was to take

charge of a farm or plantation of mine in the island of St John; and you being to contract with servants to go out with you; I hereby impower you to enter into agreements with them in the terms specifyed in our articles and oblige myself to relieve you of all the obligations you come under in such contracts.

Having signed the formal contract on October 30th 1769 to take charge of lot 34 as "grieve or overseer", Lawson was entitled to half of the profits of the farm, during the seven years of the contract, deducting servants' wages and money advanced by Sir James for stocking the farm. Lawson was also to

hyre in Scotland such number of servants as he judged to be necessary, to whom such wages shall be given as shall be thought reasonable, to commence from the time of their landing upon the Island of St John, and whose freight and expences of going their shall be advanced by the sd Sir James Montgomery.[6]

Lawson engaged 60 men, mostly from Perthshire, who were to serve a four year indenture; after their service each man was to have from 200 to 500 acres of uncleared land without rent for four years, then to pay three pence an acre per year for 10 years, six pence per acre per year for the next 10 years and one shilling per acre yearly ever after in a lease for 1000 years. A cow or two was to be given to each man and some money to help him settle. Lawson received an account dated April 1770 for £1220.6.4 from Sir James "To cash advanced to you in Scotland and paid for sundry goods delivered to you per particular account and invoice signed by yourself".[7] The men sailed on the *Falmouth* which left Greenock on April 8th 1770 and arrived on the island on June 8th.

This emigration to the island is remembered by their descendants as being as historic as was the voyage of the *Mayflower*. We are fortunate that a detailed diary of the voyage was kept by Rev William Drummond who was to minister to his pioneer flock for just a year before seeking greener pastures in Canaan, Connecticut. On April 8th 1770

Drummond spent "the forenoon in Greenock buying several necessities. At midday went on board... at 5 afternoon the Captain came on board, anchor weighed and set sail".

Although the master had intended sailing north about Ireland, the winds forced him to sail down the Irish Sea and along the south coast of Ireland, bidding farewell to the British Isles at Cape Clear on the 12th. Sailing southwards in poor weather the passengers were seasick for eight miserable days with their leader, David Lawson, suffering more than most. By 30th April when they had reached latitude 45° 06' south the captain set his course due west, calculating each day's progress by dead reckoning, that is the distance sailed each day. Navigation was still a fairly inexact affair. The approach to American waters was confirmed when 60 fathoms was sounded, which in the case of the *Falmouth* occurred on May 19th. The fact that they had indeed reached the Grand Banks was born out by meeting several New England fishing schooners during the next few days. Yet the most perilous stage of the journey was still to come for they had to sail through fog, pack ice and the unpredictable gales of the Gulf of St Lawrence. On June 2nd the men set foot on St John's Island but their voyage was not yet over for they still had to sail along the coast to Stanhope Bay. They were met by other Scots, Irish and French families and were entertained by Indians who showed "their manner of dancing and scalping". The voyage ended on June 8th with the discharge of provisions and cargo.[8]

Sir James's emigrants were appalled at what they found, for the land which had sounded such a bargain in Scotland, leased at one shilling an acre, "they thought it cheap until they came out and saw it; but then they found it dear enough".[9] Furthermore Sir James had demanded that they take their own provisions; all they had to exist on was some oatmeal and salt water and no houses to live in. The families were settled at Stanhope (later Covehead) on lot 34 which Sir James had bought from the heirs of the original owner, his neighbour John Dickson, younger, of Kilbucho. It was two years before Lawson could begin to feed his family as he had to spend most of that time clearing the land and building a house. He was then able to build a grist mill and dam, but it was so closely surrounded by trees that it was burnt down when the trees went on fire; the same thing happened to the next mill and the third mill he built was carried off by the river flooding. The agent, David Higgins, was loathe to give him any seed grain and when he did get some, his crop was eaten by mice; this story is confirmed from other sources. When his servants' years of indenture were over he had to honour his agreement and give them milk cows. All in all this tenant's "scheme was totally overset for profit to myself or his lordship" and so was unable to pay any rent.[10] Now war interrupted and made the settling of accounts more difficult.

As an active farmer Sir James was aware that much flax seed was imported into Scotland from Philadelphia and dressed flax from Holland and the Baltic states, so he hoped that some of his settlers on St John's Island would grow flax and hemp. In fact Lawson did manage to grow flax "middling well" but not hemp.[11] He was also able to send back to Scotland 22 loads of timber in three years off his lands.

It was not until 1788, some 18 years after Lawson's arrival, that Sir James's son William, a lieutenant of the 4th Foot in Canada, got leave of absence and went to St John's Island unannounced. The assessors who went with William found matters even worse than anticipated; Lawson was dismissed and one of the assessors was appointed overseer in his place. After all those years of pioneering the enterprise showed losses of

£11,914.16.7½ (later reduced to £9219.12.2½). In the light of the conditions Lawson had had to face, the dismissal seems harsh, but later the huge debt was forgiven and Sir James Montgomery even awarded him a pension of £12 a year. He lived out his days in a log cabin on the Stanhope peninsula, and died c.1808. [12]

In 1769 Sir James Montgomery had also engaged David Higgins, an American shipmaster who owned part of lot 59, to go to St John's Island. Sir James furnished him with implements and other necessities for starting a farm. Higgins became storekeeper at Georgetown, was also the factor and developed lots 51 and 59 for fishing and timber. He improved the St Andrew's farm and built a grist mill and a saw mill on lot 59. However there was little profit in these activities for he had to advance money and goods to the settlers but received payment in kind because of the lack of specie in the island. [13] Like David Lawson, Higgins was no book-keeper and his money affairs with Sir James became more and more tangled. Sir James recalled him to London to discuss matters in 1774. Sir James wrote off Higgins's debts of about £4000 in return for his part of lot 59 including the buildings on it which Higgins had already conveyed to his relative Joe Prince, also another third in lot 59 and half of lot 12 which Higgins had, and a bond of £2400. He was made lessee to Sir James of two-thirds of lot 59, half lot 12, all lot 51 and of Panmure Island for £100 per annum. Higgins returned to St John's Island in the summer of 1775 with a ship, probably the *John and Elizabeth*, with trade goods financed by Sir James. A further disaster overtook him as the boat was taken by privateers on the voyage out to Canada and he had to pay a ransom. Although he became a pillar of St John's Island society, rising to become Naval Officer of the Island and one of the first members of the Council, and despite all his pioneering efforts, he met with a series of disasters and died bankrupt in 1783. [14]

By March 1770 Sir James had acquired four townships without leaving Scotland. There were by then five resident proprietors among the 150 British families who had settled on the island. Sir James described his investment as having been got "by favour of the Crown, my doing something to set the affair agoing became in some measure a matter of necessity and accidental circumstances attended with a reasonable prospect of advantage led me to go farther than I intended".

On April 14th Sir James wrote:

I like not to tempt providence she has been kind to me much above my desert or expectation, but neither do I like to decline her favour when thrown upon me. 80,000 acres of good land in an island of a good climate for grass, fortunately situated for a market, whereby a little discretion in management it only costs me the fees of office in passing the grants may be called a cast of Providence, as no other person whatever has been favoured so much in that matter. My purchase was only supplemental to assist the settling the whole more easily. At the same time it is a property out of which I may probably draw very little in my life, but having the prospect of a numerous family I hold it to be a concern of theirs and not of mine and in their time I do believe it may be something very considerable. All this to yourself, for I wish my concern in the island of St John to be as little known as possible as it carries too much the appearance of a project, when circumstances are not fully known. I desired Lewie Grant to manage the affair of the white negroes in such a manner as to incur as little observation as possible. There are more of them than I wished for, that is owing to their leader. It is not out of Scotland that I wish my lands to be settled and I have not sent a single man from any part I have a concern in. It is to the continent of America I trust for inhabitants.

But by the 24th April he had changed his tune completely:

> In my last I exhibited a kind of supplication as to my conduct with regard to the island of St John's, but if I had known the state of the expense attending the expedition of my white negroes as you call them I had not been so forward in that matter. In short I am exceedingly out of humour with the transaction. The expense is enormous and above double what it should have been and I have acted like a good natured fool that attends not to his affairs or situation. I think too my friend Lewie has been less attentive than he usually is or he would never have permitted such an advance of money. I profess I would rather never have sent a man to the island of St John than to have had that matter transacted as it has been done. But I moderate my wrath which is exceedingly great until I see the particular accounts. I retract what I said in my last letter of undertaking to satisfy you as to the propriety of my conduct for I profess this transaction as stated in Lewie's letter to me looks like an act of lunacy.[15]

For years Sir James continued to speculate. He eventually reckoned that he had expended more than £13,000 on his new estates with little financial return. It appears that he had drawn lot 7 in 1769 and in due course bought lots 30 and 51 from John Murray of Philiphaugh and John Pringle who had drawn them originally. Sir James acquired Panmure Island, Boughton Island and Lennox Island (all off Georgetown) in 1774 from Walter Patterson, Governor of St John's Island by agreement of the Privy Council for his "great zeal and activity in carrying on the settlement of the island"; this new grant was recommended as a reward "for His Majesty's service and the public good". In 1775 Sir James bought more land - two-thirds of lot 59 from Aitchison Mure merchant, Robert Cathcart and Captain David Higgins. He also acquired three-quarters of lot 34, part of which he leased to Sir Peter Stewart.[16]

Although the *Falmouth* became so famous, the first emigrants to this island had been some of the officers and men discharged from Fraser's Highlanders in 1768 when a party from the regiment was reported to have embarked, possibly on the *Alexandria* which left Greenock for the island on April 19th; there they had been granted lots 38-42 by the government.[17] These men may have been going to join others of their regiment who had been disbanded in Canada. A few months after the *Falmouth's* arrival, the barque *Annabella* arrived from Kintyre, in September 1770. On board were Robert Stewart, his family and 60 other families (about 200 people) to settle half of lot 18 (Malpeque) which had been granted to his brother-in-law Lieutenant-Colonel Robert Stewart. John Ramsay with his six sons and two nephews were on board, along with other families with the names McGowan, McKenzie, McIntosh, McArthur, English, McDougall, Sinclair, Murphy and McKay. The boat was wrecked just off the island but though the cargo was lost all the people survived. "Though they arrived late they are well housed, happy and contented ...". It is possible that Sir James and Robert Stewart arranged the passage of another 120 families that year, to settle Covehead and Three Rivers, while the *Edinburgh* carried a further cargo of about 100 passengers the following year (1771).[18]

Captain Dugald Stewart of Campbeltown brought home a settler's report from St John's Island in July 1771:

> He will tell you what a fine farm I have and what a neat house I have built, with barns and every other conveniency ... The settlers sent over by an honourable gentleman are doing very well; they indeed brought a good farmer with them also a very good man, a minister. When these people write to their friends I dare say we will have more sent over, as we are told they are

oppressed by their lairds; and here they will be lairds themselves. We are a distinct government, tax ourselves, and make our own laws. Our governor is a good sort of man, the lieutenant governor is soon expected with about 200 from Londonderry, but we like the Scots much better.[19]

Two advertisements were circulating in Scotland praising the island. In 1772 the Lieutenant-Governor of the island, Sir Thomas Debrissay circulated a handbill extolling "the most pleasant situation either near the metropolis (Charlottetown), or adjacent to an exceeding fine fishery". Rents would be very low, the land was well stocked with profitable game and the sea and rivers abounded with many varieties of fish. In short, "a man at his leisure hours may supply his family by his gun and fishing". Every tenant and family was to find his own provisions and each to pay one guinea passage money, at the time they signed the articles.

This St John's Island lies within four leagues of Nova Scotia; so that if the tenant does not like his situation on this island, he can in a short time cross over to the continent, for which their will be a full liberty in the tenant's lease for that purpose.

The Governor was bold enough to claim that he would forfeit £200 if his description did not correspond with the general survey sent to the Board of Trade. Although this advertisement was aimed primarily at the poor people around Dublin, from where a boat would sail, it was also hoped to inveigle Scotsmen, who might apply to an agent in Glasgow.[20] It is not known how many accepted this invitation.

A year later an advertisement was inserted in the *Aberdeen Journal and North British Magazine* of July 26th 1773, although no response to it has been discovered:

"The choice estate of GEORGE SPENCE in ST PETER'S parish is to be disposed of in the following manner: the tenants paying their own freight over, and finding everything for themselves, viz.

the first year after Arrival, at one penny per Acre
three year, at sixpence per Acre
five years, at one shilling per Acre
tenth year, at two shillings per Acre
and so to continue for ever, to them, their Heirs or Assigns;
each family to have one hundred acres.

N.B. Mr Spence, as being the first Adventurer, had his Choice of the land, which is excellent: with a deal of Meadow Land, and good fishing of all sorts at the door; his son who hath been on the Island with his Family these four years, and carried on a great Farm, has now a fine Water Mill, will be of great service to the tenants in assisting them. And Capt. George Thomson can witness all this, having been often there, and know the truth of all. Enquire for Capt. George Thomson at his house in Old Aberdeen.

Wellwood Waugh of Lockerbie, a joiner aged 33 from Colvend took some, perhaps 67, Lowlanders from Dumfries and Kirkcudbright to St John's Island on the *Lovely Nelly*, in 1774; but they later moved on to Pictou. The boat sailed again from Carsthorn for St John's Island on 1st May 1775; on board were two joiners, two weavers, seven labourers, one blacksmith, all with families; also five single labourers and five other single men. Two more families boarded at Kirkcudbright, one more at Whitehaven and another at Douglas, Isle of Man.[21]

Peter Stewart

Nearly 300 Scots had been sent out to lot 18 in 1760 which had been allocated to Lieutenant-Colonel Robert Stewart and settled by his brother-in-law, also Robert Stewart, son of Charles Stewart the minister of Campbelltown. By 1775 the population of the island was 1300 of whom about half were Scots mainly from Perthshire or South Uist (for details of the latter see chapter 6). In June that year Peter, another son of Rev Charles Stewart, who had trained as a law clerk, was appointed Chief Justice of St John's with the help of his brother Robert, who was already in the island. Peter Stewart was to take settlers over for Sir James Montgomery, but Sir James did not want to send families. The men were to pay their own freight, and were to be paid much lower wages than David Higgins expected to pay them (£5-7 a year). Stewart was also, however, going to take over three or four servants on his own account:

> These I know will be expensive but I engage the men only in the view of entering into possession of a farm immediately on my landing and as I have always lived a pretty active life and been a good deal concerned in rearing and grassing cattle and in farming I hope the long experience and tolerable success I have had in affairs of that kind may be of use to me on St John's and that I shall in a short time raise so much grain and rear so many cattle with the servants I carry with me as will encourage me to enlarge my operation in that way. From the passion the lower sort of people here have for emigration I can have no doubt of getting out next year or as soon as I may find it convenient with any number of servants I may require. Upwards of 600 people quit this country [Argyll] this season for different parts of America and from the situation of the country in general ..there remains no doubt with me but many will emigrate annually for years to come .

Stewart expected to find so many people to go with him that he would have to charter a vessel unless a Clyde ship were going to Quebec. But only a month later the intending emigrants were so alarmed by the news from America that most of them decided not to go, and so Stewart and his wife, nine children, two maid servants, a man and a boy, together with three other young men who "went on their own account" picked up the snow *Elizabeth* from London when she called at Cork.

Although Stewart held some land in the island he was unable to live there as it was considered by the authorities to be too far from Charlottetown. He was therefore pleased to lease part of lot 34 from Sir James. Sir James's agent, Higgins, alleged that Stewart's predecessor had lived on this lot, that he had died without issue and so the lot was vacant; that there was a dwelling house with 15 acres of cleared land and an extensive marsh nearby which could easily be improved into meadow; that there was also good access to Charlottetown by both land and sea. However when the man who was to be Chief Justice arrived he found that the farm was more than seven miles, not three miles, from Charlottetown and was not accessible by land, there was no dwelling house or other building save a small hovel, not two acres of cleared land and only a very small piece of marsh. The agent had also let two farms on a new tract of land which should belong to Peter Stewart. He argued that he had written to Sir James before the first rent was due, so Sir James should allow him to exchange his lands for some nearer to Charlottetown and that he should also take other lands off his hands.[22]

After taking up his appointment, the now Sir Peter Stewart continued to lease the lands and in 1779 increased the acreage by a further 1000 acres in the name of his son Charles.

However by 1796 he was deeply in debt to Sir James and begged that he would not have to fulfill the lease as it would "compleatly and immediately ruin me".[23] He died in 1805 still heavily in debt.

Thomas Curtis was also a passenger on the snow *Elizabeth*; he came from Hampshire in the south of England and was probably typical of many fairly well-to-do young men who enjoyed "fishing and shooting and could use the Gun as well as most". He was persuaded to try emigration for the

Expense of going ther, and returning, would not be more than £20, if I went a Steerage passenger ... Rbt Clark Mercht (a Quaker) who had large possessions, on the island of St John's, he said (that) as I had been accustomed to Timber, and Sawing, I might make a Good fortune presently ... and that I might purchase of him as much as I pleased at 4d per Acre, for life, or 1s pr Acre free-hold, that the Captain's or masters of ships which were frequently coming in, would purchase all I cut for Ship or House Building, & that Sawyers were better paid for their labour, than in England, that the Rivers abounded with fish and the Country with game which were free for anyone

So Curtis spent his all on clothes and guns

the little money I had left I thought it would be better to give to R. Clark, and have a draft to the Amount on his agent on the Island, which I did to the Amount of Eight [?] Guineas, least by any means I should lose it.

When the day came for his departure Curtis and his friend J. Compton reported to Clark who asked "lads what stock of provisions have you for the winter"? We reply'd "none", "what", said he, "do you mean to go there to be starved"? They were fortunately able to procure some victuals.

The *Elizabeth*, set sail on 17th August 1775. Curtis took his manservant with him and there were 17 other steerage passengers. The boat called at Cork for provisions and some cabin passengers - Mr Stewart and his party. Curtis gives some insights into conditions on board. After recovering from sea-sickness our appetites now begin to increase and in want of Something better than Ships allowance being Salt Beef and Pork and puding twice a week for us in the Steerage. In the Cabbin I believe their was no Want having Fowls and fresh meat every day. This we had no right to expect as we did not pay for it.

Not all the passengers were friendly, for some "I believe thought themselves mutch above the Steerage Passengers". As they neared Newfoundland the crew and passengers were able to fish and one night "brought up a Codfish that weighd forty two pounds and a half. This was drest for the Cabbins use". Later more fish was caught and was served for dinner for all hands. The *Elizabeth* foundered on a sandbank just off St John's Island; all the passengers and all but one of the crew got off safely. The vessel was broken in half but with the onset of winter she was frozen into the ice and the men were able to save a small part of the cargo which had contained supplies for the inhabitants of the island. Mr and Mrs Stewart lost their goods, including her clothes and jewels to the value of £1000.

Curtis reflected in his journal that Robert Clark had deceived him about the island - New London compared very unfavourably with London, England; there were only about 16 houses and the people were very badly off for provisions; he was unable to get a job; the sport was not what he had been led to expect; and when he bought some clothes and presented his note he

> expected I should have rec^d the ballance in **Cash** as Robt Clark inform^d me I might have Cash or goods to the Amount; But the Agent told me **Mr** Clark new very well their was no cash in circulation that they did not see so mutch money in a year.

Curtis stayed on the island about seven months and after some delays found a ship going to England. "I can't express the Joy I Felt when I got on my native Country the 2nd Feb. 1777".[24]

However, in spite of the privations, the population continued to increase as groups of people made their way to the island. The *John and Elizabeth* arrived in the summer of 1775 with seven families (52 persons) for the proprietor of lot 57. On the vessel were William Simpson and his wife Janet Winchester from Morayshire, who were reported as "landing near Flat River as a result of shipwreck".[25] Captain Allan McDonald of Borrodale bought half lot 25 from Sir Alexander Campbell and intended going but was drowned off Skye; his son Alexander sold the lot but went himself with a few people.[26]

Later assessments

The island was not populated as quickly or as easily as perhaps government officials had hoped, for it is evident from the wording of the original grants that the grantees were expected to take or send the new settlers to their lands. Discussing the early settlements Donald Harvey has commented that Lawson's people at Covehead had the best start, the immigrants having landed without incident and thus saved their provisions, clothing and utensils. They had not been entirely destitute, nor driven from their homes through poverty, rather, they had sought to improve their condition and acquired land in a new world as yet uncrowded. Sir Peter Stewart's people at Malpaque had lost their supplies at their very door; later settlers who had arrived at St Peter's with Wellwood Waugh and those at Covehead had been plundered by an American fisherman and privateers. The people whom John McDonald had taken to Tracadie and Princeton and the seven families on lot 57, were reasonably settled.[27]

By 1797 the Assembly of St John's Island realised that many of the townships had not been settled. Some of the original proprietors had made no effort to settle their lands, others had speculated and sold, including Governor Patterson who in 1781 had rashly sold some of the unsettled grants (eight whole townships and six half townships) of those proprietors in arrears with their quit rents. Individual settlers, including a number of American Loyalists had been allowed to settle without assistance. The excuse for not sending emigrants was the American war, but as Stewart rightly pointed out the original grants were dated 1767, eight years before the start of the war. A survey was ordered in 1799 by which it was discovered that there were still 23 townships with no settlement. A further 12 townships had 36 families between them, five more had 31 families, while 26 townships each had its full quota of 100 families. Thus there was probably a total population of about 22,000. The Island Assembly, of whom both Peter Stewart and his son John, who became known as "Hellfire Jack", were at different times Speaker, thought that if the problem of settlement had been handled properly the population should have been half a million, which would have made a good self-sufficient colony. The original proprietors were furious at the way the problem of the unfilled townships had been handled and stirred up trouble so that the general political and economic condition of the island became unstable.

In 1801 the Government demanded all the quit rent money that was outstanding, which amounted to over £59,000 and on many lots the sum demanded amounted to more than could be expected if the land was sold. The lots were divided into several classes - the best developed paying least quit rent and the least developed paying most. This led to an immediate upsurge in development, nearly one-third of the lots were sold and the new proprietors brought in more settlers in a relatively short time. One of these activists was the Earl of Selkirk who settled a large body of people in a potentially good area in 1803. John Stewart commented that these new Highlanders were

> much more industrious and enlightened than the original Highland colony who first settled in the island, they have besides got rid of more of their ancient prejudices and customs, and appear to think more like the rest of their fellow subjects than those who emigrated 35 years ago.

Stewart estimated that of the original 67 townships in the island only six had not begun to be settled and of these several had earlier been at least partially cultivated by the French Acadians. There is no estimate of the total population at this time, 1804.[28] While the strong measures taken by government produced a considerable improvement, the later waves of settlers resulted in the hoped for increase in population.

6

"Good Creatures in the Main"

A South Uist emigration

The Reformation introduced new doctrines and new forms of worship into the church and caused much disruption in public and private life. Over a long period the Scottish Parliament passed a series of Acts depriving the Roman Catholics of their religious and civil liberty. The legislation culminated in an Act passed in 1700 by which papists could not become "governors, chaplains, pedagogues or schoolmasters, tutors or Curators, Chamberlains and Factors". Protestant relatives were to ensure that all children were brought up in the Protestant faith; no Roman Catholic could inherit property or lands. A further Act of 1708 prohibited Roman Catholics from acquiring movables or recovering just debts. Pressure to conform thereafter was severe and many priests did so. There were a few influential families such as the Earl of Huntly and the Maxwells who could not be persuaded and they and those priests who continued in their old parishes were able to keep alight the faint flame of Roman Catholicism. Those priests who became Presbyterian ministers were particularly officious in seeking out dissident Roman Catholics.

The Roman Catholic Highlanders suffered under a further disadvantage *vis a vis* the Lowlanders and Protestants: the majority of them spoke only Gaelic. King James VI and Parliament thought that this language was another cause of the "barbaritie and incivilitie" in the Highlands. Schools were to be set up in every parish- English Protestant schools funded by the Roman Catholics. To escape them those Roman Catholic families who could, sent their sons abroad for their education.

It has often been assumed that the Jacobite armies consisted largely of Roman Catholics, but this was not the case. Like most Episcopalians the Catholics continued to believe in the Stuart divine right of kingship and hoped that the Pretender's return would bring freedom of worship and the repeal of penal legislation. In the army of the '45 70 per cent of the men were Episcopal but only 30 per cent were Roman Catholic. However after the '45, in a relatively short time the Roman Catholics began to make a considerable contribution to the British army. This was finally recognised by General Burgoyne who unsuccessfully urged the House of Commons in 1770 to accept the fact that he had commanded 500 Roman Catholics who had pretended to be Protestants so that they could take the necessary oath of allegiance.

Although the English Penal Acts against Roman Catholics were repealed in 1778, the Scottish Relief Act was not passed until 1793. This finally allowed Roman Catholics freedom to worship as they liked and to inherit and purchase lands and property freely. Priests were permitted to say Mass openly but were still barred from certain appointments.

Final barriers were not broken down until the Catholic Emancipation Act was passed in 1829.[1]

The simmering persecution of Roman Catholics was kept within bounds after the '45, but pockets of covert oppression remained and occasionally more open forms were indulged in. In the Western Highlands and Outer Hebrides there seemed to be

> a general design in all these countries to root out Religion by discouraging Catholics all they can, dispossessing them of their lands at the end of their tacks and giving them to Protestants.[2]

It is against this background of oppression and intolerance that we can set the emigration from South Uist. South Uist was owned by Ranald Macdonald of Clanranald and his cousin Colin Macdonald of Boisdale, (Fig. 6.1) who also held in tack part of Clanranald's lands, so that he, Boisdale, had up to 300 families as tenants on his lands. Boisdale was brought up a Roman Catholic but became a Presbyterian and some time in 1768 felt obliged to convert his Catholic tenants to Presbyterianism. In a series of letters to Bishop Hay the priests in the Highlands recounted the nature of the suffering of the islanders by the hand of their laird. Boisdale

> kept a schoolmaster in his house as a loyal man both as to his spirituals and morals, the greatest number of his scholars being Catholic he did all he could to bring them to his own way of thinking, and as he did not succeed in that he caused fleshmeat to be brought into the school in Lent and forced it into their mouths and whoever did not take it was severely punished. Mr Wynn [their priest], being informed of this persuaded the parents to call home their children from the impious school where nothing was taught but was contrary to religion and morality ... Boisdale sent word to Mr Wynn never to perform any function in his bounds; Mr Wynn answered that he would not forsake his charge without the consent of those who had given it to him, upon which Boisdale gave a legal warning to all our poor people to the number of 1000 souls; soon after they were all called together and Boisdale told them he would remove every one of them unless they would make a solemn promise never to hear a priest any more, and as the people would not come to these terms against their conscience so they are all to be dispersed without knowing where to go.[3]

Boisdale continued to threaten the priests and wrote them scurrilous letters if they performed any of their duties within his lands, indeed Mr Wynn, had to flee for his life. Bishop Hay later reported that:

> Boisdale after having got his poor people fixed for another year has used every means in his power to harass them because they will not allow their children to be brought up as he pleases.

Boisdale was astonished at this temerity and retorted that he would cause his tenants no trouble if they allowed their children to become Presbyterians; again they refused; so he gave them another year to repent of their stubbornness. There was some mitigation of harassment during the winter of 1770 while Boisdale was away from the island, but when he returned in the spring the persecutions started again and he even threatened to bring in the military.[4] By the end of 1771 Boisdale had monopolised

> the products and imports of the island, giving only for the one and setting on the other what price he pleases, always taking care that no cash be returned from the balance when there is any, and throwing the merchandise into the poor peoples' hands to involve them in debt in order to have their effects in return at destruction ... They are afraid to meet him in the high roads; the best

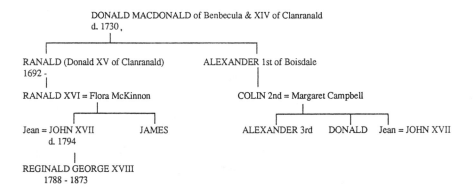

Fig. 6/1   Some members of the Clan Ranald

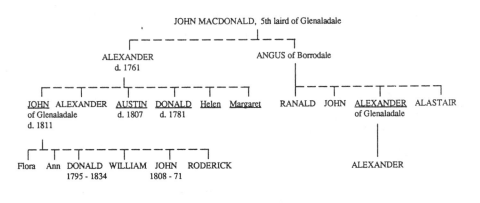

Fig. 6/2   The family of John MacDonald of Glenaladale.

appellation he gives them is "You devil". the blasphemous terms in which he mentions every article of our Holy Religion to them are intolerable to human ears.

The priests were also disturbed that the island was so far from the nearest justice of the peace to whom people might turn in the last resort or to "save a person from bastinadoing".[5] Nevertheless they reported that the people stood firm in their faith, indeed

the more they suffered the more it seemed to rivet them in their principles ... for it's more difficult to make a proselyte now of a child of only eight years of age than it was at first to pervert the whole country.[6]

In November 1771 Bishop Hay addressed a memorial to all Roman Catholics, hoping that they would assist their oppressed fellows in South Uist. In it he set out all the persecutions that Boisdale was inflicting on his tenants.[7] Monsignor Peter Grant in Rome gave the original memorial and a translation to the Pope and to the Duke of Gloucester who was then in Rome. It was hoped that on his return to London the Duke would report the situation, in the first instance to the Secretary of State for the Northern Department (the Earl of Suffolk) and the Lord Privy Seal (James Steuart Mackenzie).[8] By the following April the Bishop was able to report that the memorial had had some effect, not only through money (about £500) raised by Bishop Chaloner in London, but also in convincing some of the persecuting lairds that their tenants were willing to emigrate rather than suffer further for their religion.[9] Every landlord feared an empty farm, for that would mean loss of rent. Inevitably Boisdale was very angry at the charges against him in the memorial. He was clever enough to obtain signed proof of certain of his statements but chose statements that were not in fact charged against him. Other statements he "seems not flatly to deny but would extenuate them by calling them sudden fits or transports of passion, though they lasted full two years".[10]

Captain John McDonald of Glenaladale (Fig. 6.2) was a Roman Catholic whose father had fought for Prince Charles at Culloden and whose brother Hugh was a priest; they were kinsmen of Boisdale. John McDonald was factor on the Clanranald estate. Aware of the harassment of the islanders, he became disillusioned with his dependence on the family of Clanranald.

Glenaladale advised Bishop Hay that even the minister and other Protestants were shocked by Boisdale's behaviour and he believed that because of the tacit harassment of Catholics in general throughout the country, it would be foolish to repudiate Boisdale's denials of ill treatment as he could easily stir up more trouble.[11] It is possible to trace the course of events in the actual organisation of the emigration, which the Catholic hierarchy had decided was the only solution to the crisis. Bishop Hay encouraged this move after the conquest of Prince Edward Island by the English because, although most of the French inhabitants had left the island, the 50 families who had remained were very keen to have a priest amongst them. The bishop saw this as a good opportunity for cooperation if a Gaelic speaking priest could be sent with the Uist party.

Not everyone thought this was a good plan - Bishop James Grant thought that only about half the number of people affected by the persecutions would actually be prepared to leave everything and go, these would inevitably be the younger and more promising men who would leave their friends and relations to bear the brunt of further persecutions. He also doubted whether the government would approve a "set of Highlanders looked upon as disaffected and Jacobite should go to these parts with a design, it might be alleged, to augment disturbances". Bishop Grant would have preferred Glenaladale to go to Edinburgh or even London to try "to procure the interest of some powerful friends at court" to try to discourage Boisdale.[12]

However Glenaladale had already in 1769 started negotiations for a tract of land in St John's Island with Sir James Montgomery, who "though a man so much of the government is willing to give them all encouragement, and their being Roman Catholic far from being an objection to him". The purchase was completed and also some time before December 1770 he bought lot 36, Tracadie, from George Spence and John Mill, merchants in London.[13]

From the start, all involved in this emigration were aware of the large sum of money that would be needed before the expedition could sail in 1771:

£2000 which alas! is not easily got, Glenaladale is willing to borrow it upon his own estate if no other way can be found to raise it; but even that will not be easy, money is so scarce here especially as it must be had by next Whitsunday.[14]

Glenaladale was unable to borrow additional money from the Catholic Church in Scotland; Bishop Chaloner's £500 could be used to help the Uist emigrants, but not those from the mainland who had been offered passages on the boat provided they could pay for themselves.[15] The latter were from Ardnamurchan, for large numbers of tacks ended there in 1771 and the new proprietor, Sir James Riddell, was "so extravagant in his demands that most of the people were determined to leave the country". Glenaladale was still hoping to attract some of the more well-to-do farmers to his land in St John's Island. Quite aware of the magnitude of the task Glenaladale wrote to Bishop Hay in November 1771 offering to take the Uist party at his own expense if all else failed. He perceived the people as

good creatures in the main, yet some of them may be ignorant and a little overbearing in their way or, of inconstant peevish temper which will give more disagreeable work than can easily be imagined, to one who will have to take them immediately by the hand, help to sell their small effects in a remote island from markets, for paying their debts and purchasing necessaries, conduct them through a troublesome voyage over the Atlantick, settle them in a country almost a desert, and there to rear them till they shall have made a footing, with the same care wherewith a gardener manages his plants, add to this fatigue and dangers one encounters in the execution of the whole, and loss of other business together with expenses, all of which if I were to value them I would not gift to any man for £200 St more.[16]

How right these forebodings were to prove! He saw so many of his friends and relatives leaving the country that he feared

the whole tribe of us Macienoigs are going off at this time to a man excepting your two brothers and old Lochans and his son Donald and I will not answer long for these ... For my part it is necessary for the scheme that I should continue at home for some time as yet, supplying my brother in the best manner I can and receiving such oppresst people as offer themselves to us from all corners, but certain it is I cannot be fond of the country after all those I love best are away.[17]

Meantime Glenaladale had bought a boat, possibly the *Argyll* and sent his brother Donald at the beginning of May 1771 with 30 people to prepare a place for the greater number who would follow the following spring. This expedition cost nearly £400. Early reports from the other side suggested that the party went out with a drunken shipmaster and that the voyage took nearly twelve weeks but that they had got the second or third best lot in the island "which is saying a great deal".[18] Donald settled this small party and returned to Scotland in February 1772 in the brig *Murders*, which was wrecked off the coast of Argyll.[19] However he was able to give a first hand account of the situation he had left. One of his points was that only families should go who could maintain themselves for a year or more until they had raised crops: under the laws of the island it was incumbent upon the leader of such an expedition to maintain everyone he took over and not let them fall a burden on the host island. Bishop Hay supported him but laid down that as long as the contributions lasted all were to go, including families.[20]

In October 1771 two men from South Uist had been sent as a deputation to ask Glenaladale to carry out the promises that they had heard about. 36 families had definite orders to leave at Whitsun and about another 600 people were being harassed on lands leased from Clanranald, lands which were plenished with Boisdale's own cattle so that Clanranald could not afford at that time to turn him out.[21] Although Boisdale was the most notorious of the lairds others were also harrassing their tenants. The bishop wrote:

> no people on earth, not even the negro slaves excepted, suffer so much oppression and nuisance of every kind as well under Clan[Ranald] as under Boisdale, saving only that the former does not persecute on the score of religion.[22]

At the turn of the year Glenaladale and Bishop John Macdonald, who had ministered there, crossed to South Uist, a journey which Glenaladale had earlier described thus:

> I shall be in greater danger in my voyage to Uist in a tempestuous winter sailing in an open boat among rocks for 30 leagues, than if I were to go to St John's in summer.[23]

These two men went to interview all the intending emigrants to see just what was their situation and to make sure that they would be ready at the prescribed time. Bishop Macdonald was appalled at the condition into which families he had previously known to be reasonably affluent, had now sunk. Only two had about £12 or £14 free, another two or three had £10, the rest from £4 to £7 and some nothing at all. So not one person was able to pay the freight for himself and his family, let alone something to live on for the ensuing year. In spite of their distress and the fact that Glenaladale offered to take them away free and to support them, still the families were loathe to commit themselves until they had tried yet again to come to reasonable terms with Boisdale. In the end, of the 36 families said to be in the worst straits 10 or 12 had agreed a new lease just a few days before Glenaladale and the bishop arrived. Although they had not insisted on being allowed to call a clergyman to their farms yet they were determined to call one in time of need, nor did they consent to any degree of apostasy, but would exercise their religion as formerly.

Clanranald disapproved so strongly of Boisdale's conduct that he had offered to receive on his lands all people who were dispossessed by Boisdale.[24] These people may have been some of those already removed by Boisdale at the May term and who now rented farms from Clanranald. But they failed and had to return to Boisdale's continued bullying and threatening; he was content for a time with preventing any priest from going near them "though indeed he does not keep for a month together by the same mode of vexation".

Only nine families committed themselves firmly to going, others had been persuaded by their womenfolk to believe Boisdale's propaganda that they would be sold into slavery on the other side. They soon repented their decision, but were assured that they would be helped on the same terms whenever they did want to go, provided that they remained constant in their religion. The bishop was sure that when the time came all would want to go and feared that the situation would be worse in a year's time.[25]

Glenaladale chartered the *Alexander* of Greenock from John Buchanan and Company and it sailed north towards the end of March 1772, collecting 110 passengers at Loch Arisaig and another 100 at Loch Boisdale; 11 families were from Boisdale's estate and some from Clanranald's. Donald McDonald was again in charge of the party and was accompanied by his sisters Helen and Margaret. The freight charged was £3.12.6 for each person over seven years of age, £1.6.3 for those between three and seven years and nothing for children under three years, of whom there was a great number. The victualling consisted of 6lbs of bread and 5lbs of beef per week for every full passenger, with barley broth three days a week and pottage and molasses every day to breakfast, with a Scots pint of water per person every day. Along with each family were sent some implements of husbandry, clothing and blankets, money for a cow and meal for a year's provision. In all, about £1500 was spent on freight and provisions by Glenaladale.[26]

The *Alexander* sailed on the 3rd May and arrived at Stockfort, St John's Island on the 7th June. Among the families that sailed was that of Angus McDonald of Retland, in South Morar, who had a good property in feu to John McDonald of Morar. Angus could no longer maintain his own and his sons' families and so wished to sell. Because Boisdale was the only prospective purchaser, he was urged rather to set it in wadset, but had difficulty in finding anyone able to raise the necessary £600 or £700 sterling. John McDonald of Boisdale eventually bought Retland. In a contract between father and son Angus McDonald agreed that one-third of the selling price should be used for buying land in America, the land to go to Allan, being the eldest son and heir, except for 200 acres to each of the other four sons and 1000 acres to the father Angus. The other two-thirds of the selling price was to be divided between father and eldest son.[27]

The whole expedition had cost Glenaladale a good deal more than expected, firstly because the Uist people were so poverty stricken and needed more help than anticipated, for instance extra clothes and blankets had to be provided because recently there had been so few sheep on South Uist that no wool was available for weaving materials. Secondly, conditions on St John's Island were more difficult than were envisaged before brother Donald's visit, so that they had to take much more reserve food and clothing with them. They could expect little help from the settlers already there, not the first party from Uist but ex-soldiers with little interest in farming and with poor servants to help them, for they had not prospered, and the Frenchmen who were still there were loathe to settle down and cultivate. Also markets such as Nova Scotia and Quebec were distant.

Glenaladale's problems continued to increase. The tenants from the mainland had not paid their passage money and the man who was to buy his kelp neither took the kelp nor paid for it. He now considered the possibility of selling his estate to raise funds to pay for his expedition. Then came the collapse of the Ayr bank in which he had money; and the claim for insurance on his lost vessel was now stopped because of the financial troubles in London. Also some money that his cousin had in Jamaica could not now be recovered. He was desperate for cash, so was everyone else around him, they were all in the same state and mid-summer was not a good time for "turning to cash the commodities of the country", i.e. cattle. Against the advice of others, but for the sake of his tenants and sub-tenants Glenaladale sold his estate of the Glens to his cousin, Alexander Macdonald of Borrodale, in trust for his brother, so that Clanranald could not buy it. He and Boisdale were said to be considering further harassment of the remaining tenants as a result of Glenaladale's actions. Glenaladale kept his tack of Keppoch from Clanranald so that Boisdale would not claim it.[28]

John McDonald (no longer Glenaladale) and his family sailed for Philadelphia in July 1773, probably in the *Matty*, and then travelled overland to Boston by October. Although he had intended staying the winter in Massachusetts the reports from St John's Island forced him to go there as soon as possible. He had to buy £200 worth of goods from Archibald Wilson in Boston to take to the island. The draft he wrote was payable at 30 days' sight of Bishop Hay and his lawyer Mr Macdonald in Scotland. To forestall the embarrassment of these gentlemen refusing to accept the draft, Glenaladale wrote beseeching the bishop to find the money in any way he could:

If it is refused my ruin follows inevitably as well as theirs which I regret most, my credit and character will be gone here irretrievably; an honest man [Wilson] will be ruined who is in no opulent circumstances and transacted this affair for me without knowing me or any possible view of advantage to himself but purely to serve a countryman upon solemn assurances of his occurring no damage therefrom. It will make a prodigious sputter and I shall never after have the assurance of showing my face to the world. Therefore I am firmly determined if it is returned under protest to give myself some desperate turn and to abandon myself so entirely that none who ever knew me shall know what shall have become of me ... Of all these consequences of this step thereafter I will hold me discharged to myself.

The mental stress overwhelmed this good man for he

had undergone for three years now almost past all the anxiety the mind of man is capable of bearing, dun'd with various accounts pro and con of that island and distracted with noise, clamour and disappointment for near a year and a half under the aggravation of the inability to form a judgment of the place from my own view of it. This could be borne while under a character of honour and integrity, but once this last is buried and lost under the appearance and suspicious circumstances of fraud intended, as will be my case in regard to this man if the draft returns protested without the chance of proving one alleviating circumstance, although God knows I mean no fraud, then indeed I confess my fortitude sinks and I yield myself to the resources of despair.

He reported that his people on St John's Island were not finding it easy to settle; their first year's crops were not good except for the potatoes and garden stuffs. Fortunately 1773 was a better year for although they had had to sow a second lot of seed a good harvest was secured, which they hoped to keep for seed as long as he arrived with provisions to see them through the winter.[29] Although McDonald organised immediate relief after his arrival his colony began to disintegrate for some of the men were stirring up unrest and trying to persuade people to move on: some did, but soon regretted their move. He lost many tenants who disliked the idea of continuing to live under the power of a landlord, even one who granted leases for 990 years. They were only satisfied with outright possession and years later it was reported that conditions were still difficult, and that it was impossible to pay rent, not through indolence but through misfortune. Throughout, he charged minimal rent though his expenses ran to "several thousand pounds". McDonald retained 500 acres of land at the head of Tracadie for himself and was said to be one of the few proprietors who really tried to fulfil the terms of the original grant. He was later, in 1792, able to buy the neighbouring lot, lot 35. During the War of Independence John McDonald served with the 84th Highland Emigrant Regiment, while his sister Helen looked after his affairs and worked the farm. After his return he was offered high office in the Island Councils but was unable to accept because of his religious affiliation. He was a man of high principles who practised them in both Scotland and Canada.

Although Boisdale seems to have moderated his actions somewhat after some of his people actually left, another 50 families had determined to leave South Uist by July 1773. The island suffered from the very poor harvest of 1772 and many people died in April 1773. The harvest that year was also disastrous so that families were in a desperate condition. There is evidence that a further 200 people went from the island and Arisaig that year though not apparently helped by Glenaladale or their church. Moidart also suffered a further loss of population when two parties, one of about 50 people, went to the island in 1775 but they too soon moved on to Pictou. They were said to have sailed in the "Big Ship" which landed at Canso, Nova Scotia; a smaller vessel that sailed at the same time apparently turned back.[30] In spite of his past actions Boisdale apparently still expected people to want to come on to his land, though when he invited 60 families from Skye to take tacks with him "he was laughed at". He did however agree to allow his tenants to follow their own religion if they stayed a further three years.[31] It was reported in the autumn of 1774 that Boisdale was a reformed character and that Catholics were given unlimited toleration in their religion, priests were allowed to perform some of their duties within his own house; in general the Protestants

> no longer look upon us as a set of execrable wretches destitute of friends and the abomination of king and government, so that the consequences of Boisdale's foolish attempts have in the end proved salutary and beneficial to religion and are likely to continue to do so.[32]

Most of the other superiors in the neighbourhood were very worried about the consequences of large scale emigration, and amazed that the families had been so generously assisted; many decided to be more tolerant, though some, for instance Maclean of Muck, continued to harass their people.[33]

Patrick M'Robert reported in 1774 that about 30 families, mainly MacDonalds, were doing well after two years at Tracadie. The settlement of about 40 families at Three Rivers begun and supported by the Lord Advocate, was also prospering although the fishing there had failed. He wrote that new settlers

> had been ill for provisions, few had any to spare; but the worst time for that is over, as the first settlers can now spare a little; yet I would advise settlers who go there, to take a year's provisions along with them.[34]

The settlement of Pictou

The account of the early years of the Pictou settlement gives a good description of the fortitude and hardship faced by early settlers in Canada.(Fig 6.3) The saga, however, began with a Virginian living in Philadelphia.

Alexander McNutt, whose greatest gift appears to have been that of exaggeration, determined to acquire as much land as possible in the empty wilderness of Nova Scotia. By badgering the British government and by dissimulation he persuaded several hundred Irishmen to settle in Nova Scotia about 1763. About the same time the 10 million empty acres were being divided into 16 townships. Sixteen companies, each one associated with McNutt, applied for land. Almost half the granted land went to McNutt and his associates; but within 40 years these companies had lost all but 1000 acres to the government for failing to meet the terms of the grants. One of the companies associated with McNutt was the Philadelphia Company (one of eight companies of this name). The 14 partners were influential lawyers and merchants in Philadelphia and were granted some 200,000 acres of not very good land in Pictou County. The Philadelphia Grant consisted of Pictou Township, part of Colchester County, part of New Annan, all Earltown, Kemptown and part of Stewiacke. The land was not, as expected, along the shore line and far short of the supposed 200,000 acres, but the boundaries were redrawn to include part of the shore line of Pictou harbour.[35]

The original intention of the grantees was to settle Americans, but there were few volunteers. However on June 10, 1767 the brig *Betsey* carried six families from Philadelphia to Pictou harbour, including the company's agent and representative, Dr John Harris, and Robert Patterson, a native of Renfrew who had settled in America after the war and who became the company surveyor. These two men were to play an important part in the life of the young settlement. By some deception Alexander McNutt persuaded the Philadelphians to put down their roots not on the choicest waterfront land, but rather on an inferior stretch of shore. The families managed to raise a few potatoes in their first autumn and in 1770, working with hoes among the stumps, raised 64 bushels of wheat, 60 of oats and seven of barley, six of peas and some flax. Families began to drift in from older settlements until the population reached about 120, but the company's failure to attract any more settlers from Philadelphia forced the directors to turn their attention to Scotland.[36]

Paradoxically, the new Scottish connection can be traced back to the problems of Princeton College, New Jersey. The first five presidents had died during the twenty years since the inception of the College and the work was also severely hampered by theological disputes and lack of money. The trustees turned to Scotland for a new president. The Rev Dr John Witherspoon, minister in Paisley, was a leader of the evangelical party in the Church of Scotland and knew and corresponded with many influential American churchmen. It took two years to persuade Mrs Witherspoon to cross the Atlantic, but eventually Dr Witherspoon sailed from Greenock in the *Peggy*, with his wife and five children, leaving on 8th May 1768. In his luggage Dr Witherspoon carried a copy of the current *Edinburgh Almanack*, in which he had made a note of *things to be remembered in America*; these included the names of five men wanting information about going to America and a document binding a young man to him as servant for two and a half years. The family arrived in Philadelphia on 6th August to a very warm reception.[37] Behind this warmth lay the hope that the new president would heal the theological rift, encourage the building up of financial resources and broaden the education of young American Presbyterians.

It was not long before Dr Witherspoon joined the St Andrew's Society of Philadelphia

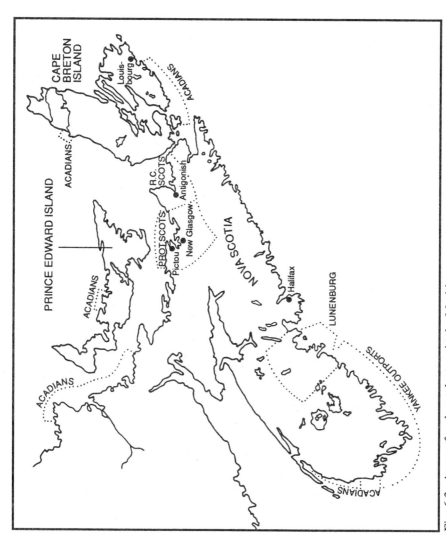

Fig. 6.3 Areas of early settlement in the Maritimes.

and became a prominent public figure. Later he went as a delegate to the Continental Congress between 1776 and 1782 and was a signatory of the Declaration of Independence. He also became involved in the contentious matter of emigration. He and John Pagan bought the controlling interest in the Philadelphia Company from three earlier directors. Witherspoon had become a member of the Philadelphia Company rather by accident than intention, but having been pressed hard he hoped that by his acquiesence settlers would feel more confident of better treatment. One condition of his joining had been that he should agree with the price of the land sold to Scotsmen, because some advertisements were blatantly misleading. John Pagan was a Glasgow merchant associated with Robert Lee and Joseph Tucker, timber merchants and shipbuilders in Greenock.

Pagan and Witherspoon appointed John Ross as their agent in Scotland. Ross was a merchant in Dingwall, Easter Ross, and also manager of a linen station in Loch Broom for the Forfeited Estates Commissioners. Thus he was in a sensitive position in the heart of an area where ancient methods of farming were being overturned in favour of modern estate practices. Ross already had experience of emigrations for he had accompanied a boatload of 200 emigrants on the *Hector*, which left Port Glasgow for Boston in February 1770.[38]

A single advertisement was inserted in the *Glasgow Journal* on September 17th 1772:

Lands to be settled in North America

To all farmers and others in Scotland who are inclined to settle upon easy terms in the province of Nova Scotia in North America ...

That the Rev Dr Witherspoon preses of the college in New Jersey, North America, with some other gentlemen in that country, and JOHN PAGAN mt in Glasgow have obtained an extensive grant of lands ...

And as soon as a sufficient number of settlers are procured for one vessel to carry out the said John Pagan will take care that she be a good sufficient ship and engages to transport the said settlers to Nova Scotia at the easy rate of £3.5s per freight for each full passenger 8 years of age and upwards to be reckoned a full freight ... There will be 3lbs beef, 4lbs bread and 4lbs oatmeal allowed a week, with barley broth and burgue [a kind of oatmeal porridge] twice a week and one Scots pint water each day to every full freight. The passage money to be paid before the ship leave Scotland. Twelve weeks provision will be laid in for the voyage which in a general way can be made in four weeks the distance from Scotland and Nova Scotia being little more than half that to North Carolina.

All persons in the west and north Highlands who incline to go and settle upon these lands in Nova Scotia are desired to apply to Provost James Campbell in Inverary, Mr Archibald Gray in Maryborough, Mr James McDonald at Portree in Skye, Mr Dougald McTavish at Fort Augustus and Baillie Alex Shaw at Inverness who will receive a signed list of the families names and numbers; and agreeable thereto the settlers will be intitled to their quantities of land in Nova Scotia according to the rule established above. There will also be lodged in those gentlemen's hands an obligation to the proprietors for obtemperating these proposals for settling their lands, as a security to all those who may agree to go over to Nova Scotia for that purpose.

There are about 20 families already settled upon these lands and make up a school of about 30 children. The proprietors propose making an application to the Governor of Nova Scotia for procuring a charter to a Presbyterian church and a school and will give to the first minister 500 acres land and to the first schoolmaster 300 acres in fee simple to them and their heirs ... also 500 acres more to the minister and 100 to the schoolmaster.

All those who propose to settle on these lands in Nova Scotia must for that purpose leave Scotland some time in the month of April each year so as to be upon the lands as early in the summer as possible, to clear grounds and prepare their different settlements for the ensuing winter. If any number of families who incline to go over and settle upon these lands have additional proposals to make, which they judge may be for the interest of their settlement, if found reasonable, they will be agreed to, upon applying to the said John Pagan by letter or otherwise, who will also be ready to treat with any persons, that for the sake of making separate settlements by themselves may want to purchase a large quantity of these lands, not exceeding 5000 to 10,000 acres.

Baillie Shaw was upset at seeing his name included in the advertisement because he had not been consulted and, as agent for the Board of Trustees for Fisheries and Manufactures, he did not wish to be associated with the scheme. There was adverse criticism of the scheme in the press from a "Well-wisher to Old Scotland" who was much more realistic about what any intending settlers would find at the end of their sea voyage. He also questioned Dr Witherspoon's part in the proceedings. The correspondence continued for several weeks.[39] Even some Americans were concerned at Dr Witherspoon's participation, so that he was stung to reply in a letter addressed to the *Scots Magazine*. He argued that his detractors reasoned that migration from Britain to America was hurtful and tended to the ruin of the kingdom and that by urging people to settle in America he must be an enemy to the country. He suggested that there was no need for alarm back home because the numbers emigrating were small compared with the total population and the numbers were soon made up by natural increase; immigrants made up only 2_ per cent of any new settlement in America. It was also said that the flow of people from America, particularly New England, back to England was twice as many as those going to America. He could not understand how he could be called an enemy to the emigrants by telling them where to find happiness and relief from their oppression; nor to those who stayed behind because there was now more room for them in the overcrowded land; nor to the landowners who might have to reduce their rents a little for a time but whose happiness depended on the misery of their tenants. If he had wanted numerous Scotsmen to go to America Dr Witherspoon suggested that he would have engaged authors to write against emigration for then people would want to find out more, also the people were perverse enough to want to go if the landlord wanted them to stay.

Since Providence has sent me to this part of the world, and since so much honour has been done me, as to suppose that my character might be some security against fraud and imposition, I shall certainly look upon it as my duty, to do any real service in my power to such of my countrymen as shall fall in my way, and shall either desire or seem to need any assistance.[40]

The *Scots Magazine*, which was opposed to emigration, saw no reason to publish the letter.

After all this controversy Witherspoon and Pagan signed a contract with John Ross dated Glasgow June 3rd 1773. The owners agreed to survey 40,000 acres and lay it off in lots of between 200 to 1000 acres. Ross received 20,000 acres, with a quit rent of two shillings sterling for each 100 acres and was obliged to settle 250 persons that same year. The proprietors would find one year's provisions

at first cost, the persons to whom the same are furnished paying ready money therefore, and the new settlers are to have every accommodation in the power of the proprietors untill they build houses for themselves.[41]

The customs officer at Inverness reported that 300 people had emigrated in 1772 and 1773 and that of the 39 emigrants from Lochbroom parish, 26 had gone from the Forfeited Estate of Coigach and another eleven families in Coigach had quitted their possessions and sold their cattle and effects to be ready to set out for America at the first opportunity.[42] Pagan fitted out the *Hector*, an old Dutch vessel which began an infamous voyage from Greenock on June 5th 1773 when the ship sailed north to Loch Broom to pick up its passengers; 14 families from Sutherland, 10 from Invernessshire, five from the vicinity of Loch Broom, one from Banffshire, one from Dunfermline and one other family. They were all Protestants save one family. One of the leaders, Roderick Mackay from Beauly had a brother already in Canada and had himself seen service in the New World with Fraser's Highlanders. A month later the boat sailed with about 200 people on board. The stoic nature of the Highlanders can be gauged from a report that the emigrants were said to have expressed their satisfaction with the voyage in spite of the fact that 18 children had died and the boat was so rotten that one could pick the wood out of the sides with a finger. A gale off Newfoundland blew the boat some distance back into the Atlantic so that it took another 14 days to recover their position; provisions and water were finished. The emigrants arrived on September 15th too late in the year to be able to raise any crops that season.

Because the short harbour front at Pictou Harbour had already been settled the new arrivals were not given houses provided by the proprietors as they had expected, but were to move away from the coast into the uncleared forest where they were not even able to fish. When the *Hector* returned from Boston with supplies for the new settlers before going on to Scotland the already despairing people were told that because (through no fault of theirs) they had not settled at Pictou Harbour they had broken their contract and so would get no food unless they moved to the forest lots or paid cash. Understandably there was trouble between the newcomers and the agents, Dr Harris and Robert Patterson.[43] Many of the immigrants were unable or unwilling to settle in the forest so went to the townships along the coast, some returning later to Pictou Harbour to work for the fishing industry and to look for land. Unexpected help was given to them by some of the Americans who had arrived on the *Betsey* in 1767 and by the Indians, so that in the following summer some men began to settle in the forest and were making barrel staves to send back to Scotland.[44]

Patrick M'Robert reported in 1774 that the land at Pictou was pretty good and that about 30 families, mostly from Scotland, had settled there. The majority of these very poor families were doing well in the short time they had been there.[45] Pictou began to thrive. The first cargo of squared timber was shipped to Britain in 1775 and from that time onward trade increased until by 1803 50 boats a year were carrying timber across the Atlantic Ocean. In 1784 the population was substantially increased with the settlement of 30 families of soldiers discharged from the army at the end of the American War of Independence. The waterfront gained notoriety with drunken sailors and periodic pressgangs from His Majesty's ships of war.[46]

On the voyage across the Atlantic many of the families must have bitterly regretted leaving home. Many died on passage or in the first months after arrival, and only the strongest survived the first harsh winters in Canada.

7

"Beggars in their Native Land"

Sutherland

In the extreme north, the vast Sutherland Estates which were to be the scene of the infamous Clearances of 1806 and 1821 came under new management after the death of the Earl in 1766. It is from that date that the deep tensions between the landlord and the tenants can be traced as new policies to increase revenues were introduced.

In the next few years nature conspired to add to the difficulties of the farmers. There were very severe storms in the spring of 1770 so that many cattle starved to death, the price of cattle fell, disease was rife and the sub-tenants were unable to pay their rents. The guardians of the Countess of Sutherland felt it necessary to advertise the fact that they had several times supplied victuals to their needy sub-tenants. Although herrings had been caught in Lochinver Bay in the early months of the year, Thomas Pennant noted that the people were still starving in July for there was no corn to be had in this area which usually had a surplus. Many substantial farmers in the Highlands were said to be ruined. In February 1772 the weather was so cold that "even our gentlemen and gentlewomen are heating themselves with the hand at the corn or Highland mill". In other words they were turning the querns because the water mills were frozen.[1]

The new policies to exact higher rents and to eliminate the tacksmen understandably produced a strong reaction from the tacksmen themselves, some of whom turned to developing large scale plans for emigration. It has to be said that these tacksmen had up till then been as much responsible for abusing the poorer sub-tenants as the landlord himself. Few leases had been renewed to the former possessors at a rent "they voluntarily offered and now cheerfully accept". It was now stated that because some tacksmen had been liable "to abuse their tacks and oppress their sub-tenants", subletting in future tacks was to be severely reduced. This policy of the landlord in allocating farms and giving leases from the estate directly to the poor sub-tenants not only removed the authority of the tacksmen, but was part of a fundamental social and economic upheaval throughout the Highlands. The reforms were not as advantageous to the sub-tenant as might appear. Many were worse off, some complained that their small farms had been engrossed by more opulent farmers and that they had been turned adrift. However, Captain James Sutherland, superintendent to the Countess of Sutherland, later reported that the poorer sort of people "are much pleased that they are to have no tacksmen over them, and no wonder, for they have been squeezed to their last shilling by some of the tacksmen". Captain Sutherland was sceptical of tacksmen such as George Mackay at Mudal who was organising an emigration:

tho I do not believe any of our Assynt tacksmen will go, yet their saying that they will go may increase that flame that I have in a great measure stifled... All I shall observe on the list of arrears is that Ken Scobie [a tacksman who backed George Mackay] has money to buy the emigrants' cattle which enables them to put their dreams about America into execution, yet he has not money to pay the Countess her rent.

The Countess of Sutherland and her estate officials were strongly against any loss of population through emigration. Only one person from her estate was amongst those 'who had emigrated lately' [ie up to 1772]. However it was later reported that 735 persons emigrated in 1772-3. In due course, under the new sett (rental) of Assynt in 1775 each tenant was allowed only one farm but many farms were still held conjointly by two or more tenants. As there was no appreciable rise in the overall rental the implication must be that the tenants had previously been rack-renting their sub-tenants.[2] It at least can be suggested that the Sutherland family at this time was working for the benefit of the poorer people in a deteriorating situation and has been blamed for the actions of their tacksmen.

Captain Sutherland reported in February 1772 that

there is an emigration going on in this country in imitation of the Isle of Skye...I have appointed all those who intend to leave the country with the tacksmen under whom they have lived for some years past, to meet me at Kildonan. I do not hear of any embarking in the scheme by the subtenants of those who have large highland tacks except George Mackay at Mudal and a young lad of the name of MacPherson. I wrote to George Mackay who is the ringleader but I have no answer from him as yet. I guess that their great argument in support of the migration will be the want of victual and the oppression they meet with from their masters the tacksmen.[3]

Strathnaver was in an uproar as about 200 people declared their intention to emigrate, (a figure that was to rise to about 400 by the summer months). Families set out on foot for Glasgow during May and passed through Edinburgh on 2nd June. It was reported that they had been turned out by opulent drovers who had engrossed their farms. It was considered

very remarkable that none was prevailed upon to inlist in the army, chusing to try their fortunes abroad rather than starve at home, although all the recruiting sergeants were exerting themselves to persuade them.[4]

Bishop Hay wrote that the 21 families, (another source suggests 48 families) had no money. They included large numbers of children many of whom had smallpox, and many of the women were pregnant. Collections were made for them.[5] Captain Sutherland reported that "our emigrants have made very false report in regard to the cause of their leaving the country". The magistrates in Edinburgh apparently offered to employ them and give them meal until they could pay for it, but the emigrants refused and hoped that the Lord would open the magistrates' hearts to help them on their way to Carolina. "When the magistrates would not listen to them, they got a Mr McPheal to preach a Sermon, and the next day they proceeded for Glasgow".[6] They sailed to Philadelphia early in July, possibly in the *Magdalene*, or the *St Andrew*.[7] (Fig. 7.1)

In mid June George Mackay at Mudal travelled south to Burntisland to charter the *Adventure* to carry 200 people to Cape Fear at £3 5s per head; he paid £300 to £400 to

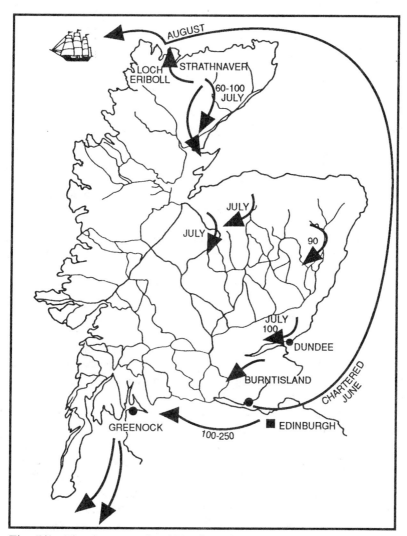

Fig. 7/1 The drove roads of Northern Scotland showing the routes taken by emigrants in 1772.

the master to victual the ship. The stores purchased consisted of 33 bolls oatmeal, 10 bolls peas, 20 cwt barley, 5 cwt cheese, 62 cwt biscuits, 10 cwt butter, 1 cwt vinegar and 4 tierce beef. The ship took on a full complement of emigrants at Loch Eriboll and set sail for Cape Fear on 19th August 1772.[8] Captain Sutherland wrote to James Campbell of Turrerick, factor on Dunrobin, on 20th June,

> I was a good deal surprised to find he, [Mackay] has a letter signed by Lieut. Walter Gray [tacksman of Rhian near Lairg], Kenneth Scobie [tacksman of Achmore], Mr Forbes the sherriff and one Mackay, who I take to be George's brother in law binding themselves for the freight of these people.

Here we have the full evidence of the influence of the tacksmen in supporting emigration, although all these gentlemen stayed behind in Scotland. Campbell replied to the Captain on July 26th:

> 350 or 400 were engaged and paid their freight for that Strathnaver ship and there is 60 to 100 that is to travel on foot to Glasgow that cannot get a passage in the ship for want of room.

In July Captain Sutherland reported that another ship anchored in Loch Broom was offering passages to America for as little as £3 per head.[9] The ship has not been identified but was probably waiting for emigrants from Skye.

Groups of people from different places moved slowly southwards. The band of 60-100 people formed from those unable to take passage on the *Adventure* wound their way south, following other groups such as one of 100 which passed through Dundee and another of 90 which passed Kincardine O'Neil, a village 24 miles west of Aberdeen, at the beginning of July. "Several detachments of these voluntary exiles past the Spey" at the end of July on their way to Greenock. Little more is heard of these groups, but large numbers of Highlanders trudging through the countryside spread the awareness of emigration widely. These Gaelic speaking people were very poor and many blamed the enormous price of provisions for their departure. Some people had had to indent and on being asked how they would manage on the voyage an emigrant replied that "they hoped the King would do something for them".[10] Captain Sutherland was vexed to meet people on the road to Edinburgh who had been inovlved in the estate work that had been set up for the unemployed; works such as building dykes and planting trees. He saw one group "lying all over the country and those that can work are dispersed everywhere, some of them I saw in Fife and I suppose the greatest part of them will return after the harvest is over". These were some of the men and women who joined the annual migration from Strathnaver to find seasonal work further south.

"The spirit of emigration spreads like a contagion over Ross and Caithness" and this included Sir John Gordon of Invergordon's estate. Some of the people there were said to be preparing to emigrate in 1773, but nothing more is known about them.[11] In September 1773 the *Batchelor* sailed into Thurso harbour to pick up 280 people from Caithness and Sutherland, a few coming from the Sutherland estates. Another group of people was boarding the *Nancy* at Dornoch; this was said to be the third ship loading in Caithness at the time. (For the detailed story of these voyagaes, see chapter 9). Meantime a group of five families, some 50 people from Sutherland, trudged towards Greenock during October 1773.

The disquiet felt by contemporary observers can be appreciated as it was estimated that in the years 1772 and 1773 1500 people out of a total population of about 20,000 had left the county; and it was calculated that if 1000 of them paid £3. 10s for their passage and took £4 in cash with them, some £7500 was taken, an amount exceeding a year's rent for the whole county of Sutherland.[12]

Robert Gray of Creich was the largest single tacksman in Assynt and was believed to have organised a visit to Dornoch by an agent of some Glasgow merchants who wanted, "a cargo of servants for America next summer". The agent was one 'Angus Sutherland's son' whom Captain Sutherland castigated:

> I wish with all my heart it had been contrived to have got him or any of those enemies to the country a hearty drubing for tho' they cannot carry off the tenants they will with their own lies debauch the servants which must distress the country and for my own part I think the plan Robert Gray and Angus Sutherland's son is on is a really rascally one ... those who shall drub the American agents, deserve the thanks and goodwill of all the country from the Countess to the smallest tenant in the country.[13]

Yet another group of about 200 people from the northern Highlands arrived in Greenock in May 1775 to look for a boat to take them to America.[14] In addition to the loss of labour due to emigration Captain Sutherland was soon to find that he had lost more men to America but they were marching off to the war.

Lochaber

The Duke of Gordon and the Commissioners of the Annexed Estates were large landowners, with many thousands of people in Lochaber and Badenoch. The weather played a prominent part in sending people out of this region - the poor harvests and resulting disease decimated this population also and only those who were comparatively healthy were able to pack up and go.

William Tod, factor on the Duke's lands of Badenoch and Lochaber, kept James Ross, the principal factor to the Duke of Gordon, informed of the distress in his districts in 1772. In February Lochaber had its worst ever storm, with the snow lying and the cattle dying by the dozen so that Tod expected

> One third of the poor people to die of mere want before the new cropt was available due to a shortage of meal, seed and provender and still the weather making it impossible to start labouring.

By March extra supplies of meal had to be imported to the area and Mr Butter (the factor for the Annexed Estates Commissioners) "gives universal and unlimited credit in that article - meal being with them the debt of honour". In May they were sent some meal though Mr Tod warned that the people would be unable to pay for it at Martinmas though he thought they would agree to pay interest from then until such time as they could pay; nor could they wait for the meal to be supplied until Mr Tod could ascertain such niceties as who was to hand out the meal and what credit was to be given. He also warned that the local horses would be too weak to carry the meal back so that those from the neighbouring district would have to carry it.

A number of the sub-tenants wanted to be "off" at Whitsunday, but Mr Tod hoped that some of them could pay a little more rent while others were good tenants and the place so poor he felt that, however bad the precedent, it was worth giving a year's discount until the new sett of the estate. He considered that certain rents were too high and that a discount should be given, if not a reduction in rent, in the new sett and talked of "the extravagent rent and the total bankruptcy of the tacksmen". If the men went, several places would be waste. One of the improvements most needed in the district was the introduction of the linen manufacture in all its branches. There were 1500 women "quite idle for want of employment in that way and who would all willingly work if they could get lint etc and persons to pay them for it".

Five tacksmen had already renounced their leases before they were out so that they could sell their few remaining cattle before it was too late, and go. Strathmassie and his brother Crubinmore, for instance, were to go to St John's in 1772 to look for a settlement. These people had doubtless been encouraged by hand bills such as those sent out by Lt Gov Debrissey and by Dr Witherspoon and John Pagan. Another four or possibly five farms would be vacant at Whit 1773 and if times did not improve by then the tacksmen of Brae Roy would not "be *able* to keep their possessions, but they have not renounced".

Mr Tod had managed to dissuade the Lochaber folk from going, at least for the time being, hoping that the next season would be more favourable, but he knew it was only a holding operation for, as he said:

> the truth is Lochaber is at present such a scene of every species of misery and distress both of man and beast that the poor people can hardly know what to offer or how they shall be able to keep possession upon any conditions. Many of their sub-tenants have already left the country, and hundreds of them are carried off by a feverish disorder which rages violently thro' the country at present, and is particularly fatal to the young and vigorous.

The Lochaber folk were not alone in going, for:

> the tenants of all the neighbouring heritors are giving up their leases fast and if the spirit of settling colonies in America is only kept up two years longer, you will certainly see waste lands in the Highlands, and who can blame the poor people to push their fortunes elsewhere rather than live as slaves and beggars on their native soil.

One laird, Mr Hall," brought a removing" against his tenants, in other words notice to quit, which they at first disputed, but they were determined to go to America, although Glengarry

> whose tenants they also are, and at whom they are most offended, has offered them any terms they choose to ask in case they will desist, but it's feared they have already put it out of their own power to stay.

Another group of tenants, from MacDonald of Keppoch's estate was also emigrating "being no longer able to bear the insolence and rapaciousness of their master"; this would mean there would be only one MacDonell left behind who would be worth retaining as a tenant.[15]

William Tod did not mention other known emigrations from the western Highlands. In July 1771 Kenneth Reoch, a merchant in Georgetown, Maryland, had organised 80 men and women to embark at Loch Broom, 23 of whom were indented, the rest were "adventurers".[16] A further 835 people were reported to have left Rossshire in 1772-3, of whom 438 were children.[17] There was yet another emigration from the area south of Fort William in 1773. Little is known of this event except from the report in the *Scots Magazine* that 425 men, women and children had left from Lochaber, Appin and Mamore, which were under the control of the Annexed Estates Commissioners. They sailed from Fort William on September 1st to an unspecified destination in America and were said to have taken £6000 in cash with them.[18]

William Tod argued that rents were still too high in 1775, particularly in Lochaber, but that by giving a reasonable discount of rent, he had prevented a single man from leaving the Duke of Gordon's estate while many of the neighbouring ones were laid waste. Many of his people were still prepared to go if they found the least difficulty in making a new bargain for their farms. Mr Tod still insisted that it was essential to prepare a new sett even though the times were unfavourable and that the Duke would have to be more generous as the concessions made by Glenmoriston and the Chisholm had made the inhabitants of Highland estates "very sensible of their own consequences".[19] Although strenuous efforts were being made on these estates to halt the outflow of people, Tod knew that migration was inevitable from an over-populated and not very fertile area.

Strathspey

As early as 1767 an "incomer" had acquired a lease of one of the farms in Aberarder, on the eastern bank of Loch Ness, from Henry Butter, factor on the forfeited Cluny estate. The new tenant tried to clear the farm of its 80 inhabitants, but they resisted. Their final appeal to the House of Lords failed two years later (except for one tenant) and the people emigrated to America.[20]

To the east of the Great Glen the clan Grant held sway in Strathspey and faced a similar situation to that found in Sutherland and Lochaber. The people there were so poor as a result of the very bad harvest of 1772 that the factor begged James Grant, younger of Grant, to let them delay paying their rents until after the summer market of 1773 when they might be able to sell their cloth and cattle. "If you are pleased to desire me to fall upon them sooner it will hurt them and make bad payment to you".[21] Mr Grant was only able to keep some of his people in Strathspey by agreeing to them having their possessions at a price agreed by two knowledgeable gentlemen of the country but

all these people were formerly the sub-tenants of one or other of the gentlemen and were only set at liberty a few years ago ... The truth is that these poor people were so elated at the thoughts of getting free of the tyrany of their former masters that they agreed to pay more than the real value rather than submit to it.[22]

A father in Strathspey wrote to his son in America in July 1773 that:

we cannot entertain you with any news from this country, which is still in the same situation as when you left it excepting that it is much poorer. Our crop this last season was exceeding rained and scanty. The whole nation is threatened with a general famine.[23]

It was feared that emigration would soon become general in Strathspey for 250 emigrants sailed from Fort George on the *David and Ann* in September, and another 240 on the *Concord*.[24] The following year some of Grant's tenants decided to emigrate and one hundred people set off to walk to Glasgow, where they arrived on 21st April 1774. The party boarded the *George* at Greenock and sailed for New York on 20th May; of the 172 emigrants 140 were from Strathspey. The passengers included Mr and Mrs Cumming and family, Captain McPherson and his family and Rev Mr Addison. They arrived in New York on 15th July.[25]

Robert Grant commented from Downpatrick in Northern Ireland:

I was sorry to see a paragraph in the Edinburgh paper the other day that mentioned the arrival of 100 emigrants from Strathspey at Glasgow ready to embark for America. I hope it is not so. In the meantime I shall be sadly uneasy till you write me as I am much interested in everything, when I think the consequences may be attended by inconveniencys to the family of Grant I own to you that I do not take the idea of your losing your people, it is dangerous to the country in general but more particularly to a Highland estate therefore every prudent method should be taken to prevent them.[26]

Sir James Grant of Grant (the good Sir James), who succeeded to the baronetcy and chieftainship of Clan Grant on the death of his father Ludovick in 1773, was considerably perturbed about the deteriorating political situation in America and the contribution that these disgruntled emigrants could make there. On March 30th 1775 his clerk wrote to John Grant of Tulloch,

Sir James desired me this day to write to you to beg you would be so good as make strict and particular enquiry as to Macpherson in Drumullie in such a manner as the same as follows may be authenticated as fact to Sir James, viz. Macpherson's name, birth and occupation, from what part of America he came last, how long he has been in this country, what people he has persuaded to leave their native country, the copy of the terms of indenture, when they take shipping, at what port and for what port of America? All the above he hopes that you will go about as secret as possible and let no one know you have any particular reason for so doing or that Sir James wants such an account.

One question he did not ask was why the people were leaving. The reply must have increased his fears for on April 19th 1775 Sir James Grant wrote to the Lord Advocate, Henry Dundas:

As yet my country has been little affected, (by emigration), but I am confident the frenzy will extend universally, if proper means are not taken to prevent it. It is in the power at present of any little pedling merchant to carry off hundreds and as the Highlanders are so connected by intermarying you will easily see how far thay may extend.[27] (See chapter 11 for the full text of this letter and the Lord Advocate's reaction).

Towards the end of May 1775 Mr Tod heard that the Duke of Gordon had intercepted a body of people from Strathspey and "was so good as to attempt to dissuade them from leaving their country" by offering to accommodate them with lands.[28] This group of over

200 people was gathering at Aviemore in preparation for the long march to Greenock. In May their arrival was announced in the *Edinburgh Advertiser*. On June 6th it was reported that in the preceeding two weeks four vessels containing about 700 emigrants sailed from Greenock and Port Glasgow while two more vessels were sailing north to pick up more passengers.[29] A convoy of five ships scheduled for Virginia and one for New York left Greenock on May 26th and a further three boats for Virginia and one for New York sailed on June 2nd. Those boats identified as carrying passengers did not include people from Sutherland or Strathspey. However we know that a party of 24 people from the Inverness area must have trudged down the Great Glen and crossed the sea to Stornoway. They were among those who boarded the *Clementina* for Philadelphia. The company consisted of 90 men, of whom roughly half were farmers and the rest "servants", with 68 women and 54 children. This is the only known emigration from the area around the Moray Firth.[30]

James McIntosh was probably on the *Monimia* one of the ships in the convoy. He became schoolmaster at West Chester, Pennsylvania, and wrote to his father, in Gaigh, Kingussie:

> We arrived here safe the 26th of July, having a passage of nine weeks, two days excepted which time were enjoyed a double portion of health, (thank God for it), we had no sea sickness but about two hours and an half, we got 232 passengers on board and lost none of them but Thomas McPhails youngest child, who died of the jaundice through excess of sleep, in stead of whom our cook's wife brought furth a child. Indeed our passage had been very long, yet I would not scruple to go to sea tomorrow, because I know that the Lord is to be found there as well as any else where, and that I very well know that seldom any misluck happens to any who come here; and indeed I must own that we came over, in a very troublesome time, as the Americans and the Government are so enraged against one another; they had several battles fought at Boston and the adjacent colonies that by the American Continental Congress we are informed that no less than 1300 of the English army were killed in the field, and no more than 400 of the American army. The Americans are so obstinate that they will all chuse to die by the sword than condescend to the slavery the King intends to bring them under, they are daily under arms, and can rise by one beat of the drum.[31]

Hector McLaine was not so fortunate. He sailed in an unknown ship which appears to have been wrecked, and in February 1776 wrote a somewhat garbled account to his father who lived in Rossshire. Hector was badly injured during the shipwreck but managed to reach shore by hanging on to a spar of a boat. There he was picked up and looked after for nine weeks before being fit enough to travel to New York where he hoped to become a ship's carpenter. McLaine declared that he had lost his family, but his father told him, after he got ashore, that his mother was ashore and two of his daughters "badly hurt and brused on board". Perhaps the family survived but were separated after the disaster.[32]

During the years 1772-5 there was an almost continuous movement of hundreds of people walking to the port of embarkation from the remote corners of Scotland on the start of their journey to America. Yet there are few accounts of the trek from home to port; the distance from Strathnaver to Glasgow is about 300 miles.

A.R.B. Haldane has pointed out that although General Wade constructed nearly 250 miles of military roads south of the Great Glen between 1723 and 1740, "the first properly constructed roads to be made in the Highlands, they did little more than touch the fringe of the problem of Highland transport". There remained a network of tracks, pack horse trails and drove roads. Roads were to become a force for economic change only after Telford's engineering triumphs in the early nineteenth century. The Highlanders appreciated the opening up of markets as a result of Wade's roads, but some critics complained that they opened the country to strangers and weakened the attachment of the clansmen to the chieftains, while remote districts were laid open to invasion.[33] Most journeys were on foot for roads that could take wheeled traffic were few and far between. Although they could have hired a chaise between Inverness and Fort Augustus, Dr Johnson and James Boswell were among the 'elite when they were able to hire relays of ponies for their celebrated tour; horses with men running beside them to lead the way. It was along these tracks that the emigrants had to walk, carrying their children and all the baggage they were taking with them to America, for it is doubtful if even sledges, let alone carts, could be drawn along many of them.

William Gilpin has left an account of the progress of one party from Breadalbane. "The *word was given*, as it was phrased" at the beginning of March 1775 and a rendezvous at Killin appointed for May 1st. About 30 families, 300 souls, from the Breadalbane estates, gathered. There they slept in barns and other outhouses which they had previously engaged.

> Early next morning the whole company was called together by the sound of bag-pipes and the order of march was settled. Men, women and children had all their proper stations assigned ... they were a jocund crew; and set out, not like people flying from the face of poverty; but like men who were about to carry their health, their strength and little property to a better market.

All the people wore their best attire, the men were armed, many had as much as £200 or £300 in money, few had less than £30 or £40 and all had provisions with them. Some of the men were able to hire carts. That day the party marched to the head of Loch Lomond, about 25 or 30 miles, where their hired boats were ready to take them down the loch for their last short march to Dumbarton; there they waited until their boat was ready at Greenock.[34] Only one ship has been identified as carrying these people- the *Commerce* which sailed for New York in June with 116 people from Breadalbane. The company consisted of 21 farmers and 12 servants, six wrights, five taylors, three smiths and three masons, two shoemakers and two pipers and one schoolmaster, one weaver, one founder and one tiddler. 15 wives and 43 children accompanied the men. An advance party of about 40 people had sailed in the *Lily* in April.[35]

The Atlantic Seaboard

As noted in chapter 4 most of the emigrants from Scotland in the 1730s and early 1740s went from Argyllshire. In May 1768 the *Scots Magazine* reported a further emigration from that area. Some 40 or 50 families, including some persons "of good circumstances" went from Jura to Cape Fear, North Carolina; they possibly sailed on the *Bell* from Port Glasgow on June 1st.[36] The following year Hector McAlester wrote from Islay to his brother Alexander, who had settled in North Carolina in 1736, that he was returning to North Carolina as

> their are some hundreds of families in this island and our neighbouring county Argyleshire,

determined to leave their country, and have applyd to me to goe with them to Carolina.[37]

When the *Mally* sailed from Islay for North Carolina on 21st July 1769 with a full load of emigrants, the *Scots Magazine* reported that this was the "third or fourth emigration from Argyll since the conclusion of the late war". Another boat, the brig *Helen*, sailed from Campbeltown on July 31st for Cape Fear with 84 men and women and 60 children. The passengers carried their belongings in "20 chests and 11 barrels of mens' and womens' apparels and bed cloathes, 60 axes, 60 edges, 30 hand borers and 20 handsaws". 100 families of Highlanders arrived in Brunswick, North Carolina in September and two more emigrant boats were expected any day.[38]

In 1770 the *Scots Magazine* reported that a further six large vessels with 1200 people aboard "at a moderate computation", had sailed from the Western Isles and other parts of the Highlands between April and August.[39] Robert Forbes, the Episcopal Bishop of Ross and Caithness, believed that 800 were from Argyllshire and about 500 from Islay, all going to North Carolina.[40] So far only two of these vessels can be positively identified. The *Neptune* was advertised for North Carolina in February by merchants in Campbeltown and sailed from Port Glasgow on 17th July with 360 people. The *Edinburgh* sailed from Campbeltown for North Carolina on August 29th with 120 emigrants on board.[41] Governor Tryon of North Carolina confirmed that 1600 settlers from Arran, Jura, Islay and Gigha had settled in the colony, most of them in Cumberland county, in the previous three years.[42]

Both the *Glasgow Journal* and *Edinburgh Advertiser* reported that in February 1771 some hundreds were preparing to emigrate from Islay and Skye to go to Georgia and New Caledonia (Nova Scotia). In June the *Scots Magazine* reported that 500 from Islay and adjacent islands were preparing to leave.[43] Referring to Islay, the *Edinburgh Advertiser* hoped that

> some proper plan will be thought of to encourage our natives to cultivate their own country; there are abundance of improvements still wanting in this part of the kingdom and the loss of useful hands must soon impoverish any country.[44]

The only known boat to have sailed was the *Elizabeth*, which left Campbeltown on July 27th with 70 (or 100) passengers; their luggage was contained in "27 barrels and seven parcels of household furniture, apparel and cloaths". Governor Martin commented in March 1772:

> Near 1000 people have arrived in Cape Fear River from the Scottish Isles since the month of November with a view to settle in this province whose prosperity and strength will receive great augmentation by the accession of such a number of hardy, laborious and thrifty people.[45]

By 1772 a correspondent from the Western Isles was complaining that since 1768 the people who had emigrated from this poor corner of Scotland had carried with them at least £10,000 in specie.[46](Fig. 7.2)

Godfrey McNeill from Argyll was said to have sailed on the *Brunswick* from Greenock to Virginia in August 1773, to look for a suitable settlement for a number of families from Argyll.[47] Daniel McLeod of Kilmorie, in Arran, set off from Williamsburg, Virginia, to view the lands in Beekman township on Lake Champlain that he had already bought in order to allow a considerable number of families to settle there and indeed

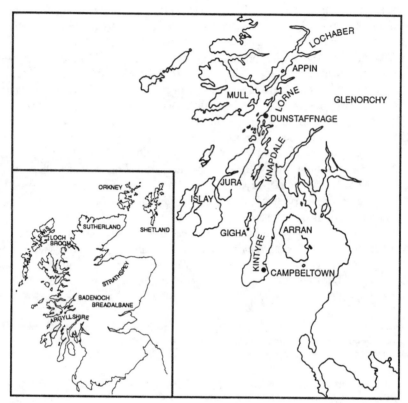

Fig. 7.2   The districts in Argyllshire from which emigrants departed.

he did take across 58 men and 43 women.[48] The brigantine *Carolina Packet* sailed from Greenock on October 13th 1774 for Cape Fear, calling at Lochindaal in Islay to pick up 62 emigrants from Islay and Mull, "only five of the passengers were people of any consequence, the rest were of a lower class, servants of the Gentlemen, or labourers who could pay for their passage". The ship had to put into Campbeltown for five days at the beginning of December, but reached Cape Fear safely by 17th January 1775.[49]

Emigrants were being encouraged by authors such as the anonymous *Scotus Americanus* who wrote a tract from Islay in 1773 recommending North Carolina. This man blamed the landowners for shaking the "iron rod of oppression" too much over the tenants. Absentee landlords, if they visited them only oppressed more, they were accompanied by minions and sycophants, and if the poor reached them

> they find such an awful distance and state kept, that they are spurned away with looks expressive of the utmost contempt, or dismissed with a volley of oaths and curses, in a language strange and unknown to most of them.

Landowners, he wrote, also railed against their tenants for not improving but did nothing themselves. In North Carolina, he continued, the land was easily cleared because the trees were tall, not too near together and there was little undergrowth. The method of settling was to find a space of King's land or commons, or unpatented land and get an order from the governor which was given to a surveyor. This plan was returned to the office for recording patents, signed by the governor and was then good for ever. The expense was 10 guineas and 2s 6d per annum quit rent per 100 acres. Once 70 or 80 acres were opened up it was enough for the support and employment of one family. New emigrants were far more independent than the old settlers; and if a man could take £500 in cash into the country he could live as well as a proprietor in Scotland could on £500 per annum. However, some people were unable to pay their passage to Cape Fear so went as redemptioners, and if, 40 days after landing, they were unable to find the money from friends or by work they were bound to serve for three years. Some of the first settlers had big tracts of uncleared land, but no labour, they therefore rented for 12 months' provisions, the use of implements and livestock, and sometimes black slaves. In return, the labourer gave the produce of the land, one third of a bushel of grain, the third hog etc, but could sell as much turpentine and staves for his own use as he pleased. Finally, the author warned immigrants not to overeat on arrival.[50]

On the other hand some newspaper correspondents hoped to discourage emigrants by quoting unfavourable reports of conditions in America, such as this picture of life in North Carolina:

> A captain of a vessel lately arrived [1772] in Clyde from Charlestown affirms that many of the poor deluded farmers that went away some years ago from Islay etc to the back settlement of Carolina were heartily sorry for having been so easily imposed upon and that they applied to him in numbers to obtain a passage to their native country. It is a pity that our people should be sent to cultivate the waste lands in America and such large tracts of ground lying uncultivated in our own country. Were the waste lands throughout the kingdom portioned out in small parcels and given to poor and industrious families, at a small quit-rent or no rent; it would not only be a very charitable expedient by providing for many hundreds who are now in want, but might be a means of preventing such emigrations and would ever most effectually and certainly prevent the necessities of life from being at such exorbitant prices. The cottagers with the small

farms would be obliged constantly to supply markets with poultry, butter, eggs, cheese etc in order to procure for themselves such necessaries as they would from time to time be in want of, besides a great part of the country which now lies desolate and useless would be inhabited and rendered beautiful by cultivation.[51]

A group of 92 people sailed on the *Ulysses* on 13th August 1774 for Wilmington, N.Carolina, where they arrived on 17th October. Another party of 36 sailed on the *Diana* on 15th September arriving at Brunswick in the autumn. There were two Glaswegians in the party, all the rest were from Kintyre, of whom nine were farmers with their families.[52] The shipping agents - John Buchanan senior, merchant in Greenock, George Buchanan junior, merchant in Glasgow and Alexander Mowbray, merchant in Edinburgh - advertised in May 1774 for any young people willing to indent for America. Their boat, the *Sharp*, sailed from Greenock for New York in the middle of June. On board were Alexander Campbell, son of Duncan Campbell of Glenure, with his wife and family and 160 other people, probably from Appin.[53]

In May 1775 it was reported that another 500 people from Kintyre were preparing to go to America. The families from there, from Knapdale and the nearby islands assembled on Gigha where two boats were waiting to embark them. The emigrants were said to be in high spirits and in "no way intimidated on account of the many informations they receive concerning the commotions in the British colonies and the danger of emigrating at this time".[54] One of these boats may have been the *Jupiter* of Larne which sailed from Dunstaffnage in September with 200 passengers from Argyllshire for Wilmington where she arrived on 14th November. The party, of whom only six were over 50 and 47 were under 10 years of age, included an officer, four farmers, one shipmaster, four tradesmen and ten labourers from Appin; two tradesmen, seven labourers and five female spinsters from Glenorchy; and two labourers from Lismore, with their respective families.[55] The *Edinburgh Advertiser* commented on the passengers in the *Jupiter* that:

> though formerly among the first to take up arms against the reigning family they now declare their readiness to support government in case they find it necessary on their arrival in America. They advance for their conduct in emigrating in these troublesome times, that it is better to confront an enemy in the wildest desert in that country than have to be beggars in their native land; that the oppressions of their landlords are such, that none but the timid will bear them while an asylum can be found in those wild but happy regions of America for those that have a spirit to seek for it. Many of them are amongst the best in circumstances in this neighbourhood, one of them went away with his seven sons. In short, the migrations of the sheep graziers from the south and the uncharitable exactions of the proprietors of lands will soon banish the old inhabitants and depopulate their poor but once happy country, which, as Ulysses says of Ithaca, is, a barren clime, but breeds a generous race. Our readers will observe that the above emigrations happened before the orders were issued by the commissioners of the customs for stopping them. It is expected these orders will prevent the infatuated people from ruining themselves.[56] (see Chapter 11 for the orders).

Once the decision to leave had been forced upon the Highlanders, the hardships of a land journey often of hundreds of miles, on foot and carrying their scanty possessions, were followed by the miseries of the Atlantic voyage. Many then faced years of indentured service. On the outbreak of war, before they had received any benefit from settling in a new land those who remained loyal to the government found themselves on the move again - this time to Canada.

8

"The Infection is Catched"

The Isle of Skye

Dr Johnson left the mainland of Scotland to visit some of the Hebridean islands. Although he was horrified at the condition of many of the houses, he enjoyed hospitlity and the intellectual qualities of many of the men and women, including some in Skye.[1] The impetus for mass emigration from the Isle of Skye can be traced to the actions taken by Norman McLeod of McLeod in his attempt to avoid imminent bankruptcy. He forced upon his tenantry a massive increase in rents when he leased the estate for 23 years from Whitsunday 1769. He made no provision to assist the tenants with agrarian improvements and consequently denied them any possibility of increasing their productivity and their capacity to pay their increased rents. McLeod's callous policy was taken up by Sir Alexander McDonald of Sleat, the Duke of Gordon and other proprietors. (Fig. 8.1)

There can be no doubt that there was considerable unrest among the people of Skye, including some of the very substantial tacksmen. Reasons given for their dissatisfaction included the haughty behaviour of the lairds, high rents, excessive grassums and the fall in the price of cattle. The proprietors thought that their tenants were indolent and stubborn; that the Skye men showed a spirit of independence, or at least resistance, to alien ideas of unremitting labour.

> The spirit of the inhabitants of that part of the country was not so pliable and easily moulded as in the interior and more civilised parts of the kingdom where the inhabitants were inured from their infancy to toil and fatigue.

It was suggested that because the tenants disdained taking farms in the low country, where Highlanders were held in contempt, they preferred to launch out into a new world where they believed they could get farms cheaply, even, if necessary, conquering Indians to do so.[2]

Bishop Robert Forbes reported that 2000 emigrants were preparing to leave Skye in 1771, for St John's Island, all from the estate of Sir Alexander McDonald of Sleat.[3] (Donald Mackay gives the date as 1768 for this emigration but no evidence has been found to support this view.) By February 10th 1771 ten of the most substantial gentlemen had signed a covenant to leave and had engaged 100 families to go with them. Then at a meeting in Portree, on 5th March (the meeting has also been dated 11th March), the tenants of Sir Alexander McDonald of Sleat drew up a scheme of emigration to go to America. In about two days some 300 people had subscribed at least £20 sterling, one man subscribing £120. Each subscriber was at liberty to engage some of the lesser

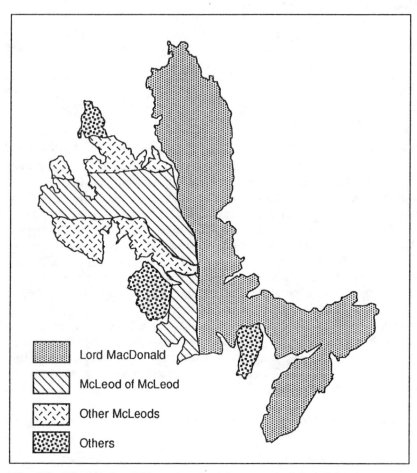

Fig. 8/1   The lairds of Skye showing the extent of their island estates
in the 18th century, with boundaries generalised.

tenants to accompany him to the New World. Thirty tacksmen from Sir Alexander's estate signed and more were joining every day "like a disease the infection is catched from one person to another". They proposed emigrating as a single body to North Carolina where they would buy lands and settle near each other. After the meeting they drank to their late landlord who "always studied to make them an easy and happy people". It was suggested that "they despise toil and trouble or any hardships they may suffer themselves as its working for a perpetuity to their descendents".[4] The *Glasgow Journal* of 28th March 1771 reported in these terms:

> Many more are daily following this example having transferred their attachment from the proprietors to the farmers. There will be a great quantity of black cattle to be sold in Skye this summer.

Norman McLeod wrote to Thomas Pennant that 270 people had left Glenelg on the mainland opposite Skye. Several people were actively soliciting for emigrants. For example, Alexander Morrison of Shinidin, a tenant on the McLeod estate, made plans to leave from Bracadale and sent a circular inviting people to go with him to America. Other islands, too, were in turmoil as Maclean of Muck had given notice to 20 to 30 families on Eigg to quit at Whitsunday 1771.[5]

There was much discussion of the problem between the landlords. Sir Alexander McDonald wrote to McLeod of McLeod in June 1771 saying that his small tenants were very poor and unable to take enough land to maintain themselves and their cattle and that his tacksmen had thrown up their tacks before he was able to reach the estate to talk with them. He hoped that McLeod would serve his people better as "they have been civiller than mine" because they were waiting peaceably for his arrival, so he should "explain the length that you can go, unless you find them very refractory".[6]

A neighbour thought that even if Sir Alexander had tried to pacify his people and given them their lands as they had held them formerly, he would have failed as "the people have such a universal hatred against him". Alexander McLeod, natural son of the clan chief McLeod of McLeod, reckoned that Sir Alexander McDonald would have £1500 of laigh lands without tenants and on his own estates the people would see Sir Alexander's lands

> waste or at best inhabited by tenants which will destroy the breed of cattle so much as will depreciate the character and prices of Skye cattle in general and the land rent will fall when it's too late for them to carry themselves away.[7]

Indeed it was Bishop Hay's opinion that the Highland gentry would "very soon have more than cause to repent the repressive measures they have followed for some times past".[8]

The papers reported that hundreds of people were embarking in February and September 1771. Customs officials noted that Captain Chivers in the *Nancy* of Londonderry made journeys from Loch Tarbert in Skye to North Carolina in 1770 and 1771, each time with 300 passengers, some of them being men of property. The boat reached Carolina on January 5th 1772 after fifteen weeks at sea, "suffering much by bad weather and want of provisions". Confirmation came from Hector McCaraig who wrote to his brother "some hundred famylies [are] goeing this year from the island of Skye".[9]

In 1772 the Privy Council refused the petition of James MacDonald of Portree and Norman MacDonald of Sleat in Skye for themselves and Hugh MacDonald, John Betton and Edmund and Alexander MacQueen of Sleat, the Rev William MacQueen and Alexander Macdonald of Skye, for 40,000 acres in North Carolina which had been referred to the Board of Trade on 14th June. The Board of Trade had reported that

> the emigration of the inhabitants of Great Britain and Ireland to the American colonies is a circumstance in their opinion which cannot fail to lessen the strength and security, and to prejudice the landed interest and manufacturers of the kingdom, and the great extent to which this emigration has of late years prevailed, renders it an object well deserving the serious attention of Government.[10]

The winter of 1771/2 was extremely harsh and the tenants lost around one third of their cattle. The financial problems of the Clan McLeod became critical and the aged and infirm clan chief passed over his authority in 1772 to his 18 year old grandson Norman, who was assisted by John (Coll) McLeod of Talisker. On McLeod of McLeod's estate of Dunvegan the tenants were restive but not yet at the point of preparing to leave, though they were complaining of the high rents and not only of being deprived of wood, but of having to pay for any wood they did manage to collect. The young Norman McLeod suggested that it would be shocking to proceed against them by law, but he said that the insolence of their behaviour justified any severity,

> If they will not be satisfied with reasonable terms, leave them; and if they stop payment any messenger in Scotland will execute dilligence. Our constitution is now so well established that any part of High Majesty's dominions is as acceptable to law as London or Edinburgh.[11]

At first the young McLeod appealed to the ancient bonds of clanship:

> I called the people of the different districts of our estate together; I laid before them the situation of our family - its debts, its burthens, its distress; I acknowledged the hardship under which they laboured; I described and reminded them of the manner in which they and their ancestors had lived with mine; I combated their passion for America with a real account of the dangers and hardships they might encounter there; I besought them to love their young chief and to renew with him the ancient manners; I promised to live among them; I threw myself upon them; I recalled to their remembrance an ancestor who had also found his estate in ruin and whose memory was held in the highest veneration; I desired every district to point out some of their oldest and most respected men to settle with me their every claim; and I promised to do everything for their relief which in reason I could. My worthy relation ably seconded me, and our labour was not in vain. We gave considerable abatement in rents; few emigrated and the clan conceived the most lively attachment to me ...

Later in life General Norman McLeod recalled these difficult days:

> In the year 1771 a strange passion for emigrating to America seized many of the middling and poorer sort of Highlanders. The change of manners in their chieftains since 1745 produced effects which were evidently the proximate cause of this unnatural dereliction of their own, and appetite for, a foreign country. The laws which deprived the Highlanders of their arms and garb would certainly have destroyed the feudal military powers of the chieftains, but the fond attachment of the people to their patriarchs would have yielded to no laws. They were themselves the destroyers of that pleasing influence sucked into a vortex of the nation and

allured to the capitals; they degenerated from patriarchs and chieftains to landlords; and they became as anxious for increase of rent as the new-made lairds, the *Novi Homines*, the mercantile purchasers of the Lowlands. Many tenants, whose fathers, for generations had enjoyed their little spots, were removed for higher bidders. Those who agreed at any price, for their ancient *Lares* [resting places] were forced to pay an increased rent, without being taught any new method to increase their produce. In the Hebrides especially this change was not gradual but sudden, and sudden and baleful were its effects. The people, freed by the laws from the power of the chieftains and loosened by the chiefs themselves from the bonds of affection, turned their eyes and their hearts to new scenes. America seemed to open its arms to receive every discontented Briton. To those possessed of very small sums of money, it offered large possessions of uncultivated but excellent land in a preferable climate; to the poor it held out high wages for labour; to all it promised property and independence. Many artful emissaries who had an interest in the transportation or settlement of emigrants, industriously displayed these temptations; and the desire of leaving their country, for the new land of promise became furious and epidemic. Like all other popular furies, it infected not only those who had reason to complain of their situation or injuries, but those who were most favoured and most comfortably settled. In the beginning of 1772 my grandfather, who had always been a most beneficent and beloved chief but whose necessity had lately induced him to raise his rents, became much alarmed by this new spirit which had reached his clan. Aged and infirm, he was unable to apply the remedy in person; he devolved the task on me, and gave me for an assistant our nearest male relation, Coll McLeod of Talisker. The duty imposed on us was difficult, the estate was loaded with debt, encumbered with a numerous issue from himself and my father, and charged with some jointures. His tenants had lost, in that severe winter, above one-third of their cattle, which constituted their subsistence; their spirits were soured by their losses, and the late augmentation of rents, and their ideas of America were inflamed by the strongest representation and the example of the neighbouring clans. My friend and I were empowered to grant such deductions in the rents as might seem necessary and reasonable; but we found it terrible to decide between the justice to creditors, the necessities of an ancient family which we ourselves represented, and the claims and distresses of an impoverished tenantry.[12]

By April 1772 the *Edinburgh Advertiser* reported that nearly 700 Skye men were preparing to emigrate - one vessel was ready to set sail with 300 people on board, and the remainder were to follow in June and July. On July 17th the same newspaper recorded that

a large ship had been freighted at Greenock to carry 300 passengers from the Isle of Skye to Carolina, this is the emigration mentioned some time ago; they will sail next month. They are from a different quarter of the island from whence last year's emigration went.

The paper next reported that the *Pearl* had sailed from Greenock on August 10th for Skye to pick up 300 passengers for Cape Fear.[13]

Flora MacDonald (protector of Bonnie Prince Charlie) thanked her man of affairs, John McKenzie of Delvine, on August 12th 1772, for his repeated kindness to her and her family of whom

there will soon be no remembrance in this poor miserable island, the best of its inhabitance are making ready to follow their friends to America, while they have anything to bring there, and among the rest we are to go, especially as we cannot promise ourselves but poverty and oppression, having last spring [ie 1771] and this time two years lost almost our whole stock of cattle and horses. We lost within these three years 327 heads so that we have hardly what will pay our creditors which we are to let them have and begin the world again, anewe, in a othere corner of it.[14]

Flora MacDonald's husband, Allan MacDonald of Kingsburgh, recorded on 2nd March 1773,

The only news in this island is emigration. I believe the whole will go to America ... This year they have already signed and preparing to go above 800 souls and all those from Skye or North Uist. It is melancholy to see the state of this miserable place. The Superiors summoning the tenants to remove for not paying the great rents etc, the tenants charging the Superior for oppression, for breaking the conditions of his tacks and wrongeously turning them out of their lands in the months of May and June without previous warning. No respect of persons as the best are mostly gone stealing of sheep, etc constantly, and picking and thieving of corn, garden stuffs and potatoes perpetually, lying, bankrupting and slandering, honesty and integrity fled, villainy and death supported by downright poverty in its place. Most miserable is the state of this once great and good family. When this next emigration is gone only old Aird and other three old men will be all that will be in Sleat and Trotternish of the name MacDonald.[15]

Flora, her husband and family sailed with her brother-in-law Coll McCallister on the *Balliol* in August 1774 from Campbeltown to Wilmington, where her step-father, Hugh, had gone in 1771 or 1772 with other members of the clan. Kingsburgh was no more successful in America than in Skye, though he might have succeeded had he not been caught up in the war. Flora returned to Skye in 1780 where she spent many anxious months waiting for news of her husband and five sons, all of whom had enlisted with the government forces; only one son survived. Allan returned to Scotland in 1784 where he and Flora stayed for the last few years of their lives, dying in 1790 and 1792 respectively.[16]

There was such a shortage of cash in Skye that year that rents had to be paid in bills given by the drovers; when Dr Johnson and Boswell tried to change a bill their messenger was only able to get the money from the master of an emigrant ship.[17] The islanders were desperate and many left during the next few years. Their loyalty was sorely tested when war finally broke out, for the governor of North Carolina enlisted 1600 Highlanders into the Loyalist force which was routed at Moore's Creek Bridge, near Wilmington, on February 26th 1776.[18]

The record is somewhat deficient in regard to the number of ships leaving Skye. The *Nestor* was seen by Dr Johnson on his travels in September 1773, lying in Portree harbour. A few days later Boswell saw the *Margaret* pass the island with emigrants on board. Donaldson maintains that the *Margaret* sailed annually from Portree. This ship is noted in the customs books in 1774 and 1775 but without reference to passengers; she was owned by the merchant family of Buchanans who certainly carried passengers in some of their other boats. Two unnamed boats delivered 244 and 280 emigrants from Skye to Brunswick, North Carolina in 1773 and a third boat from Greenock delivered 102 emigrants. The *Cato* was chartered and sailed from Skye in August 1774 with 372 people for Brunswick where they arrived on 1st December. Alexander McAlester in North Carolina wrote to his brother in January 1774

we have had com this year upwards of seven hundred soles from Skaye and the neighbouring isles and great many expected nixt year.[19]

Rev John Bethune, who went to North Carolina in 1773 and became chaplain to the Royal North Carolina Militia and then the 84th Regiment, later reckoned that 128 people left from Bracadale alone between 1771 and 1774. Dr Johnson summed up these emigrations:

> whole neighbourhoods formed parties for removal; so that departure from their native country is no longer exile ... they change nothing but the place of their abode; and of that change they perceive the benefit.[20]

The people of Skye expressed their feelings in dance as well as in sorrow as James Boswell discovered one evening:

> In the evening the company danced as usual. We performed, with much activity, a dance which, I suppose, the emigration from Sky has occasioned. They call it *America*. Each of the couples, after the common *involutions* and *evolutions*, successively whirls round in a circle, till all are in motion; and the dance seems intended to shew how emigration catches, till a whole neighbourhood is set afloat.[21]

Lewis

The folk on Lewis had also suffered from dreadful weather and a succession of bad harvests. The consequent loss of many cattle and recurrent epidemics of fever added to their burdens.

> The pestilential fever that has rag'd in this part of the country for some time past, is greatly abated. We were afflicted with this disorder, much about the same time last year, but it did not prove so fatal. It is thought to be owing to the vast quantities of fish and herrings that are daily eat [sic] by the inhabitants, the greatest part of whom live entirely upon herrings and potatoes during the fishing months, owing to the scarcity of corn and want of bread.[22]

Between 700 and 800 sailed from Stornoway in July 1772, complaining of the oppression they laboured under.[23] In the following July a further 840 were preparing to cross the Atlantic. The proprietor of the island, Lord Fortrose, hurried from London to treat with the remainder of his tenants.

> What are the terms they asked of him, think you? The land at the old rents; the augmentation paid for three years backward to be refunded and his factor to be immediately dismissed, I have not yet learned whether he has agreed to these terms; but he must soon or his lands will be left an uninhabited waste.[24]

The flow of emigrants continued the following year when the *Friendship* sailed on the 2nd May 1774 from Stornoway for Philadelphia with 106 people on board. In November 1774 the *Peace and Plenty* of New York sailed from Stornoway to New York with 59 people from Lewis and Loch Broom.[25] One of these passengers was twelve year old Alexander Mackenzie who was on his way to join his father in New York. In later life he engaged in the fur trade and explored the great Mackenzie River, which was given his name.

Orkney

The people of Orkney had had long and bitter experience of grasping landlords. It was many generations before they recovered from the rule of the Earls of Morton, the most notorious of whom was Earl Patrick. At his trial he was convicted of having had the weights on the pundlar (steelyard for weighing) increased, thus raising the rents and dues which were paid in kind by weight. He had sentenced and banished his richer subjects and then escheated their lands and goods; he had bound his tenants to serve only himself and not to seek redress of him from the king, council or court of session; of stopping all passages and ferries without his leave; of binding his gentlemen tenants to servile works; and of prohibiting all the inhabitants of Orkney and Shetland from buying or selling anything without his licence. He was executed for treason in 1610.[26] Relations between landlord and tenant were not much improved in the eighteenth century.

Orcadians had for many years sought their fortunes abroad. From 1722 the London directors of the Hudson's Bay Company ordered their ships' captains to call in at many ports on their way north to collect servants for the Company. If they had not enough volunteers, they were to make up the numbers at the last port of call- Kirkwall in Orkney. Orkneymen were well regarded by the Company. Lists of company men are missing before 1774 and the place of origin of the men was not noted before 1790 so it is difficult to know how many Orcadians served in the Company- one estimate is 4-500 by 1790.[27]

By the 1770s Orcadians were emigrating to areas farther south; the dearth of 1772 took its toll in th Orkney islands as a correspondent wrote despairingly:

> The excessive high price of provisions, especially oatmeal, which has been uncommonly dear for two years past, is not the least of many causes to be assigned for this depopulation; the more so, when it is taken into consideration, that the linen manufactory, in all its departments, has greatly decreased; in so much, that many thousands who were formerly supported by this branch alone, cannot, even by the greatest application, earn a scanty subsistence.[28]

Another Orcadian wrote that the people were "in a miserable condition for want of bread and this is the second crop here which threatens nixt to a famine. This one is much worse than the last".[29] But it was not until September 1774 that the first ship called at Orkney with the intention of picking up emigrants for America. Fifty-five people sailed in the *Marlborough* from Stromness to Savannah, Georgia, all being indented servants to Messrs Brown and Gordon. The owner of this vessel, Jonas Brown, indented a further 53 emigrants for their passage in the same vessel the following year. A correspondent wrote from Orkney in September 1775 saying that copies of a printed paper were circulating there, trying to persuade people to emigrate to Georgia, but which, to the sad experience of many who had left that part, had been found exceedingly unhealthy and had proved the burial place of some hundreds of the unhappy people who had been induced to leave that and the neighbouring counties.[30]

Shetland

The Shetlanders were not unaware of the sufferings of the Western Highlands, though few were themselves tempted to go to the New World. Several vessels on their passage to America, entered Shetland harbours, usually when they had been driven far off course. A large emigrant ship was believed to have been wrecked near Hesta head about 1765 but nothing more is known about it.[31] In the winter of 1773-4 the local population entertained about 300 stranded emigrants off the *Batchelor*, which must have put an enormous strain on the limited resources of the islands. (See chapter 9 for details of the voyage.)

One man who did go was John Harrower, a Lerwick merchant. He left his wife and family in 1773 because life was so difficult for them at home. He confided in his diary that he nearly engaged on a boat going from Leith to Carolina (28th December 1773) but instead went on to London. However he was no more successful there so eventually engaged to go to Virginia for four years as a schoolmaster for "Bed, Board, washing and five pound during the whole time". On board the snow *Planter* Harrower met friends from Orkney in equally dire straits. Seventy-five men had indented themselves for four years to Captain Bowers, after being given a medical examination. When the ship arrived in Virginia in May 1775

severals came on board to purchase servts Indentures and among them there was two soul drivers. They are men who make it their business to go on board all ships who have in [them] either servants or convicts and buy sometimes the whole and sometimes a parcell of them as they can agree, and then they drive them through the country like a parcell of sheep untill they can sell them to advantage, but all went away without buying any.

Harrower went to a good master but died suddenly in 1777 without seeing his wife and family again.[32] About 20 Shetlanders travelled to North Carolina below decks on the *Jamaica Packet* in 1774 and a similar number went the following year.[33] All in all, while events in the Western Isles broadly followed those on the mainland, there was little emigration from these Northern Isles.

9

"Accommodation on Very Moderate Terms"

There are few detailed accounts of emigrant voyages across the Atlantic Ocean in the 18th century. This chapter attempts to provide some insights into the privations endured by the emigrants by following the misfortunes of four vessels. They embarked about 800 people in Caithness and Sutherland in August 1773. Groups of people from the Great Glen embarked on the *David and Ann* and the *Concord* at Fort George; another group boarded the *Nancy* at Dornoch; the *Batchelor* picked up more passengers in Thurso Bay. The vessels soon ran into trouble, both man made and natural; their problems became a byword for the hazards an emigrant might suffer. A violent storm blew up in the Minch which scattered the vessels and there were grave fears that two boats had been lost and that the emigrants from the third boat had returned home to Caithness in a most miserable condition. The *Nancy* was not apparently with the other boats. A few days later the newspapers refuted the report, suggesting that the three ships had been spoken to by a boat returning from Grenada

> far beyond the British coast, all well. If any people had left the ships in Stornoway some of the families would have returned home by now. Such accounts as those from Stornoway must come from persons interested to stop the emigrations which perhaps they have been the occasion of, but such low methods always produce a contrary effect than what is intended.[1]

Further reports suggest that the *David and Ann* took on fresh supplies in Stornoway. Conditions on board were terrible with 16 dying at sea although help was obtained from other vessels including a French Guineaman. The emigrants finally arrived in Bermuda about 1st March 1774 in a very weak condition. After recuperating for a fortnight they continued their journey to New York, where they arrived on April 13th.[2]

The Batchelor

James Hog was a native of East Lothian but for some years lived at Borlum, in Caithness, on a farm belonging to Mr Innes of Sandside "who did everything ... to render my possession convenient and profitable ... But by the barbarity of the country where I lived I was in a manner forcibly expelled". Hog was an improver but unpopular because of the way he had cleared sub-tenants and cottars from his farm. His crops were stolen and when he dismissed some of the worst offenders among his sub-tenants they were taken in by others, and even after the offenders had been prosecuted and served their sentences they were welcomed back into the community. In the winter of 1771 a ship was wrecked nearby and though Hog tried to save some of the cargo from plunderers he was unsuccessful and he himself was persecuted for his efforts by having his house set on fire; the culprits were protected by the sheriff-substitute. Hog decided to join his brother Robert, a merchant in Wilmington.[3]

Hog therefore set about finding people to accompany him to America and organised their transport. He chartered the *Batchelor* from James Inglis, junior, merchant in Leith. In the contract, dated 24th August 1773, Inglis agreed to pick up Hog and his family and servants and 200 emigrants "and more if the vessel can stow them" in Thurso Bay or Scrabster roads. Inglis

> would provide and maintain the emigrants with good and wholesome provisions, viz each adult to receive 4lbs meal, 5lbs bread biscuit, 2lbs beef, 2lbs barley and pease and 1lb molasses, with 6 gallons of water weekly; those under eight years to receive half rations. On the other hand Hog was to pay £6 each for himself, his wife and mother-in-law, £3 each for his children, all of whom would use the cabin, and £1 10s each for up to six servants; he would furnish provisions, except fire and water, for all, though the servants were to be restricted to the same quantity of water as the captain and crew. The freight rate was £3 10s per emigrant and £1 15s for children under eight years old; the emigrants to furnish their own bed and bedding. Half the passage money was to be paid before the ship left Leith, the other half to be paid before anyone boarded in Thurso Bay or Scrabster. Hog was to assist the captain in the management of the emigrants and the division of provisions during the voyage. Finally, it was agreed that if the vessel was detained in Thurso or Scrabster for more than ten days Hog was to pay £3.3s a day during the delay.

The ship, with 280 people on board, sailed from Thurso on September 14th 1773. Hog travelled with his wife, five children all under eight years old and ten servants; there were also 174 passengers over eight years, 30 children under eight and 30 "sucking children". Bad weather forced the *Batchelor* into Stromness on the 19th and on setting out a second time on 26th September got as far as Lewis when they were blown back to Shetland and put in to Vaila Sound, Walls, on 3rd October.[4] The local minister, Rev John Mill, recorded in his diary "The smallpox at same time carried off severals, and some of their children crammed in the hold were said to be stifled to death and thrown overboard into the sea before they landed". The boat was repaired and ready to sail again by 24th October but another gale caused further and worse damage. The ship dragged her anchors and was so badly damaged that the passengers were put ashore and confined to the parish of Walls by order of the sheriff-substitute and Vice-Admiral-Depute of Shetland, William Balfour of Trinaby.[5] They were not allowed to travel through the country looking for help because of the smallpox scare; but the kirk sessions in Shetland "being well acquainted with the distressed circumstances of such people" sent £13 2s for their assistance and the moderator of the session donated a further £24. Two lispunds of oatmeal and 15 (?lbs) of potatoes were also given for the emigrants although the local people were already suffering severely as a result of several poor harvests.[6]

William Balfour thought that the ship should already have been moved to a safer place and made fit for sailing to America by the spring. On 7th November he reported to Hog that the *Batchelor's* master, Captain Alex Ramage, was prevaricating about the repairs to the ship and the welfare of the emigrants and although he had protested to Inglis and Sir Laurence Dundas's commissioner he urged Hog to protest again, but warned that if he left the country he would give up his claim to damages.

On 10th October John Bruce Stewart of Simbister and other heritors petitioned the vice-admiral depute of Shetland shewing that Hog had agreed either verbally or in writing with the emigrants to have a vessel ready at Thurso Bay or Scrabster Roads by the 1st July to go to Wilmington, North Carolina and that he had stipulated that the owner provide and maintain the emigrants ashore as well as at sea till the voyage be completed. In other words, Inglis was to maintain the emigrants during the whole period of the voyage and until they landed at Wilmington. Besides their passage money each emigrant was to pay 1s 6d per person over eight and 9d under eight years for his trouble in finding and entering into a contract with the owner; so that between them they paid £731 passage money and £15 9s for his trouble.

The ship did not arrive until the 28th August so the emigrants had to stay in Thurso for the extra eight weeks which reduced them to a state of indigence and want. As a result of the shipwreck the families had been in Shetland for a month and had been refused help by both Hog and Captain Ramage so that many would have died of hunger and cold had it not been for the humanity of the gentlemen and the hospitality of the people of Walls. The petitioners argued that the emigrants should have been given the provisions, some of which were still on board ship and some stored in the house of Mr Henry of Torralwall where Hog was staying. Hog had petitioned Inglis and Ramage in October to no avail to help the emigrants as they were bound to do by the contract. The heritors also suspected that Cpt Ramage would get the ship declared a wreck so that he would not be bound to take the people to Wilmington, that he and Hog would desert the emigrants and leave them an insufferable burden on the country which had already been greatly distressed for want of bread for the past three years and did not expect a good harvest from the present crop. The petitioners wanted Hog and Ramage to be ordered to remove the emigrants or at least to provide for their welfare while in Shetland. Some of the orders and judgements craved were illegal and unwarrantable and such matters as were competent were already *sub judice* upon the petition of the emigrants against Hog and Ramage. The case was dismissed as no title was produced in the person of the petitioners to insist in the petition on behalf of the emigrants.

Meantime the emigrants filed a petition against Hog. Replying, Hog swore under oath that he had not undertaken to bind the owner of the ship to find provisions for them while in harbour and that he had warned several of the emigrants of this fact. The emigrants also asked whether Hog had told them to expect a ship in Thurso by the end of June or the beginning of July and the ship to be victualled with Lothian meal not Caithness meal. Hog agreed that he had expected a ship to arrive during July but had not undertaken a specific time. He did not remember any agreement about a particular type of meal. Hog also swore that the half freight paid to him by the emigrants before setting out for Edinburgh was not for buying provisions for the journey but that Inglis had insisted on the money being paid before fitting out the ship. This case was also dismissed.

While stranded up north John Will determined to go home and so signed a document at the home of John Henry, Torralwall, dated November 30th 1773:

> Though you have agreed to let me go south, I acknowledge it is at my own desire and that I have no intention to break my indenture, but will certainly upon your giving me notice come to any place you shall desire at my own expense to go in the same ship with yourself, or with any other, bound for North Carolina you paying my freight, in order to fulfill my indenture.

Nothing more is heard of him.

When the ship's anchors dragged it was believed that her bottom was damaged and she could not be careened for inspection without anchors. Hog and Cpt Ramage wrote to Inglis about the 6th December. As soon as Inglis heard of the trouble he sent a carpenter with the necessary equipment on a sloop which left Leith on the 2nd or 3rd Janaury, but it did not reach Shetland until the end of the month and Vaila Sound until the 10th February. Because of bad weather and other accidents it took several weeks before it was decided that the *Batchelor* could not be repaired locally.[7]

Captain Ramage finally sailed the *Batchelor* out of Vaila Sound on 20th April and arrived in Leith, the only port on the east coast with drydock facilities, on the 25th April. He had told the emigrants that he was to land them at Thurso to await the refitting of the ship which would pick them up again on the return journey. However, as they were destitute they decided to go to Leith in the hope of recovering some money from a Court Action against Inglis.

Inglis wrote to Hog on 7th May intimating that he refused to proceed and alleging that he had fulfilled his part of the contract, but offered to submit the case to jurisdiction. Hog therefore commenced an action in the courts for the recovery of passage money and damages. He stated that

> All this time not the most distant hint was given to me from Mr Inglis or Captain Ramage that the contract was fulfilled. On the contrary we were all along made to believe that the ship was to proceed with us as soon as she could be refitted.

The emigrants hoped for a speedy decision from the sheriff court which had however, been adjourned till the 3rd June, so they agreed to submit, then when Hog warned Inglis of this decision "I think on Friday last", Inglis refused to agree to the submission.[8] The court case, decided in favour of Hog, was reported in the *Edinburgh Evening Courant* on 29th June 1774.

Inglis appealed but died before the appeal was heard in 1777. Inglis's representatives stated in the appeal that Inglis had sent a sloop to Shetland with materials for refitting the *Batchelor* but as the men could not make a proper job the boat returned to Leith for further repairs which took rather a long time. Inglis's representatives claimed that Hog had misinterpreted the letter, that he had not withdrawn the vessel but got it refitted, though tardily. Hog also claimed that by the time he had contracted for a passage in another boat many of his emigrants had dispersed. It was stated that Inglis had sent another boat. Inglis's representatives argued that he was not responsible for restitution of freight because much of it had already been consumed and many of the emigrants had dispersed. Inglis's case was lost again.[9]

While the emigrants were stranded in Leith Hog quickly arranged for himself and his family to sail from Greenock and left his party to fend for themselves as best they could. Faced with this group of wretched people, the churches in Leith raised at least £40 for them. Some of the families were then able to return home, but the *Edinburgh Advertiser* urged that it would be "kind and humane for the people in the different places and countries they pass through to give the necessary subsistence".[10]

James Hog had made a detailed list of his emigrants, noting the name of the head of the family and the number of dependents over eight years and under eight, their parish and how much money had been paid for each family. In all there were 57 families which included 158 persons over eight and 52 children under eight years. The families had come from 13 parishes -

Caithness		Sutherland	
Reay	14 families	Kildonan	11 families
Wick	3	Farr	7
Thurso	3	Tongue	6
Halkirk	1	Eddrachillis	2
		Clyne	2
		Rogart	2
		Lairg	1

Total that have not discharged	181
Discharged 18 full and 10 half freights	23
	204

Died in Zetland 8 half freights	4
Died in Zetland	4
	8

besides sucking children.[11] (Fig. 9.1)

From the customs house record of Lerwick, it appears that 127 men, women and children who were on Hog's list sailed in the *Batchelor* from Lerwick to Leith. This list details only 31 heads of families; the majority of the men were farmers, although there were also four servants, three shoemakers, two tailors and one shopkeeper, one schoolmaster and one clerk. Nearly all the respondents mentioned high rents, poor crops and loss of cattle leading to high prices as the chief reasons for going to America. Several farmers complained of the heavy burden of the services demanded -

> up to 30 or 40 days of his servants and horses each year, without the least acknowledgement for it, and without victuals, save the men that mowed the hay who got their dinner only.

Others complained that the distilleries were taking so much grain that the consequent scarcity led to high prices. Almost all the families were hoping to join either family or friends in North Carolina.[12]

It is known that some at least of these emigrants did reach America. Later, Hog wrote, vindicating his actions:

> The loss of so many people, and the number they may in time draw after them, will probably be missed by the landholders; but let them learn to treat their fellow creatures with more humanity. Instead of looking on myself as an enemy to the country, in being accessory to the carrying off so many people, I rejoice in being an instrument in the hand of Providence, to punish oppression, which is by far too general, and I am glad to understand, that already some

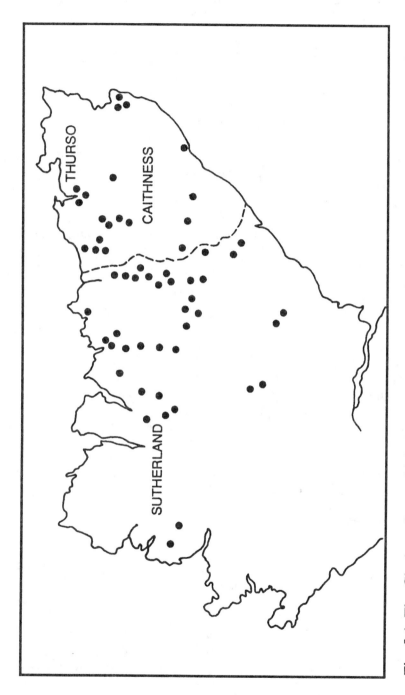

Fig. 9.1 The Clachans from which the passengers of the BATCHELOR left before emigrating in 1773/4

of these haughty landlords now find it necessary to court and caress these same poor people, whom they lately despised, and treated as slaves or beasts of burden.[13]

The Nancy

A second miserable voyage has been well documented. The *Nancy* of Sutherland had been victualled in Leith before sailing from Dornoch with 250 people in the middle of September; it is not known whether she was caught in the storm in the Minch. But the voyage was badly mismanaged from the very beginning if one can believe the allegations and counter allegations. The emigrants complained that nearly 100 of them had fallen victim to the "avarice and inhumanity" of the captain, George Smith. The bare figures hide a tale of misery and heartache: more than 50 children under four years old died; six of the seven women who gave birth while on board died and with them their new born infants. The accusations continued: the master wished their deaths from the beginning and the boat was never properly fitted out; the master did not give them all the provisions and much of what they were given was stinking; the water was certainly foul. On the other hand, the captain kept a large hogshead of good meal and water for himself and the crew.

It had been agreed that each passenger should get 1/2 pound of beef a day, which would amount to 17 1/2 pounds per person for a voyage of 5 weeks and supposing that the boat had taken 200 passengers some 4500lbs should have been provided. In fact 1200lbs were supplied for the passengers and 720lbs for the crew. The rest of the passengers' food consisted of 15,120 lbs oatmeal, 6720 lbs peasemeal, 1120 lbs biscuits, 672 lbs cheese and 224 lbs whole pease; for the crew 672 lbs bread, 448 lbs whole pease, 60 lbs butter and a barrel of flour. The voyage lasted 12 weeks due to bad weather; though the emigrants turned sickly the storm had prevented the opening of the hatches for fresh air. The captain not only acknowledged his failure to victual adequately, but admitted that it was his normal practice. He declared that as for the charge of cruelty he never saw man, womam or child struck and had never heard a complaint from them against any member of his crew; nor could be believe any of the survivors drew up the account published, because, he argued, the survivors consoled each other and did not exaggerate their misfortunes.[14]

The owner of the *Nancy*, Mr George Parker of Burntisland, also hoped to vindicate himself by telling his side of the story- according to him, the terms of the agreement were that half the freight was to be paid at the port of outfit by 27th July and the remainder either in cash or negotiatble bills when the people were put on board in the Highlands. But as no part of the sum was paid at that time the vessel was delayed till the beginning of September and obliged to sail with less than half of the stipulated sum paid. This was laid out to procure as much wholesome food as possible, "though the quantity of provision was not nearly so great, nor the kinds they would have had had the terms of the agreement been observed". Because of the unhappy situation in the Highlands, more people were ready to go than the vessel could contain. Therefore the usual quantity of provisions and water was reserved for the ship's crew and all the rest was set aside for the people, and each article was noted down. Those who accepted the agreement went, and those who chose not to go had their money returned to them without hesitation. Not only he but they knew before they sailed, as they do now, the exact position regarding them, except the weather they might have and the length of the passage, both of which were no doubt uncommonly bad.[15]

On arrival in New York in December the captain narrowly escaped the vengeance of the law by sailing out of the port during the night.[16] Dr Ezra Stiles commented that there were 300 people on board the *Nancy* reckoned at 188 passengers and that they had agreed to pay £3 6s sterling apiece for their passages except for 35 "to be disposed of as servants for three years". Their miserable state on arrival in New York excited public charity and £80 was collected at the Presbyterian Church there, thanks to Dr Witherspoon who happened to be in the town at that time and preached a sermon on the subject.[17] In a letter home a gentleman of New York wrote concerning these people and others who had recently arrived:

I wish the gentlemen in Scotland would take measures to put a stop to the frequent emigrations from the Highlands and other parts of the country, by doing so they will be the means of saving numbers of their unhappy countrymen from misery and ruin. The unfortunate situation of such of these unhappy emigrants as have of late been brought to this colony is beyond description; almost the one half died on the passage, owing to hunger and the bad accommodation on board the vessels that carried them. Most of those that remain depend for their support on the generosity of the public who are now become tired of this burden. Such of them as go back into the woods under their chiefs that came out with them find themselves still in a worse situation, and the hardships they undergo are infinitely greater than at home. They have a long winter to struggle with and a very hot summer, and it will be five years before they can earn a subsistence for themselves, and by that time they and their children will become slaves for life to pay off the debt contracted for a miserable subsistence during the five years. Such as are at liberty to think for themselves have sold their service for four years for a small sum, and to be found in clothes and victuals, of which they will receive but a scanty provision. It is said that some of the MacDonalds are going over to bring out more, but though it may be an advantage to the rich who have estates in the colonies, to get people, yet the poor emigrants cannot be placed in worse circumstances than by being brought to any of our colonies, where they may expect the very worst treatment without the least hope of getting back to their native country. I hope therefore some means will be used to undeceive them, for I am persuaded it is the hopes of better things which tempt them to come here in such numbers. I give you leave to publish this and if it should be the happy means of preventing my countrymen from leaving their native country, to encounter the dangers and distresses they meet with, it will make me very happy.[18]

In October 1773 Mr William Parker, who was possibly George's brother, was on his barque *Carolina* which was bound from New Orleans for Burntisland. His lady and four children were also on board. The boat

was driven by stress of weather about 10 o'clock in the night time, upon the west part of Fair Isle, twixt two rocks, by which merciful and wonderful interposition of Providence they were all saved, being about 20 souls, with the provisions and some of the cargo. Next day the ship sank.[19]

The Parkers must have hoped to persuade future passengers that they would have a more successful voyage for they inserted the following advertisement in the newspaper; the brigantine *Harriet*, Thomas Smith master, was expected to sail to New York and

Cape Fear in July 1774:

> Any moderate number of persons that the vessel can conveniently carry that are wanting their
> passage to either of the above places, may be accommodated on very moderate terms, and the
> ship well victualled and manned; and for their better accommodation, as great inconveniences
> have arisen from want of fresh air in bad weather the vessel will be fitted with air ports and
> grating hatches: a surgeon also goes passenger, in order to settle in N. America who will be
> ready to give his assistance to anyone whose situation may require it.[20]

The *Harriet* duly sailed but it is not known whether she carried emigrants.[21]

The Jamaica Packet

In reality the Parker voyages continued to be mismanaged. We have a first-hand account
of the passage of the *Jamaica Packet*, owned by George Parker in Wilmington. Miss
Schaw was one of the five cabin passengers with their two servants, who lived in some
comfort, having taken amongst other things a spinet with them. According to Miss
Schaw there were a smith and his family, two tailors and a handsome young cooper on
board. These people were going voluntarily to the West Indies to mend or make their
fortunes, "so had no claim to that pity the others had a right to". The others consisted
of 53 emigrants from Shetland smuggled aboard privately and battened down in the hold
in case they were discovered by the port authorities, and of whom Miss Schaw was
unaware until they had been under sail for some days. The boat sailed from Burntisland
about the 25th October 1774, bound for Jamaica.[22] The Kirkcaldy Port Book states that
the boat was carrying 30 passengers; the official list details three families from Shetland
consisting of 15 people, a single man, a blacksmith, a family from Burntisland and two
young spinsters from Edinburgh.[23] The emigrants had originally gone to Greenock for
a boat, but had had to return to Burntisland, where they were lucky to find one not yet
sailed. They were charged double fare, but as they could only pay half they had to
indent.

The boat sailed close to Fair Isle where the passengers hoped to buy fresh provisions;
several small boats laden with goods rowed out from the island but no transactions took
place because a fracas broke out between the captain and the natives, possibly because
the previous winter the captain had lost another boat off Fair Isle, (the *Carolina*
mentioned previously). Shortly afterwards the *Jamaica Packet* ran into a severe storm
which lasted for ten days; considerable damage was done - the main mast split and some
property, including food, was lost. The cabin passengers lost the food they had taken
with them and so had to rely on the boat's provisions which were not as stated on a list
provided by the owner and paid for by his passengers. The provisions actually consisted
of

> a few barrels of neck-beef and a few more of New England pork (on the third voyage across the
> Atlantick and Hot Climates), oatmeal, stinking herrings and, to own the truth, most excellent
> potatoes.

These people suffered little compared with the emigrants who were below decks
without fresh air except what entered

down the crannies, as did the sea, to such a depth that they could not lie down for several days but had to sit supporting their little ones in their arms to save them from drowning. No victuals could be dressed and no fire got on, so that all they had to subsist on was some raw potatoes and a very small proportion of brisket.

The emigrants had for a grown person per week - one pound of neck beef or spoiled pork, two pounds of oatmeal with a small quantity of biscuit not only mouldy but absolutely crumbled down with damp, wet and rottenness. Half the quantity was allowed a child, so that if they had not had potatoes, they would not have survived. Their only drink was a very small portion of brackish bad water and even this scanty allowance was grudged them. The owner, to save expense, had taken the water for his ship from a pit well in his own back yard, although fine springs were nearby.

The ship made landfall at the Azores but did not stop. There was another severe storm in which all the rigging sails etc were destroyed; although they met a naval ship it did not give help. They arrived in Antigua after seven weeks, on December 12th. Miss Schaw and her party stayed in the islands for some weeks. She confided to her diary:

> our emigrants are all disposed of to their hearts contentment, except two families, who steady to their first idea, persist in going to America. As to those who have stopped here, they are already so entirely changed as not to be known.

Miss Schaw and her party put their gear on board the *Jamaica Packet* again but the captain and the drunken mate sailed for America without them, so they had to follow in another ship and arrived in Brunswick, North Carolina on 14th February, a few days after the *Jamaica Packet*.(Fig. 9.2) She stayed in North Carolina for several months, but with war clouds massing eventually left in a hurry and was lucky to get a passage on the *George*, going to Lisbon and Greenock. On that boat our "cabin and state rooms are large and commodious, our provisions excellent and our liquor tolerable".[24]

Miss Schaw appears to have travelled in relative comfort but the hardships and tragedies of the emigrant families are beyond imagination. The privations of such a long voyage in small sailing vessels would have been bad enough, but on top of that they were cheated in every way. Gross over-crowding of inadequate accomodation and insufficient provisions and water were normal.

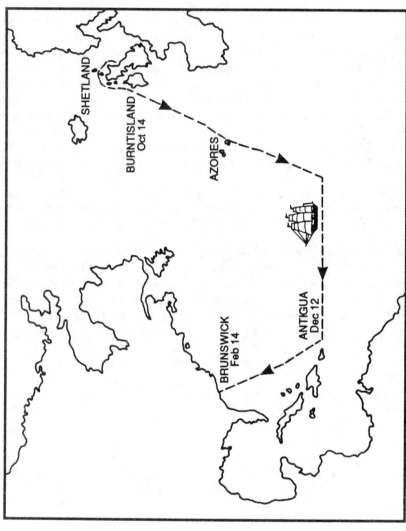

Fig. 9/2   The voyage of the *Jamaica Packet*,   October 14th 1773 to February 14th 1774.

10

"Eight Years Without Rent"

"To the southern inhabitants of Scotland", wrote Samuel Johnson after his tour of the Highlands in 1773, "the state of the mountains and islands is equally unknown with that of Borneo or Sumatra; of both they have only heard a little and guess the rest".[1] This sweeping generalisation has a certain validity but it cannot be extended to include ignorance of the mass emigrations taking place, for they were amply reported in the *Scots Magazine* and other papers of the time. Processions of pathetic people had also been seen moving towards the major port of embarkation, Greenock. Although the emigrations between 1770 and 1775 were largely a Highland phenomenon, they did inlcude a proportion of Lowlanders. The 1788 census for Prince Edward Island, for example, shows that of the Scots residing there, five-sixths were from the Highlands and one-sixth from the Lowlands. This accords with the Scottish evidence available so far.

An example of the general awareness and concern is found in a sermon preached by the Rev William Thom of Govan parish, Glasgow, who gave "seasonable advice" to the landholders and farmers in Scotland in 1770, presumably before a congregation about to emigrate. He was outspoken in condemning proprietors for raising their rents, in some cases higher than for rich lands in England, thus causing many tenants to leave and much cultivable land to be wasted. Tenants were not blameless for some outbid others needlessly when they themselves were in fact unable to pay the rent promised. Mr Thom argued that mass emigration was preferable to staying under oppressive landlords and that emigrants should go on the short voyage to America because it was part of the British Empire. America was a large country where land was cheap and there was little taxation, where there was civil and religious liberty; a land that could become the seat of the British government. He continued that it was the duty of afflicted people to pursue the means of deliverance for the sake of the elderly and the young children; but also they were to have compassion on those who might be left behind and on their oppressors in the hope that they would repent.[2]

Emigrations from the Lowlands in the early years of the 18th century are not well documented. Many who went as farmers, doctors, teachers, merchants or servants went for a term of years, fared well and stayed for life; others returned to Scotland at the end of their contract; many died from malnutrition or disease.

The merchants who traded between Scotland and the American colonies did so at first illegally in breach of the English Navigation Acts; nevertheless a substantial business was established. By the time relations with England were relaxed after the Union of Parliaments, the merchants of Glasgow had a base for increasing their trade. Tobacco became the mainstay - companies such as Buchanan, Hastie and Co and John Glassford and Co, sent young men out to Virginia and the Carolinas as merchants and storemen.

Some arrived before 1740 but many more were sent between 1750 and 1775 as a response to the westward expansion of the tobacco plantations and the consequent increase in the tonnage available for export. These men played a very important role as middlemen buying tobacco from the planters and giving them credit when buying goods from the store, goods that were imported on the ships returning from Glasgow. Although the storemen were discouraged by their employers from marrying for fear of lessening the time and interest available for their work, many did settle in America. Some of the older men did not come to terms with the American Revolution and returned to Britain leaving their sons to carry on the businesses as best they could. Although the tobacco trade was resumed after the war Glasgow's dominance was never recovered.[3] Thomas Loudon Macadam, later to find fame as a road-builder, was one of the merchants who had to leave America after the war. He had been the British agent in New York for the sale of prizes.[4]

Although the most important port for the emigrant trade was Greenock, its immediate hinterland, the emerging industrial region of Western and Central Scotland sent few emigrants. Yet through the years small but significant parties did emigrate. In 1753 Samuel Waldo advertised land rent free for 19 years and a quit rent of 10 to 40 shillings a year; and certain craftsmen were offered free transport and employment. About 70 people from Glasgow and Stirling answered the advertisement and settled in the new town of Stirling, Maine.[5] In 1764 15 men and two wives sailed on the *Douglas* from Greenock to Boston. In 1765 47 young men indented to go to Florida and another 300 tradesmen went there two years later. Meanwhile an unknown number of sawyers had gone to Nova Scotia in 1765. In August 1767 the *Pearl* sailed from Port Glasgow to South Carolina with at least 50 indented servants who complained on arrival of ill-treatment by the master.[6] In 1771, 18 young women were reported to have indented to go abroad in order to try their fortunes in some of HM plantations and had set out from Glasgow for Greenock.[7] That year William Cunningham and Co, tobacco merchants in Glasgow, sent across hands and materials for their two ships building in Boston.[8] Perhaps the biggest exodus of tradesmen was that of hundreds of linen makers who went to North Carolina in 1770 and 1771. It is not known from which area these people came.[9]

During this period there was considerable unrest in the textile industry. The manufacturers were also threatened with disaster by the collapse of the Ayr bank in 1772. They bitterly opposed the labourers' attempts to improve their lot by introducing combinations which sought to regulate wages and to prevent the masters and weavers who refused to submit to this regulation from giving out or receiving any work. The combination was enforced by "many riotous proceedings" which interrupted the manufacture of Paisley for several weeks and reduced many of the journeymen to a state of beggary. As some thousands of weavers were concerned and threatened to leave for America in a body the trial of 12 of the town's journeymen weavers became very delicate. After the verdict was returned against seven men, the Lord Justice Clerk (Lord Miller) commented:

> I have reason to hope that peace and good order is now restored to that place, and all thoughts of going over to America are laid aside. I pray God for the sake of this country, that such ideas of migration to America may not become epidemical amongst the most useful of our people ... In this part of the kingdom transportation to America begins to lose every aspect of punishment.[10]

But the hard core of Lowland emigrants appears to have been, not a people in distress taking flight into the unknown, but a competent and pragmatic community determined not to accept economic ruin but to be masters of their own fates. Alexander Thomson, who had farmed Corkerhill in Renfrewshire, wrote from his farm, Corkerhill, in Franklin County, Pennsylvania, giving what must be considered a typical description of a more prosperous lowland tenant farmer making his way in the New World. He had stayed on his father's farm near Glasgow and had tried to find suitable farms for some of his numerous sons, but though he found many vacant, the lairds were all asking double the rent he thought they were worth. He had decided to emigrate with all his family save the eldest son Robert who presumably hoped to take on the family farm of Corkerhill. The voyage of the *Friendship* on which the family sailed, lasted just two months and all arrived in Boston in perfect health in September 1771. Thomson had decided to sail to Boston because he hoped to meet family friends who had settled there some time previously and others from Paisley who had gone "very lately".

Thomson contacted Dr Witherspoon who advised him to rent at first, but he decided to buy a plantation of 430 acres and while he was waiting to take possession he and his family gained valuable experience working on nearby estates. Although some of his land had already been cleared, Thomson and his family set to work and cleared a further 50 acres in just over a year, finding the job easier than they had expected; he then planted 200 trees. He recommended tradesmen and farmers to come to America for they would undoubtedly succeed if willing to work hard. Although many had been indented they had paid off their debts and were now prospering on their own account. Thomson enlarged on the benefits of a new country - no tithes, no general taxes or mill multures or such grievances as tended to detract from the industry of the farmers. They could choose their schoolmasters, ministers and parish officers "we have no character hereabout which answers to the Scotch justice of the peace, which we who come from Scotland look upon as a very great blessing". The law was impartially administered by people who were really, not nominally, their representatives. Thomson asked that his letter be published because he wanted to refute the charge that he was discontented and because he hoped that people back home would be helped to dispel their fears by what he had written about his new country.[11]

As is shown in the following examples great care was taken by potential emigrants from the Lowlands. Many set up emigration companies with written constitutions and publicised their activities through pamphlets. Members went over to America to look at possible land; and they had good contacts over there.

Inchinnan Company

In 1772 some tenant farmers in the shires of Dumbarton and Renfrew printed a pamphlet, costing threepence, of a plan "for purchasing and improving of lands within HM dominions in North America, in such manner as is or shall be comfortable to the Laws and Priveleges of HM subjects of Great Britain". They claimed that:

their sphere of life did not afford them a liberal education, whereby they are sensible that the learned can easily perceive defects in form, order and address. They therefore send it abroad stript of the ornamental embellishments of learned pens, only in the common language ... preferring utility to dress. And if any of better learning should please to join the plan it is hoped that unelegency of style will give no offence, as no loss can accrue to them thereby, especially since by the writing out of the bond of association, whatever is defective or superfluous may be greatly amended, it being proposed that the same shall be done by some able hand.

These working farmers called themselves the Scots American Company of Farmers, or the Inchinnan Company as it later became known because so many of the members came from that parish. They agreed at once that some might emigrate while others might stay at home and speculate in the land. At their first meeting it was agreed that a share in the company would cost £2 10s and anyone holding four shares would be entitled to two votes; anyone joining after the first input was to pay interest as if he had joined at the start, so that all would eventually have an equal share. All money was to be banked immediately so that it could accumulate interest, but anyone could remove his stock at any time. Two men were to be sent to America to look for land as soon as there were sufficient funds; if they could not find land they were to return home and the subscribers repaid. If they purchased land they were to send word home but stay on themselves so as to get on with the job of settling. They were to lay off land for the public use of the company, such as houses for the managers, and lots for the members. They were to start clearing the ground and building houses for the managers and any members who sent money, but were to try to keep a little ground cleared on several lots rather than spend all their time on the whole of one lot. The first houses built were to be retained in favour of the company at home until the second round of clearing should start.

As this was a business proposition proper accounts were to be kept - a general account which would pay for the clearing and building on the public land and which would receive money from the sale of timber and turpentine from the forests cleared from the public land. The particular account would draw money from the sale of the produce of the lots and this would pay for the concerns of those staying at home, for instance for labouring the land. The land would be lotted for in Scotland and anyone intending to go over was to give six months' notice; when they arrived they would receive subsistence from company stores for a year at prime cost.

Another clause recognised the fact that people in different circumstances might join the company; some would be able to have assistance to the tune of nine-tenths the value of their lot, to be repaid in annual instalments; others might go over as servants for normal wages until they could acquire their own lots; those in reduced circumstances could be helped by the managers in America.[12]

Of the 129 men who signed the original bond of association, 33 came from Erskine parish, 28 from Inchinnan, 21 from Kilpatrick, 12 from Glasgow parishes and the rest from other nearby parishes. By occupation, 38 men called themselves farmers or tenants and another 35 probably worked directly on the land; there were also eight textile workers.[13](Fig. 10.1)

James Whitelaw and David Allen were sent out by the Inchinnan Company to investigate the possibilities in America. They sailed on the brigantine *Matty*, leaving Greenock on 25th March and arriving in Philadelphia on 24th May 1773. They very soon met Dr Witherspoon and later Sir William Johnson and then set out on horseback to travel through the states of New York and Pennsylvania. They stayed with Alexander Thomson, who wrote on August 6th 1773:

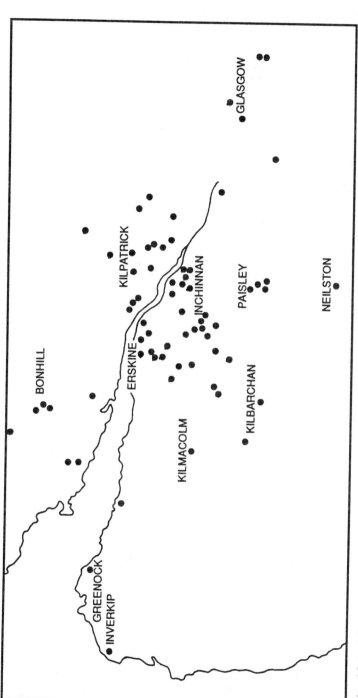

Fig. 10.1   The homes of the Scots American Company of Farmers before emigraton in 1774

In your letter you mention the American Company of Farmers in the west of Scotland, and I cannot but approve of their sending over skilled men to take up land for them before they bring their families here; and they have just taken the method which you and others advised me to take, and I

would surely follow your advice, but I could not prevail on my wife to stay a year behind me. David Allen and James Whiteland (sic), the two commissioners from that company, are now at my house, and I hope they will rest with me for a week or two, for I can easily accomodate them and their horses. They are going for North Carolina to look for a large tract of land agreeably to their commission. A large tract of land to the extent of 16,000 or 20,000 acres, all contiguous, and conveniently situated and not yet occupied, is not to be got in the middle provinces; though they might hereabout get plenty of single plantations here and there; for the farmers are, many of them, selling their plantations and going back [ie west] to take up larger tracts. I therefore advised them all I could to go to the Ohio, but they are afraid the settlers there will be too far from market or a landing place. Since I came to America I have learned to think that those who have got a rich soil in a favourable climate, and those who have got all the conveniences of life in great plenty, may be happy enough though they have but little money, and they may carry on a sort of inland trade among themselves by way of barter; but those on the Ohio will not be long under that necessity, for I hear that money is already subscribed to improve the navigation by cuts into the Ohio, and besides the farmers in that rich country may easily get money by rearing large flocks of cows, hogs, and sheep, which they may drive to Philadelphia and the market towns of New York and Maryland. By my being here I see that much of that fine land on the Ohio and Mississippi will be quickly taken up, though no person should come to it from Scotland. I see emigrants in crowds passing this way almost every week. One of my family, whom I lately sent to Philadelphia, lodged in a house with fifty of them and within these few days I saw more than three score, all of them hastening to the banks of the Ohio. Some of them came from Ireland, some from England, and some from Germany, and we hear that several ship fulls are coming from Corsica or Italy. About Fort Pitt, where three considerable rivers fall into the Ohio, the country is pretty well peopled already.[14]

Allen and Whitelaw continued their travels through Maryland, Virginia and North Carolina.(Fig. 10.2) They returned to New York by 1st October where they again met Dr Witherspoon and agreed to buy from him about 23,000 acres in the township of Ryegate (New York, but later Vermont). Dr Witherspoon had earlier proposed that if the men took the whole of the land on offer he would reserve to them 2000 acres and rent the rest at two shillings sterling per acre; if they took three-quarters of the tract then he would reserve 1300 acres and they would pay £3 3s York currency; or if half the land then three shillngs York currency, "but he advised us to be at all due pains, and if we should find a better place for our purpose, to take it, as he is very fond that our scheme should succeed".[15] Dr Ezra Stiles confided to his diary that Dr Witherspoon had sent and procured settlers from Paisley;

he agreed with them that they should cultivate etc and enjoy eight years without rent, then he would execute leases to them reserving to himself a rent of 6d per acre sterling. Allow 2 or 3000 acres for useless land and highways - raise 6d on 20,000 acres gives a rental of £5000 st per annum. The Dr seems to be taking care for this world as well as for that which is to come. Is he not laying a foundation for the ruin of some of his children and posterity.[16]

As soon as the purchase was complete word was sent home. Other members of the company had sailed on the *Matty* and disembarked at New York, for James Whitelaw recorded in his journal that, on his way to Ryegate, he had met James Henderson with tools and chests. The party set to work, surveyed the township for division into 400 lots, there being 400 shares in the company, cut down wood to start building houses and

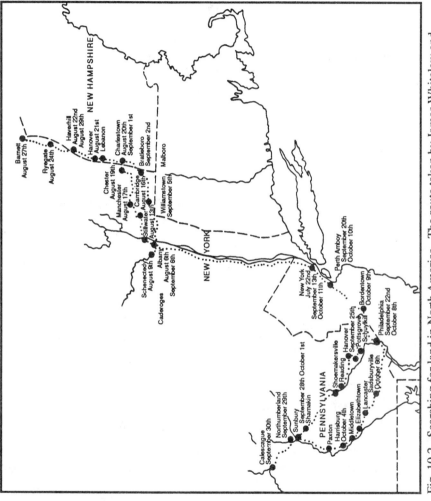

Fig. 10.2 Searching for land in North America. The route taken by James Whitelaw and David Allan during their investigation on the behalf of the Inchinnan Company in 1773.

began cultivation so that by the time the next party arrived from Scotland they had even made 60 pounds of sugar. The *Edinburgh Advertiser* reported on February 11th 1774 that about 500 manufacturers (weavers) were preparing to embark for America. 212 of them, mostly from Paisley, sailed on the *Commerce* which left for New York on the 15th. The first eight men, one of them a manager, with some of their families, arrived at Ryegate in May 1774. The next two groups of people arrived in October, they "were all hearty and had a good passage and good usage from their captain"; and another family arrived in February 1775.

One hundred and thirty-nine men had signed the Inchinnan bond of association in Scotland 11 being managers, of whom only three apparently went to Ryegate. By April 1775, 70 lots had been taken up; of the 26 men who signed for them only 15 had apparently signed the bond, they each also chose one or more house lots. These settlers prospered and James Whitelaw later became surveyor-general of Vermont.[17]

Other companies

Meetings were held in the counties of Perth and Stirling during April 1774 to form emigration societies. As the men from Campsie and Kilsyth in Stirlingshire were unable to agree about "the expence of their deputies for purchasing lands, the meeting broke up, and the parties went home to their respective abodes, without coming to any determination". The farmers from the other villages were more successful. Societies were formed at "Arnpyn" (Arnprior, one of the Forfeited Estates), Monteith and Kippen.

> Upwards of one hundred heads of families are engaged in our emigrating scheme; and if we can find a soil and climate agreeing with our constitution (under God), there is no fear of our doing well abroad: for, you know, there is not a tract of better-cultivated land in Scotland, considering the soil, and opportunities we have, than what we propose to leave; and no doubt, it is a grief to our spirits to leave it and our native land, and venture upon such a dangerous voyage: but there is no help for it; we are not able to stand the high rents, and must do something for bread, or see our families reduced to beggary.

The men subscribed £500 for purchasing land in America; and sent two of their number to choose a site for them. The money was lodged in a Glasgow bank. The *Edinburgh Advertiser* commented sourly;

> If these people would labour diligently and live moderately they might do very well at home, but many of them were much addicted to idleness and dissipation.[18]

At the age of 27, Alexander Harvey who lived in Culmoir in the parish of Gargunnock, Stirlingshire, was chosen as one of the agents for this society which became known as the United Company of Farmers for the Shires of Perth and Stirling. Harvey sailed on the *Matty* from Greenock on the 18th May 1774, arriving at Buchanan's wharf, New York on 21st July. With him sailed 35 other men, eight women and 10 children, who were not aparently members of the society. We know that four men went to Albany and one to Philadelphia.

One of Harvey's first jobs on arrival was to deliver, or post, all the letters he had brought from home, and to send back letters to his father and the Company. He quickly contacted several people who had land on offer and visited Dr Witherspoon in New Jersey. After a few days he went up north to view land in the Caderogues Patent which though good land was too small for their purposes; Cambridge was too rocky and small; Chester was mountainous and the soil not so good. He finally reached the west end of Ryegate to view Dr Witherspoon's ground; there he stayed with James Whitelaw. Harvey commented that the people, who had been settled for less than two years, had

> no orchards nor anything curious as yet but they have good grain growing on their ground they have excellent tobacco with potatoes, wheat, Indian corn, Rie and pease with special oats.

Whitelaw conducted Harvey through the east end of Ryegate, which he found rocky and bad though with some good land. Eventually Harvey discussed terms of sale with Mr Stevens, a land surveyor, for land in Barnet, which he found rocky "with abundance of pine most of it is not capable of bearing grain yet the whole of it might in time be good pasturage"; other parts appeared fertile and the deciduous woods not too thick.[19] Harvey sent home a report, dated New York 2nd September, that he and his friends had heard that lands might be cheaper in the South, but they were molested by Indians, trouble which was unknown in the North.[20]

He stayed in New York for a week before setting off again on his travels through the Jerseys, to view lands at Caliesgague, which he found broken and the best already picked. Back in New York, Harvey turned down an offer from Colonel Stone for lands on Lake Champlain, but eventually agreed, November 23rd, with Sam Stevens Esq for 7000 acres of land in Barnet, to pay 14d sterling an acre, half the money to be paid in November 1775 and the rest then or to bear interest for such time as it remained unpaid.

During the next few weeks seven men recently arrived from Scotland each subscribed £5 sterling for two shares in the Company's land. Harvey stayed in New York during the winter, organising men and equipment for the Company's new land, until he and a small party of six men set off again for Barnet on March 23rd. The men who went overland arrived in Barnet on April 20th, those going by boat with the heavy gear arrived on May 6th. Work started immediately. Alexander Harvey later married Janet, daughter of Walter Brock who had settled in Ryegate with the Inchinnan Company. Having borne 13 children, Janet, after Harvey's death, later became the third wife of James Whitelaw of Ryegate.[21]

Towards the end of March 1775

> "Notwithstanding all the rumours of disturbances in America the spirit of emigration still unhappily prevails. This week a considerable number of labourers and useful mechanics from Monteith, Kippen etc and members of the Perth and Stirling Company set off for Greenock".

The party, which included 14 farmers, five wrights and six spinsters from Stirling; and 11 farmers, four wrights and six masons from Perthshire, were among the 232 people who sailed on the *Monimia* from Greenock in June and arrived in New York on July 26th. More of the farmers from the Perth and Stirling Company and from the Inchinnan Company had sailed on the *Lily* and the *Glasgow Packet* in April and on the second sailing that year of the *Glasgow Packet*.[22]

Galloway

Substantial emigrations left from Galloway - the counties of Wigtown, Dumfries and Kirkcudbright. The movement had received a favourable notice in the *Dumfries Weekly* in 1772 when a young man in Boston wrote home to his father in Galloway that:

> I have now got a settlement and that to me and mine for ever. I have bought 1500 acres of land a good quantity of which is cleared as also a house upon it. Each hundred acres of said land is able to maintain a family of 12 persons or more, and that with all things they have need of for meat drink and cloathing. This is a country in which the farmer may make rich and the poor man live. I hope against the spring to make 10 or 12 cwt of sugar and I think if I had once got a crop I will make £300 st per annum ... he that hath the worth of £50 or £60 st may live like a gentleman; and he that hath no money may live well with moderate labour ... I would be glad to see some of you in the spring of the year. Bring testificates of your character along with you, and a store of sea provisions such as oat-bread, cheese, hung meat, sugar, rum, tea etc. Excepting these and your cloathes with a chest to secure them in you need bring nothing else, as almost everything is cheaper here than in Scotland, except shoes which are extravagently dear.[23]

Emigration affected even prosperous burghs in the area. Kirkcudbright had a population of 1153 in 1771 which had risen to 1341 by 1786 and 1641 by 1792, but:

> Although from the great increase of population in the burgh since 1771, the inhabitants in the town are become much more numerous, yet, from the constant emigration of young people, the growing population receives a considerable check. No town in Scotland sends perhaps, for its size, so many of its children abroad to foreign countries. Many of them have, by their industry and application, succeeded extremely well. Some have acquired very ample fortunes, with a fair and honourable character.[24]

In April 1773 the *Buchanan* left Glasgow for New York with some 90 passengers from Galloway, "many of whom are respectable persons" who intended going on to Quebec. Two of the young men who went on to Quebec sent money home to their father, a tailor in Glasgow urging him to take their mother.[25] An English boat, the *Favourite* from Whitehaven took a group of 140 people to New York, arriving on August 13th after a three month journey. The passengers were described on their arrival as "mostly young and all remarkably healthy, well-looking people, having had neither sickness nor death on the voyage, except a young child who was ill before it came on board". This same ship carried another 75 passengers from Wigtown in 1774 and an unknown number who were described as "of considerable property and tradesmen of different kinds" in 1775.[26] The *Magdelene* left Greenock for Philadelphia in August 1774 carrying 24 emigrants from different parts of the country; apart from two gentlemen, they were all workmen.[27]

An association of 2-300 small farmers in Wigtownshire was set up in 1773; they left Whithorn early the following year.[28] Nevertheless the customs officer at Wigtown reported in January 1774 that few people had emigrated in recent years, but that those who had had encouraged their friends and relations back home to follow; consequently an association had been formed of upwards of 160 persons, farmers and tradesmen to go in the spring or summer of 1775. Some of the farmers had disposed of their leases advantageously and others had refused to take new ones. But what was more worrying was the fact that an intercepted letter from America advised the party to take few possessions but mostly coin, which was not allowed to be taken out of the country without the King's special licence and the officer would therefore like a ruling on the matter.[29]

During the months of April, May and June 1774 six boats picked up 936 passengers from Galloway, all bound for New York. 60 people left from Dumfries and groups of 72 and 158 people left from Gatehouse while 641 people left from Wigtown. During the later months of 1774 and in 1775 at least another eight boats left Greenock with emigrants- two for North Carolina, three for Philadelphia, one for Georgia, one for South Carolina and one for Quebec. It is not known whether or not the few passengers noted on some of these boats were the cabin passengers accompanying the hundreds of emigrants packed below decks for fewer than 100 emigrants were noted by the customs officers. 87 passengers on the *Neptune* which sailed from the Clyde were mentioned only because many of them "were deprived of their arms after they embarked by order of the government".[30]

The *Edinburgh Advertiser* reported during 1775 that 500 people were preparing to emigrate from Kintyre to North Carolina; the same paper announced in August that two vessels were lying at Gigha ready to take on people from Kintyre, Knapdale and the neighbouring islands.[31] In June some 80 Wigtonshire men (four farmers and the rest tradesmen) left Stranraer in the *Jackie* to go to North Carolina.[32] These people may have been those to whom Peter Stewart referred as he was preparing to go to to St John's Island (see Chapter 5). Another group sailed from Campbeltown on 4th August in the *Lord Dunluce* of Larne, for Wilmington, having on board, "300 chests and 100 casks or barrels containing bed cloath and body cloaths, body and table linens and household furniture" belonging to an unknown number of passengers.[33] (Figs. 10.3 & 10.4)

Both rich people and poor people were amongst the emigrants; it was expected that as some on the *Golden Rule* were people of property, they would be taking several thousand pounds in cash with them. The men on the *Gale*, however, were

> mostly poor people who have little or nothing after paying their freight. A few of them are indented for three years having had nothing to defray the expenses of their passage, nor do the greatest part of them know in what way they are to be provided for after landing.

On the *Adventure* were two men, with wives, who indented for four years and two men indented for three years.[34] Patrick (Peter) M'Robert, a farmer aged 38 from Drumlanrig who went to look for land, sailed on the *Adventure*. In a letter home he described the journey as being agreeable but tedious. There was one casualty - a nine year old girl fell overboard and although one baby died another was born. The boat was followed by bonito, so many were caught and eaten that "all hands began to tire of them". The ship steered as far south as the 24th degree of latitude to benefit from the Trade Winds. M'Robert wrote that it took a good while to get established on an agreeable footing, "even in this country".

> everything is strange; you have all to seek, and as it were, to begin a world a-new; to acquire aquaintances; to struggle hard for a character etc. these require courage and resolution in the adventurer.[35]

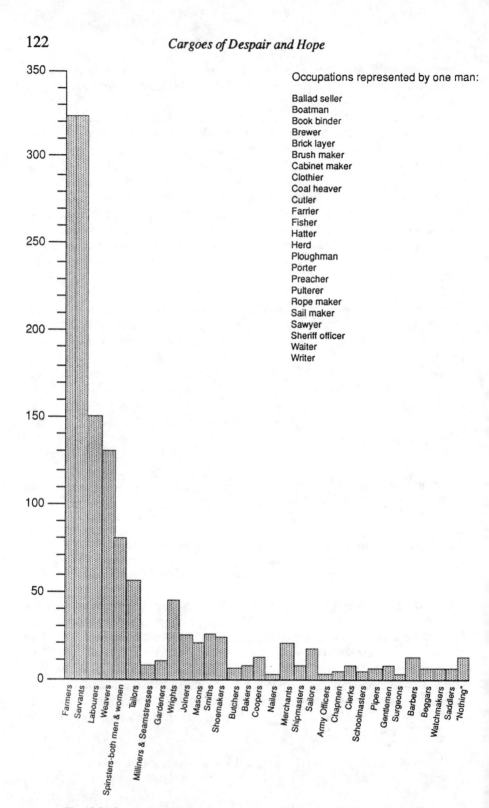

Fig. 10.3 Occupations of men who emigrated in 16 boats in 1774 and in 19 boats in 1775

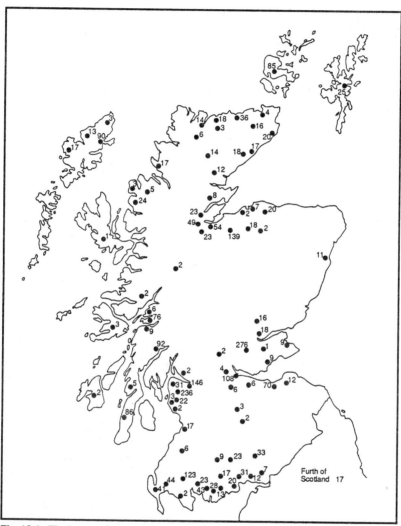

Fig. 10.4 The homes of the emigrants who sailed in the 16 boats in the 16 boats in 1774 and the 19 boats in 1775 for which there are detailed passenger lists.

Eastern Scotland

Little organised emigration has been found from Moray, Banff, Aberdeenshire, Kincardineshire, Angus, Fife, Kinross, Clackmannan, West Lothian, Midlothian, East Lothian, Berwickshire, Roxburghshire, Selkirkshire, Peeblesshire, Lanarkshire or Ayrshire. Improvements in farming on Lowland estates had been taking place from the last decades of the seventeenth century before the population explosion hit the Highlands. The development of potato and vegetable growing enabled the people in the Lowlands to cope with most crop failures. Those who were displaced from their holdings were nearer other forms of employment in the central belt of Scotland, where limestone quarrying and the woollen industry were becoming important outlets for this redundant labour force. Many men and women moved to Glasgow and the small towns in the west, which were growing fast as a result of the industrial revolution and the increased trade with America. Aberdeen, Dundee and Inverness were centres to which rural workers moved from the Lowland areas of the north-east.

There are however two accounts of movement from the North East. At the beginning of 1773 there was a move towards emigration by about 50 Roman Catholic families from the Enzie, Strathbogie and Auchindown; they went as far as Aberdeen whence they were to sail to London, but turned back because of the discouragement from Bishop Hay and others who told them in no uncertain terms of the difficulties they would face and the amount of money they would require. These people had as yet nowhere to settle but were expecting to be able to acquire land in London. Bishop Hay commented that although they had turned back this year he would be surprised if they did not try again unless their circumstances improved vastly.[36] The only emigrant boat known to have sailed from Aberdeen was the *John and Jane* which sailed with 59 passengers on the 22nd April and arrived in Halifax, Nova Scotia on the 9th June 1773.[37]

Apart from those who went to St John's Island under the auspices of Sir James Montgomery few emigrated from Perthshire although it included extensive Highland areas, a Gaelic speaking population who suffered from rapidly rising rents after the introduction of sheep in 1762. The activities of Lord Kames (Henry Home), a leading figure of the Enlightenment who wrote extensively on law, moral philosophy and agricultural improvements provided some alternative homes and employment. He had put his ideas into practice on his estate of Kames in Berwickshire and when his wife inherited the estate of Blairdrummond in Perthshire in 1766 the judge started to improve the moss there, an area of about 2520 statute acres, of which he possessed about 1890 acres. A drain was dug to float the turves of moss down to the River Teith and thence to the River Forth. Each new tenant was given an attractive lease to encourage him to work and settle on the moss. By 1791 150 tenants had settled in the area, of whom 90 per cent were Highlanders from the nearby parishes of Callander and Balquhidder.[38]

There was considerable unrest in the towns of Perthshire. Farmers had been exporting meal rather than selling it locally so that it had been scarce for some time, but now there was a "total want of meal in the market of Perth for eight or ten days and the neglect of the police to provide against this" infuriated the populace. A mob of about 400 people rioted in Perth, Newburgh and Abernethy in December 1772 because of the scarcity of meal. When the JPs and heritors met at Perth in January 1773 they agreed that the country produced a surplus of wheat and barley but insufficient oats and meal. One of the mob had been arrested and was sentenced to transportation for life, the first seven years of his sentence to be in the service of the contractor for transporting felons.[39]

Other newly emerging industrial towns in the Lowlands were experiencing a recession. Witnesses to the Committee appointed to enquire into the present state of the linen trade in Great Britain and Ireland in 1773 made it quite plain that the trade languished as compared to 1756 because of the increased amount of linen being imported with too low duty on it. The imported linens were said to be cheaper than home produced ones because of cheaper labour and materials. That is not to suggest that Scots workers were well paid, their wages had been decreased since the end of the Seven Years' War; and the number of looms had been reduced to around 25% of the previous number. Rioting was taking place, especially around Dundee. It was argued that the price and availability of corn was sufficient for the demand and the unrest was due to the conditions of the industry;

> so that it is time that the cry of such general distress should reach the throne. Is it not hard that our market should be glutted with foreign linen to the starving of our own poor?[40]

Leith, the premier port in eastern Scotland, played only a small part in the emigrations. Several vessels such as the *Concord* which sailed in August 1773 used the port for victualling. The *George* sailed from Leith for South Carolina in August 1774 with an unknown number of passengers on board. The *Friendship* sailed in May 1775 taking 88 people from eastern Scotland, they arrived in Philadelphia "all very healthy", after nine weeks and two days. After alllegations of irregularities a magistrate had brought the emigrants back on shore and had found that about 60 were properly indented, but of the other 30 some were indeed illegally indented while others were too young and "incapable of indenting".[41]

It is likely that many persons, especially from Southern Scotland, sought passages to America from English ports, but little evidence has been found. A list of Scottish emigrants on over 30 boats sailing to America from English ports during 1774 and 1775 shows that only one, two or three men went on each of them. Two exceptions were parties of eight men who left from Whitby on the *Marlborough* for Savannah in 1774 and a party of 54 men, women and children on the *Georgia Packet* which sailed from Newcastle for Georgia in September 1775.[42]

From the available information, it is clear that the pattern of emigration from Lowland and Central Scotland differed considerably from that of the Highlands and Islands, reflecting the difference in culture between the two parts of the country. The skills that the Lowlanders took with them enabled most of them to settle successfully, either as farmers or in the rapidly developing industrial society of America.

11

"Open the Eyes of the People"

This chapter details the responses of politicians and others to the wave of emigration which had started in 1760. The comments range from thoughtful attempts to diagnose the root causes and sympathetic understanding of the predicament of the emigrants. to hysterical predictions about the consequences for Britain.

The political and social implications of the emigrations were appreciated from at least as early as 1765 both in the mother country and in North America. That year John Fothergill, a Yorkshireman who had studied medicine in Edinburgh under Alexander Munro, published a pamphlet linking emigration to the maintenance of stability in the twelve colonies. He argued that the effects of the migrations to America had

> undoubtedly been signally beneficial to this country, and some degree of gratitude seems due even to those who have done us a kindness, though without designing it ... Wise and gentle methods will ever strengthen this union, ... Harsh and ungracious means will as necessarily weaken the union and will make them desirous of forgetting that they are of English descent ... Such means will infallibly kindle jealousies, spread discontent and disaffection and put a stop to industry and to every virtuous aim or emulation. People under such circumstances, impatiently look forward to that independency, which their situation favours.

That warning was printed ten years before the outbreak of the War of Independence. Fothergill was still trying to head off the split between the two countries when he drew up a scheme of reconciliation with Benjamin Franklin in 1774, but it was overtaken by the outbreak of the war.[1]

An anonymous pamphlet published in Glasgow in 1771 suggested some of the causes for emigration. The writer noted that professional men - surgeons, merchants, military men, and others - had been in the habit of going abroad in their ones and twos but always intending to return. They went to Europe, to India, to America. Now, not only these sorts of people were moving out of Scotland in greater numbers, but also many farmers and labourers. It was no longer quite such a traumatic experience to go to America as many Scots knew about life in the new country from letters of friends and relatives who were traders or farmers, or from those who had served there during the Seven Years' War and some who had settled there afterwards. The author of this pamphlet did not think that religious persecution was an important element in determining people to move. He thought that, particularly in the islands, feudal law had not been removed in practice although it had in theory; judges and sheriffs still thought of a law in terms of the feudal law so that it was rare for a baron or his factor not to get the judgement. There was now no outlet for all those young men who used to go into the militia, nor could they move easily to work in towns. Unless one actually had work to go to one was likely to starve as the town parishes would not, indeed often could not, look after all the indigent poor who were not allowed to beg without a licence, and might even be fined for so doing. Thus many in the towns starved, stole and even hanged themselves. He wondered whether cheap education was a good thing for there were so many trained surgeons and schoolmasters who were scandalously poorly paid. In fact some people thought that educating the lower classes was positively bad for they were so corrupted by education that they thought for themselves and became less dutiful and obedient.

The chief cause for emigration, according to this pamphleteer, was the difficult situation on the land. Many landlords had run into financial trouble, sometimes as a result of the laws of entail which could make it impossible to improve an estate. Some lairds had tried to recoup themselves by engrossing and by increasing rents suddenly. The new manners made men "so indelicate and openly selfish as to make an offer for any farm which one of their neighbours was in possession of". Those who could not afford the higher rents became discouraged and slothful "oppressed, debased without spirit and in a manner without hands" for if they did manage to make a profit it would all go in the rent, so there was little hope of betterment.

The writer went on to suggest that there were steps to be taken to remedy some of the evils - better police, equality before the law and more opportunity to become one of the electorate, the unbiassed administration of justice, a reduction in the number of distilleries which were using grain that should be used for making bread, the fostering of agriculture and the better security of property.[2]

Nor were the tacksmen blameless, according to another writer, for when they took large estates it was customary to sublet the "skirt" and worst parts of it to the poor people

at as high a rate as he can, and makes them obliged to perform many services, and the rent and services paid by them is generally much higher in proportion than what is paid by the principal tacksman.[3]

There was considerable discussion in the newspapers. A piece in the *Scots Magazine* revealed some underlying fears: "it is to be dreaded that these migrations will prove hurtful to the mother country and therefore its friends ought to use every proper method to prevent them".[4] A correspondent with property in the Western Isles concluded that

unless some speedy remedy is fallen upon by the government and landholders, the consequences must prove very fatal, as that part of the country is rather in the infancy of being civilised than improved; besides, the continual emigration from Ireland and Scotland will soon render our colonies independent of the mother country.[5]

Another correspondent wrote that:

Ever since roads were made and property protected by law, clanship has daily been declining in the highlands. Many of the younger sons and the sons of the wealthy wadsetters and tacksmen who got commissions or fortunes abroad have come home and inspired such a spirit of liberty among them that now in place of fighting or shifting for their chiefs, it is their chief maxim to shift each for himself like the people of other civilized countries.[6]

On the other hand some correspondents hoped that intending emigrants would be given a more realistic view of the conditions ahead of them:

> Emigrations from Scotland to America are now become so frequent that a parliamentary stop
> is talked of to prevent the depopulation of the country. The usual bait made use of on this
> occasion to induce the poor people to leave their friends and native country is the promise of
> the precarious possession of a few wild and uncultivated acres of land, upon their paying a small
> annual quit rent; but these unthinking people do not consider the many inconveniences and
> hardships attending such emigrations, and the difficulties they must undergo, not to mention
> the want of assistance, the very high price of labour and of all kinds of necessities, as well as
> the difficulty they must labour under (in subsisting themselves and families in a remote and
> uncultivated part of the country) while clearing these grounds, which require time, and which
> in most places will cost them over £30 Sterling each acre in cutting down and removing the
> woods, bushes etc.[7]

The discussion continued:

> what would ancient chiefs think of those who are their proprietors or managers under various
> denominations, and are the means of unhinging that distinguished affection? ... It is full time
> they roused themselves to examine in person into the causes of emigration ... and endeavour to
> put a stop to this ruinous practice.[8]

A Highlander writing in 1773 argued that nothing but absolute necessity made
Highlanders think of migrating to another part of the world and many who had gone
because of the high rents had had only enough money for their passages. He argued that
the conduct of the chieftains was hurtful to the state because those men with spirit fled
from the high rents and in America became a possible threat to the mother country, while
leaving few suitable recruits for the army. Many proprietors hurt their personal interests
because their Edinburgh agents sett [rented] their estates, never having seen the land or
knowing the climate, but assuming that crops that grew in the south and east would also
grow in the north and west. Many sub-tenants who knew the climate agreed to grow the
new crops though having no intention of so doing; others were unaware of such clauses
in the tacks; the new crops failed and so it was often impossible to collect the full rent.
Finally, the writer thought that because the proprietors had acted against religion the
recent bad seasons had been a warning from God.[9]

A more forceful opinion was voiced by James Grant at Castle Grant, who wrote in
February 1773 about the recruiting in the district for the East India Company:

> How is His Majesty's army when the exigencies of the state require it, to be supplied, if the
> country is to be perpetually drained by these methods which I insist upon are illegal and
> unwarrantable. And if the country is to be drained not only in time of war but by every other
> method in time of peace, how is the ground to be laboured, manufactures to be carried on or the
> poor farmers to live?[10]

The *Caledonian Mercury* printed a letter from a writer who was worried not only
about emigrants leaving Britain but about the effects they would have on the commerce
between Britain and America:

> The emigrations from the more northern and western parts of this country to America, are now
> grown alarming, and loudly call for the help and assistance of the legislature; but the task of
> preventing people from flying from a country where they are starved, to one where they have

the happy prospect of all conveniences of life in abundance, for their lawful industry, is exceedingly difficult; and, indeed, what I hope, the laws of our free constitution cannot reach to. The proposing to confine a British subject in a corner, where he has the certain prospect of famishing, (for the good of population), is a detestable idea, and unworthy the thought of a British lawgiver; therefore I hope our illustrious senate will never adopt so harsh a measure to defeat emigration. Yet some method it is necessary to take, and that soon, to prevent this country from growing a desert. The evil is gradually advancing from the wild and remote parts to the more southern; and that spirit, which at first only infected the poorest husbandman, has now taken possession of our manufacturers. The wonted wealthy and opulent town of Paisley cannot now support those ingenious mechanics who have raised it to its present greatness, but they are forced to abandon their friends and country, and seek that subsistance in a distant clime, which they cannot obtain in their own. The state by this unhappy evil, not only loses those useful members, but also their families and offspring; and what is still more alarming, they go and naturalize themselves among the disobedient children of their mother country, and imbibe their destructive notions of anarchy. The Americans are too prone to throw off the yoke, which, in my opinion, hangs gently about their necks; and every shipful of these emigrants that reaches their shores, will hasten that day when they shall throw off their dependence upon Britain altogether. Besides, the great acquisition of these manufacturers to America, will proportionally be a loss to the mother-country, as the many commodities that are in use to be exported from our markets, will cease to be demanded, these articles being cheaper furnished by what I may call their *new subjects*. But not only America will be the seat of emigration, but other countries, from whom we draw a vast balance in trade, will likewise, with open arms, receive our needy artisans, and give them such a degree of encouragement, as will greatly accelerate our misfortune. The most obvious potentate in Europe from whom we are likely to suffer, is the present Empress of Russia; her vast genius for political commerce, with the noble profusion with which she treats men of genius indiscriminately of all nations, will tempt many of our manufacturers to fly with their families to her munificence; and those articles, of which we export such quantities up the Baltic to St Petersburg, and the other Imperial ports, will daily decrease in consumpt, and the once-boasted commerce of our country will quickly decay.

But let us in time avert these dangers, and nobly rouse ourselves from our present lethargy: let us consider, that it is the interest of our country that is at stake; and that it behoves us, as Britons, to make every human effort to rescue it from its impending fate.

I am happy to hear one scheme talked of, which, if put in execution, will certainly conduce not a little to that desirable end; I mean, the re-establishing those ancient, though misguided chieftains, in their paternal properties, at a low price. It is impossible to conceive with what joyous alacrity their remaining dependents will fly under their protection; and the smallness of the purchase of these lands will put it in the power of the proprietor to set them at so low a rental that the industrious husbandman will still be able to live comfortably in his own country, without consigning himself over to perpetual banishment in a distant clime.

The next, and indeed the grand object of our legislature, to prevent the further growth of emigration, is some wise and wholesome law for the encouragement of the linen manufacture: the decrease of this branch of commerce has not a little aided the evil complained of, and I hope, by the end of the present session of Parliament, to see it remedied. Many other thoughts might be suggested on this subject, which, I hope, some of your correspondents, possessed of greater abilities, will lay before the public.[11]

The writer of this letter was referring to the estates annexed to the government after the '45. When the bill for restoring the estates was passed in 1784 it was suggested that it might help to prevent emigration. Other people thought that few had emigrated from them because the farms were so well managed and the rents were "easy", yet "from the shameful and oppressive rapacity with which rents are raised it would appear some landlords want to depopulate and form sheep farms".[12] The introduction of sheep farms could not be halted.

Government response

Government had tried to influence matters. The First Lord of the Treasury was informed of an illicit trade (the taking of cash out of the country by the emigrants) being carried on "to the detriment of the American Revenue"; therefore on 7th May 1773 he asked that the principal officers of the customs should send an account of the names, burthen, lading and destination of emigrant boats to the Board and to the principal officers of the ports in America. This instruction was issued by the Scottish Board on 24th November 1773 and a similar letter from the Treasury followed on 8th December.[13] The officers at Port Greenock replied on 13th December that they had not yet been able to learn anything about the emigrations but that in the previous week two vessels had cleared for the West Indies, carrying 22 and eight passengers respectively. The report shows that the reasons given for emigrating were the extravagent rents and dearness of provisions,

> the inducements, if any, are from the favourable representations of their friends, already abroad, give of America. We cannot learn that any means are used for inciting them to such emigrations, their chief motive being to mend their fortunes.[14]

An Inverness officer reported that no emigration vessel had cleared out from there and though he had written to "the most intelligent persons we could think of at the places where the emigrations happened" the answers had not been entirely satisfactory. However this officer confirmed that 4 or 500 men, women and children had emigrated during the previous two years. He underlined the Greenock officer's view that people so oppressed

> would grasp at any opportunity to be relieved from a condition but one degree removed from slavery ... The diseased never hear of a cure mentioned but they believe it will give relief, so is the case with the poor Highlanders.[15]

Mr Archibald Campbell, sheriff of Argyll, had been asked to enquire from the other sheriffs the causes for the emigrations from their districts. He understood why the people would "embrace the humour of deserting their native country". Firstly, military men lived well in America after having taken their discharge there. Secondly, landlords at home often started to increase rents suddenly though they might have achieved their results successfully if done more slowly, for he was sure the lands were worth the rents if properly cultivated and stocked. Thirdly, some of the tacksmen decided that they could not afford higher rents. With the prospect of a high standard of living in America, they persuaded their sub-tenants to go with them "and haunted all public occasions with drinks, pipes and fiddles to rouse their spirits to the expedition".

Lord Justice Clerk Miller commented in April 1774 that Campbell's reports had only been requested from the sheriffs of those counties where emigration had been considerable so as not to "alarm the whole country as if this spirit of emigration had already become general". However the movement was spreading from the Highlands to the Low Country and the manufacturing towns and villages "and what is more alarming, affects not only the lower class of people, but some of the better sort of farmers and mechanics who are in good circumstances and can live very comfortably at home". He was also worried that associations of people were being formed to buy lands "on the joint stock", that is by forming limited companies, as this would eventually enable people to carry money with them and

> it may in time as effectually depopulate this country as the mines of Peru and Mexico have depopulated Spain. While individuals think and act for themselves there is no great danger that many will go; but when they enter into associations, and go off in bodies for the same place with their wives, children and kindred, this removes the natural tie to their country ... they fortify one another in their resolution, and nothing can convince them of their mistake until too late.

As we have seen, there were indeed associations of Lowland farmers and tradesmen who organised their emigrations. Like other officials, Lord Miller blamed the emigrations on the recent bad crops, unemployment occasioned by the decay of manufactures and the rise in rents. He feared that people would soon go, not for want of bread "but for the motive of obtaining a better situation in America". And though some would doubtless prosper, the poorest people would be worse off than at home and indeed it seemed that there were already some who would willingly return.

> A few hundreds of such emigrants returning to different parts of the country would more effectually open the eyes of the people, and cure them of their passion for America, than all that can be said or written on the subject.[16]

The Earl of Suffolk replied to the Lord Justice Clerk, on May 13th that the emigration was "by no means so great as generally represented. But the spirit of associations is peculiarly dangerous, and cannot be too much discouraged". Members of the government discussed the possibility of bringing back dissatisfied emigrants "to undeceive their countrymen with regard to the sanguine ideas at present prevailing of the advantages to be derived from emigration". He thought it would be difficult because so many were under special contracts of service.[17] Lord Miller wrote again on May 30th that several shipmasters were finding it more advantageous to carry passengers than freight to America and were sending agents to entice passengers to go from different bays and harbours of the coast. But the people

> were crowded and in other respects miserably accomodated on board ... many must die in the passage, but while they are under this infatuation they are deaf to all advice and more particularly of the gentlemen who they consider as interested and combined to deceive.[18]

With mounting tension in the American colonies, increasing numbers emigrating and with recollections of the Covenanting wars and of the '15 and '45 rebellions the British government became convinced of the dubious patriotism of the Scots. On the one hand, a boatload of Roman Catholics who were assisted by their Church revived dormant fears of Jacobitism. On the other hand, Presbyterians were equally suspect for they could be associated in the mind with the Covenanters; many North American Presbyterians were descended from emigrants from the seventeenth century Scottish Plantations in Ulster and they were justifiably assumed to be revolutionaries to a man.

Pressure for government action continued to build up. Edmund Burke warned Parliament on March 22nd 1775 that three thousand miles of ocean lie between you and them. No contrivance can prevent the effect of this distance in weakening government. Seas roll, and months pass, between the order and the execution, and the want of a speedy explanation of a single point is enough to defeat a whole system ... In large bodies, the circulation of power must be less vigorous at the extremities. Nature has said it. This is the immutable condition, the eternal law of extensive and detached empire.[19]

Sir James Grant of Grant wrote to Henry Dundas, the Lord Advocate, on 19th April requesting action. Dundas was MP for Edinburgh from 1774 to 1802, when he was elevated to the peerage as the first Viscount Melville. During his parliamentary career he was Home Secretary, Secretary for War, First Lord of the Admiralty, President of the Board of Control for India and Treasurer to the Navy; in this last position he was impeached in 1805, but although aquitted, he never again held office. As Lord Advocate Dundas was in a supreme position to affect affairs in Scotland; by the use of his powers of patronage he put his political friends in high positions, in fact for many years he was the virtual "dictator" of Scotland. Sir James wrote:

The state of the Highlands as to emigration really deserves the attention of Government, notwithstanding the troubles in America, that spirit is daily gaining ground. It is with regret that I observe that Government amongst the other regulations in regard to America has not proclaimed that no vessels loaded with emigrants are to be allowed to sail. This as America is declared by Parliament to be in a state of actual rebellion would appear to be no more than a proper and prudent regulation of internal police for the preservation of His Majesty's subjects, and more immediately of those poor deluded people, who in great numbers I am informed, propose sailing with their wives and families this spring, without knowing to what hardships they may be exposed. My heart bleeds for them, and makes me consider it my duty to represent this to Government by your means that they may, in case it has not occurred to them before, issue such orders as may seem most proper to His Majesty and his ministers to the different ports, and particularly Greenock from whence they commonly embark. If this is done no time is to be lost, as they sail in May. Government may never have a more proper opportunity of chequing this emigrating disposition without force, and it will show the Highlanders that his Majesty attends to their safety.

When this is done, proper and effectual steps should be taken for encouraging and employing this valuable set of people when required.

As yet my country has been very little affected, but I am confident the frenzy will extend universally, if proper means are not taken to prevent it - it is in the power at present of any little pedling merchant to carry off hundreds, and the Highlanders are so connected by intermarrying, you will easily see how far that may extend. These sort of people hire a ship, and by enticing people to emigrate not only secure a free passage to themselves, but I am told make a considerable profits besides - so that it is really now become a species of low traffick.[20]

There was also a deep fear among the authorities that Britain's technological lead would be lost through emigrants taking their knowledge overseas and so customs officers were alerted. A Dumfries customs officer reported that after a fruitless search of the emigrants' baggage on the *Lovely Nelly*, which sailed in May 1775, they found

barrels containing utensils for agriculture and axes, saws, hammers etc, all British manufacture ... No utensils in the above packages made use of in the cotton, woollen and silk manufactures of this kingdom.[21]

Harsh reality

Some bleak pictures of life in North America were being put about and the authorities hoped that stories of hardhip would discourage intending emigrants. In a letter from New York dated April 6th 1774 it was argued that of those recently gone to America almost half the passengers had died of hunger and the disgraceful accommodation on board the boats.

> Most of those that remain depend for their support on the generosity of the public who are now become tired of this burden. Such of them as go back into the woods under their chiefs that came out with them find themselves still in a worse condition, and the hardships they undergo are infinitely greater than at home. They have a long winter to struggle with and a very hot summer, and it will be five years before they can earn a subsistence for themselves, and by that time they and their children will become slaves for life to put off the debt contracted for a miserable subsistence during the five years. Such as are at liberty to think for themselves have sold their service for four years for a small sum, and to be found in clothes and victuals, of which they will receive but a very scanty provision. It is said that some of the the MacDonalds are going over to bring out more, but though it may be an advantage to the rich who have estates in the colonies, to get people, yet the poor emigrants cannot be placed in worse circumstances than by being brought to any of our colonies, where they may expect the very worst treatment without the least hope of getting back to their native country; I hope therefore some means will be used to undeceive them.[22]

Another correspondent from Baltimore underlined the problems:

> Many people from England and Scotland are flocking to different parts of this continent on divers schemes; and I see many who wish themselves at the place they came from. This is a very trying climate, the two extremes of heat in summer, and cold in winter, are severely felt here. Whole families are daily arriving and travelling into the back country seeking to take up and cultivate land which, from experience, they find to be a very laborious task. It is just like setting a man in the middle of a wood, for the country in its native state is all covered with wood, and I have seen many people fatigued to death in a little time. Happy are they that can rest contented at home.[23]

A settler in Virginia complained that

> They were in the utmost distress, sorely lamenting their departure and earnestly wishing they could return home. Such as had indented for their passage were sold very cheap, some even kept so long on hand that the proprietors threw them their indentures and bid them shift for themselves. They who are tradesmen find themselves obliged to accept of very low terms for the West Indies.[24]

More details were added by a gentleman in New York:

> It is melancholy to see the delusion of your poor people coming over here. I have seen many hundreds of them that had come out who were convinced of their error; and those that had it in their power were agreeing for their passage home again. I have seen old barracks and old hospitals full of these miserable people, starving for the want of the necessities of life.[25]

A Bostonian reported against this background of growing political tension:

> Several emigrants from Scotland have of late arrived here. I wonder any persons that could

make shift to live at home would come to this infatuated continent till matters are once settled, when there will be room enough for thousands to sit down upon *estates* already cleared.[26]

An artificer in Philadelphia confirmed these scenes of hardship:

My situation here is very disagreeable, all business at a stand, merchants, traders, workmen etc starving, I am heartily sorry for leaving Scotland: all Scottish people are looked on in a very bad light unless they join the Americans. I am told that many of my countrymen in other parts of America, who have come out lately, are actually starving. I wish I could get home again, but I have no money to pay for my passage. The people who came out here some time ago from Scotland were sold like so many sheep; but now nobody will buy them as they have enough ado to maintain themselves, so that the people are left to starve.[27]

Disgruntled Americans and unhappy emigrants were producing the sort of propaganda that the government wished for in order to discourage emigration. However as we shall see in the next chapter, after the outbreak of war it was decided to bring emigration to a halt.

12

"My Bounden Duty"

Before the actual outbreak of hostilities in America Parliament, dominated by landlords, was affronted when commerical interests in several British cities, especially the tobacco barons of Glasgow, petitioned Parliament in sympathy with the rebels.

The political unrest in North America began to affect emigration towards the end of 1775. The critical skirmishes at Lexington and Concord had been fought and the bloodiest battle of the American war had already taken place at Bunker Hill outside Boston on 17th June 1775.

There had been several reports that all was not well with some of the emigrants once they landed in America. 30 or 40 families returned on a boat sailing from Boston in 1775. As Campbell, a customs officer at Greenock wrote:

> I have often seen and heard of Scots emigrants to America but never until now of American emigrants to Scotland *Tempora mutantur* ...
>   P.S. For God's sake make the news of the arrival of emigrants from America as publick as possible, to see and prevent our deluded countrymen from emigrating to a country when nothing but anarchy and confusion reigns.[1]

Nevertheless, in spite of a good harvest two vessels were lying off Gigha during August ready to take in emigrants for Cape Fear from Kintyre, Knapdale and the adjacent islands, each vessel to carry 150 persons:

> the crops of every kind are very rich in Argyllshire this season; the hay and barley harvest well advanced, but no appearance of herring in any lochs, which is much regretted by the inhabitants who have yearly great dependence on the produce of the sea.[2]

There had also been considerable disruption to shipping in the early months of 1775. The rebelling colonists had turned back the *Happy Janet* and the *James* without allowing them to discharge their cargoes. On the British side, in May and June customs officers had boarded at least two ships - the *Monimia* and the *Neptune* - and divested the emigrants of all their fire-arms, swords and daggers before they went on board at Greenock, "by which provident conduct the owners and freighters of the vessel were saved from the penalties inflicted by the Act 29 Geo II for exporting arms, gunpowder etc".[3]

On August 14th fears were voiced officially by the Lord Justice Clerk, that the emigrants might take up arms against the king once they reached America, for although they were loyal while left to themselves the American agents might deceive them from their duty. While H.M. recruiting officers in Scotland were under the restraints of law and the subjects secured against their fraud and violence

> these American agents are free to recruit whole shipfuls of men for that country without any restraint or control whatsoever and without its being in the power of Government to know with certainty the numbers transported from one country to the other.[4]

Government was so worried about the state of affairs in America that a proclamation for suppressing rebellion and sedition was issued on 23rd August. Emigration was called to an abrupt halt on 4th September 1775. Henry Dundas, the Lord Advocate, stopped any further departures with a few letters which illustrate the immense power of the 18th century administrative machinery. Dundas reported that on receiving His Majesty's proclamation for supressing rebellion he was informed of ships embarking hundreds of passengers for America, many of whom were carrying money, arms and ammunition and he had therefore required the Board of Customs, sheriffs and admirals depute to stop emigrant ships from sailing. Dundas suggested that opportunity be given to emigrants to return in transports coming back from America.[5]

The same day the Lord Advocate turned his attention to the source of emigration and wrote to the officials in country districts:

> I am informed that ever since His Majesty's proclamation for suppressing rebellion and sedition was issued, there are many of His Majesty's subjects emigrating to America and some of them with money, arms and ammunition. I think it my bounden duty to prevent such emigrations, which I am satisfied would in the end provide support to the rebels, and I am therefore to desire you to exert yourself to the uttermost to prevent these emigrations, and to prevent any ships sailing for America with more than the complement of men necessary for navigating the ship. I must also desire you will call a meeting of the Justices of the Peace of the county, intimate this letter to them and desire their aid in the execution of the same. I shall expect your answer.[6]

The prohibition was given wide publicity in the press after copies of the orders were sent to all customs houses by the Commissioners of Customs:

> There are two ships now on the western coasts of Scotland preparing to take on board a large body of persons proposing to emigrate from this country to America, and that although Government has not hitherto seen cause to take any coercive measures to prevent such emigration, it may be highly proper from the present situation of America to discourage or even to prevent the same as much as possible, and therefore desiring that directions may be given to the officers at the ports to postpone the clearing out of such ships with emigrants till further order, and to use their best endeavours to prevent their sailing without first stating the matter with all its circumstances to the Board for their consideration. And Mr Moyse acquainted the Board that he dispatched letters to the ports of Port Glasgow, Stornoway, Oban and Campbeltown, as desired by the Lord Advocate, and that in the said letters he also directed the officers to acquaint the Board with any information relative to the vessels above mentioned, or any other vessels intending to carry emigrants out of the kingdom and ... to communicate any intelligence they may receive with respect to emigration from this country. The Board approves thereof.[7]

The orders appear to have been followed implicitly for the duration of the war, for not a single reference appears in the customs records of any violation, although numerous transgressions in relation to forbidden cargoes were minutely chronicled.

On 5th September Dundas wrote privately to William Eden MP Under Secretary of State. The letter shows just how well informed Dundas was of circumstances in every quarter of Scotland and must be quoted in full.

You would receive a letter from me last night officially informing you what I had done respecting an immediate intending emigration from this Country to America, and I wrote to the same purpose to Lords North, Suffolk and the Attorney General. It gives me much pleasure to hope from your last letter that there will be an end of that relaxation of government which never fails to enfeeble it. I hope that spirit will not be confined solely to the American contest, but will spread itself thro' every branch of authoritty in this country. I am much obliged to you in what you say concerning my particular line of conduct in this country. I think, if I know myself, if I err in the execution of my duty it will not at least proceed from any inclination to relax the vigour of government.

Since you have taken the trouble of giving me your sentiments respecting the disease of emigration and the cures you propose for it, I shall with equal freedom tell you whence after the most mature consideration I think this spirit has arisen in this country, and how it is most likely to be checked, for I doubt much, if it is at all to be extirpated.

You seem to suppose that the severity of gentlemen proprietors in Scotland to those under them has been the cause of the decay of that love of country which has drove the Highlanders to seek an asylum in America. And you are so far in the right, for I do believe that the severity of some great proprietors in the North by a precipitant and injudicious rise of rents was the immediate cause of emigration in some parts of that country, but this will by no means account for the universality of the disease which prevails in many parts of the country, where such severity does not nor never did prevail. Besides I believe that many, indeed most, of those who had been injudicious in the manner you suppose have rectified their error, but the spirit of emigration still prevails and the same seeming discontent in their old habitations.

For my part I believe that the cause is deeper rooted, and is to be traced back to that system of legislation which took place immediately subsequent to the late rebellion. At that time you know that many of the Highland chieftains, whom they had been accustomed to venerate and respect, were forfeited and banished from all interest and connection in that part of the country. This of consequence produced a gloom and damp upon the spirits of their dependents. Immediately subsequent to this followed the various acts of Parliament all calculated for and tending to eradicate the spirit of clanship in the Highlands of Scotland; and they have had that effect to a very great degree. This has been attended with two consequences. Formerly a Highland chieftain naturally valued himself upon his influence in the country. He did not conceive money to be the only valuable produce of his estate but he likewise put a valuation upon what I call a rent in Men. In proportion as his clan was numerous and his estate covered with inhabitants, he felt himself great and respectable, but when that consequence was gradually wearing away, he would not put the same value upon idle men, what has always been the situation of the Highlands of Scotland, for there is no doubt that the Highlands produced more inhabitants than are necessary for the local demands of that part of the country. In short one consequence of destroying clanship in the Highlnds was to annihilate the desire of the Highland chieftains to have their estates covered with inhabitants and they were led to turn their thoughts in what manner they could employ their lands more profitably than in the cultivation of idle men.

Another consequence following from the destruction of clanship is likewise very obvious and indeed in some degree connected with what I have last said. The power of a chieftain over his clan was perhaps dangerous to the State when the chief himself was not well affected, but altho' the tendency of it might be dangerous the fact must certainly be admitted that there arose from it a strong cement and bond of union which consequently was dissolved, at the same time that the connection which was founded upon it was dissolved.

Do not conceive that I mean to find fault with those legislators who devised the system for civilising the Highlands of Scotland by dissolving the clanships. That system was necessary at the time, but I will not pay the same compliment to the judgment of those who are zealous for the continuance of that same system in all its rigour, and now that the reason for it has totally vanished - I say vanished, for it is to talk like children to talk of any danger from disaffection in the North. There is no such thing, and it ought to be the object of every wise ruler in this country, to cherish and make the proper use of the Highlands of Scotland. For it is impossible that it can now have any other object than what must tend to answer very salutary and beneficial purposes to government. If you ask me what these purposes are, I readily answer that the Highlanders were born to be soldiers and the Highlands ought to be considered as a nursery of strength and security to the Kingdom. Upon this principle I say it ought to be the object of Government to view with the most favourable eyes those proprietors in the North who value themselves upon possessing an extensive influence amongst their people, and who consequently bestow the most attention to acquire that influence. By such a connection they are at all times ready to call forth into vigorous exertion a set of hardy and brave men, who by being neglected are induced to look for protection upon the other side of the Atlantic, or to speak more properly are induced to wander there from the want of that cherishment and protection which their fathers had felt in their old habitations.

I have already mentioned that the Highlands of Scotland has at all times been productive of more inhabitants than were necessary for the local demands of the country, but this could never be attended with any inconvenience but the reverse, for they supplied the defects of the Lowlands, and everybody acquainted with this country knows that more than the half of our day labourers, of our menial servants, our chairmen, porters, of our workmen of every kind are all from the Highlands of Scotland. And upon this ground I am satisfied that altho' the proprietors in the North have taken the first alarm on account of the emigration from their country, they in fact are not to be the first sufferers. It will be felt sooner and more severely in the Lowlands, when deprived of that great supply which they annually derive from the superfluities of the North.

This was the manner in which the Highlands used formerly to empty itself of its superfluities. They have now taken the turn of emptying themselves into America. The present situation of that country has afforded us a momentary occasion of suspending those emigrations by coercive measures, but you may depend upon it, such measure can only be followed while the immediate occasion of it subsists. If there were no such pretence as that of rebellion in America, it would be wicked to think of keeping your subjects at home by force. In a free country, in a small island and where there are dayly opportunitys of getting away, such an idea is impracticable. I have no doubt that for the present we shall be able to keep them at home, and every friend of Government should seize the opportunity in the meantime of endeavouring to regain their affections to this country, so that these may operate, when pretences for coercion shall be at an end.

I will not pretend to point out to you the various methods by which this ought to be attempted. These will readily occur to yourself. In so far as it falls within my province to inspire the gentlemen of this country with the importance of being kind and beneficent to those who live under them, my endeavours shall not be wanting, but Government must likewise do its part. Why should the clamour of opposition or the scurrility of a newspaper dismay Government from allowing the old proprietors to return to their estates in the North? Their crimes were great, but their punishment has been equal to their crimes, but I do sincerely believe nothing could lend more to cherish and revive the spirits of the inhabitants of the North, than being witnesses of such a generous exertion of the beneficence of Government. In return for this they and the other proprietors of the North would give their most vigorous assistance to aid Government in levying that force from the North, which it will be able to supply, and which Government will most unquestionably stand in need of. Even if the present American conditions did not subsist, I should think it a wise measure in government to keep at all times a military establishment in Scotland to be recruited from the North. As the men would be supplied from the superfluities of that part of the country, it will be the very best militia without any of its disadvantages. If the officers were named from the different corners of the Highlands, they would recruit from their own class and thereby renew that cement of connection which my opinion leads me to think ought now to be cherished, not to be checked. This and this only is the radical cure of emigration.

I have thus thrown loosely together a few of these ideas respecting the Highlands of Scotland which at some future time will be the subject of conversation at large. If your ideas upon these subjects happen to correspond wiht mine, I flatter myself we may be able to have them carried into practice. At present you will observe that I speak confidentially to yourself, and as such you will consider what I write, for I do not recollect ever to have unbosomed those topicks so freely to any other person.

I had almost ommitted to mention a difficulty I find myself under in the execution of a part of my office, and as it must certainly have occurred in England, I could wish with your first convenience you could drop me a few lines on the subject. You know that where a crime is not of the nature to deserve a capital punishment, the punishment next in degree is transportation to America. This is necessary from the want of other species of punishment, for the generality of criminals have no funds to be the subject of pecuniary punishment, and whipping is a species of punishment which I abominate. I scarce know one good effect from it, and I am sure of this bad one that the person who undergoes it becomes more profligate than ever.

These topicks however may be more proper for future discussion. What at present I wish to ask from you is, whether notwithstanding the present situation of America, it is the practice of England to pronounce as usual sentences of transportation to the Plantations of America without any limitation. If this is done, it seems to me to be sending so many wicked and desperate men to be employed against us in that country. And yet I am (at a loss to know) what other punishment there is to substitute in its place.[8]

Not everyone approved of the Lord Advocate's action in stopping emigration as these letters to the press illustrate:

I am humbly of the opinion that without an Act of Parliament, or at least a royal proclamation, such measure must be void and null. The established law, says the great law-oracle Blackstone, is that the king may prohibit any of his subjects from leaving the realm; a proclamation therefore forbidding this in general for three weeks by laying on an embargo upon all shipping in time of war will be equally binding as an Act of Parliament because founded on a prior law. No royal proclamation has yet been issued. I should therefore humbly apprehend that no person can be hindered from going where he pleases till that is done.[9]

Another gentleman wrote:

as I am no lawyer, I know not but some old Scotch act may be found ... which may seem to justify what has been done; but I presume that if any King's solicitor or Attorney General in England had recommended to the sheriffs, to convene the justices of the peace and to the commissioners of customs to stop emigration, he would have drawn upon himself the indignation of that free people; the sheriffs would have treated his letters with contempt, and he must have felt the vengeance of an English House of Commons, tho' in Scotland liberty is less known and its manly voice is seldom heard. This coercive method of stopping emigration will be looked upon as illegal, till some new or unknown law is produced; it appears to me altogether unjustifiable, and can never produce any good effect. To compel people who are in hardship to remain at home without offering them any relief is inhuman and cruel. To prohibit British subjects, whether poor or opulent to go to the British colonies, is to act directly in opposition to Parliament. Parliament in all its late acts hath considered America as if it were a part of Great Britain. It is therefore as lawful for peaceful British subjects to emigrate to British America as it is for a gentleman to remove from one parish in Scotland to another. But besides the probibition is ill-judged, for it must defeat its own aim; the common people from the mere aversion to constraint, in a special manner, are never so desirous to change their abode as when they have been forbidden to do it; in all probability many thousands of them will emigrate to America, who, unless they had been prohibited would never have had the thoughts of leaving their native country, and if they be determined to emigrate, I suppose that no illegal orders to customs officers, sheriffs or Justices of the Peace can effectually hinder them. However as I have heard little about this affair for a week or two past, I think it may be hoped that when a lawyer so eminent and hitherto esteemed so friendly to the liberty of the subjects, shall take a little time to think of his project, he may possibly relinquish it, for he will perhaps see that it is illegal, inhuman, impolitic and impracticable.

However, in the same issue, an English supporter of the Lord Advocate wrote:

> some severe remarks appeared in the English newspapers. I think, Sir, notwithstanding the outcry that interested persons, such as contractors to send out their fellow creatures to be sold in America, may make, yet the gratitude and thanks of the whole country are due to the Lord Advocate, the commissioners of customs and all who endeavour to stop the emigrations. Their conduct has been founded on humanity and sound policy.[10]

On November 20th Lord North introduced three bills in the House of Commons which forbade all trade and intercourse with America; allowed American ships and goods captured at sea to be forfeited to the captors; and empowered the Crown to appoint commissioners to inquire into grievances, to grant pardons to individuals and to receive into the King's peace any districts or colonies which would return to obedience.

Meetings of local authorities were held throughout Scotland to consider the Lord Advocate's decree and reports of two of them have survived. The Justices of the Peace of Stirling were by no means unanimous as to the need or indeed the legality of the order:

> Johnstone [M.P. for Dysart burghs and a Stirlingshire landowner] was compleatly absurd. He spoke violently against the Justices of the Peace intefering said such a step would be illegal that we had no Power, he said he wished there were more of the Common People there that he might inform them that they were their own Master, and might emigrate if they chose it, in short it is impossible to tell you the whole of his absurdities. I proposed a motion 'that the Members of this meeting wou'd exert themselves to the utmost of their Power to prevent etc etc etc any attempts toward Emigrating' This Johnston (sic) violently opposed, and wanted to insert 'as far as we legally can' which I luckily turned into ridicule, by saying, there could be nothing so ridiculous as a meeting of the *Justices of the Peace* saying in their minutes, That they intended to act *according to law.*[11]

However the members of the Quarter Sessions of Kirkcudbright protested their loyalty to the crown in no uncertain terms:

> Impressed with the deepest sense of the Blessings we enjoy under your Majesty's auspicious Reign, we cannot help testifying our abhorrence of these attempts which are made to disturb its tranquility by our Rebellious Fellow Subjects in North America.
>
> Warmly attached to our inestimable Constitution it is our earnest wish that every part of it may be preserved inviolate. To attain this great end it appears to us an indispensible requisite that the Supremacy of the British Legislature be asserted over every part of the Empire.
>
> With such Sentiments as these, we must express our disapprobation of the principles of those men, who make British Liberty to consist in an undistinguished opposition to every measure of administration. The fatal effects of a conduct, resulting from such principles are now severely felt by the misguided Colonists on the other side of the Atlantic.
>
> We lament and pity the mischiefs which evil councils, licentiousness and a factious spirit, have produced among a deluded people. But since conciliatory proposals have been disregarded and mildness and forbearance construed into timidity we humbly apprehend that vigorous measures are now become absolutely necessary to bring back these unnatural children to a proper sense of their duty to their mother country. Being fully persuaded that these measures will be such as are consistent with the Honour, the Dignity and the Liberty of Britons, we will support them with our lives and fortunes.[12]

Mr Alexander Spiers of Elderslie, who had been in America for 20 years, considered *The present state of America and Lord North's declaration in the House of Commons:*

When the people of America are made acquainted with the declaration it is presumed that instead of healing the differences it may still tend to widen the unhapppy breach. They will consider it as the effects of fear on the part of administration proceeding from the additional strength the minority have acquired this session, the difficulty of raising supplys, the embarrassed state of the nation or the prevailing opinion that Britain is not equal to the task of conquering America. These sentiments and opinions fostered and diffused over the continent will raise the spirit of the congress and create ideas of independence and at least advance their demands beyond what Britain can grant. They will immediately adopt the idea of the inability of Britian to compel obedience and perhaps form a resolution to continue the war till they oblige the mother country to bend the knee and treat with them on their own terms. The transactions of last year have created new obstacles and raised new difficulties which will have their weight in postponing an accomodation and their nature is such that they must increase yearly so long as this unnatural contest continues. A system of government is now established in America. Great officers of state have been appointed, places of trust and emolument have been created, individuals have been invested with great power ... men filling these important offices will not easily be persuaded to abandon their power ... Military officers too who not only have places of great honour and emolument but also a great extent of power will not easily be persuaded to give up so many advantages without an adequate consideration ... Many of them perhaps men of desparate fortunes whose extistence depended on the continuation of the contest. With these I would also class the *American paymasters, agents contractors Treasurers Secretaries* and every new created office of trust and emolument ...These men will oppose an accomodation even on the terms of the congress. They will wish for a Revolution that the energy of the old laws may never be restored and the mortgages and securities upon their estates in the hands of British subjects may be rendered ineffectual ... The transactions of last year convince me that the British forces are unequal to the task of keeping possession of New York, Philadelphia and Charlestown, and acting at the same time on the defensive in the province of Massachussets Bay. Distempers arise from the change of climate. Numerous accidents and misfortunes befall an army in an enemy country which must be recruited from a nation at the distance of 3000 miles, from people who are either not hearty in the service or debauched in great towns, raw and inexperienced in the art of war. To oppose these to the Americans who are from their infancy trained in the use of arms and fired with the spirit of enthusiasm which at present prevails could scarce be attended with success. The game laws of Britain prevent the youth of this country from knowing the use of fire arms till they enter into actual service ... If therefore an accomodation is by any means to be effected on honourable terms I give it as my opinion with great deference and humility that *20,000* Russians will strike more terror in the minds of the people of America than double the number of British troops ... The Indians also are a terror and a very proper engine in the hand of government .. If government does not take them into their service the Americans will ... Hitherto the ships of war have been very deficient in their duty ... Manufactures prejudicial to those of Britian are introducing and meet with great encouragement.[13]

So emigration was halted for nine years. Military recruitment immediately mopped up several thousand men and their families, who might have been candidates for emigration. After 1783 emigration was resumed, only to be halted again on the outbreak of the French wars. The social problems of the Highlands remained unresolved and renewed pressure to emigrate developed. Parliament again had to grapple with the difficult question of freedom of movement. But never again did government formally deny the right to emigrate.

13

"Born to be Soldiers"

After the '15 rebellion the United Kingdom government began to use surplus Highland labour, at first for policing the Highlands and later and on a much larger scale for Britain's imperial purposes. Several independent companies were raised in 1725 to keep watch on the Highland Clans and discourage cattle thieving. They were known as the *Freiceadan Dubh*, or Black Watch; in 1740 it was designated the 43rd Regiment (changed in 1749 to the 42nd). The use of the Highlands as a major recruiting area had been proposed in 1738 by Lord President Duncan Forbes of Culloden who suggested that the Highlanders should be formed into several regiments commanded by English or Scottish officers "of undoubted loyalty" and officered by chiefs of the "disaffected clans".

> If Government pre-engage the Highlanders in the manner I propose they will not only serve well against the enemy abroad, but will be hostages for the good behaviour of their relatives at home, and I am persuaded it will be absolutely impossible to raise a rebellion in the Highlands.[1]

His suggestion was not taken up. A few years later rebellion broke out and ironically the decisive Battle of Culloden was fought on Forbes' own lands.

The Seven Years War

The outbreak of the Seven Years' War with France in 1756 at last forced the adoption of Forbes' proposed policy. The Highlands were scoured for recruits, and Scots were sent to fight Britain's wars in Europe and North America. According to Lenman, the avowed objective was to transport potential Jacobites to foreign battle-fields where they could be slaughtered fighting the French, rather than leave them to plot subversion at home.[2] During this war no fewer than ten line regiments, the 77th (Montgomery's), 78th (Fraser's), 87th (Keith's), 88th (Campbell's), 89th (Gordon's), 100th and 101st (Johnstone's), 105th (Queen's), 113th (Royal Highland Volunteers) and the 114th (Maclean's) were raised; all were disbanded after the war.(Fig. 13.1)

Dr Walker's Report on the Hebrides, which he compiled after his visits in 1764 and 1771 gives some information of the numbers of men from the islands who went to serve in America in the Seven Years' War. Dr Walker's "fighting men" included those men between 18 and 56 yearas old, or about half the population, and included those men who were "blind and lame or otherwise diseased".[3] His estimate of the total population for the islands is not reliable and he did not note the number of men who had returned to

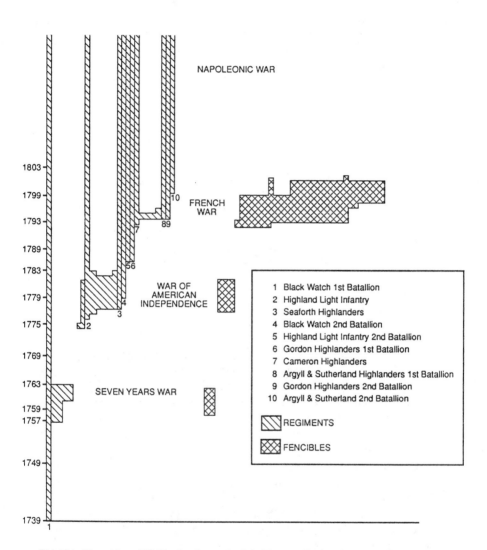

Fig. 13.1 The raising of Highland regiments for Britain's wars. Each regiment mobilised about a 1000 men with an unknown but substantial number of camp-followers.

every parish. Nevertheless the figures are of some interest. Some of the men who returned he called Chelsea Pensioners; the Royal Hospital in Chelsea had been founded in 1682 for men in receipt of a pension through service, disability, or a campaign pension, candidates had to be 55 years old unless disabled by army service. Of those men who had not returned Walker stated that "many had been killed". In fact, many of the rest settled in America on land granted by the government.

Total population		Soldiers	Returned
Lewis	c. 7000	170	34
Harris	c. 2000	118	14
N.Uist	c. 2600	60+	?
S.Uist	c. 1600	72	?
Barra	c. 1300	31	?
Islay	c. 7000	500	?
Mull	c. 5300	350	50
Coll	c. 1200	40	?
Tiree	c. 1700	57	12
Skye	c.15000	500	?

Table 13.1. Dr Walker's Estimate of the Populations and Soldiers from the Hebrides.

In his census of 1755 Rev Alexander Webster had reckoned that one-fifth of the population of each parish could be regarded as "fighting Men".[4]

At the end of the war in 1763 men of the 77th, 78th and those of the 42nd regiments who had served their time with the colours were discharged in Canada and settled in Quebec and Nova Scotia. The government argued that these loyal military men would then be ready to deal with any possible rebellion by the French Canadians. Fraser's Regiment were settled round Murray Bay and Mount Murray (Nova Scotia) which was a good site for the protection of Quebec. The St Lawrence River was an excellent means of communications and provided a regular supply of fish. After years of service in the army the men and their families were used to a harsh climate and the hard physical work in unfavourable conditions which to some extent resembled their lives in Scotland. In accordance with government regulations, captains received 3,000 acres, lieutenants 2,000 while the non-commissioned officers and men each received 200 and 50 acres respectively. Although the countryside around Murray Bay is very picturesque and rather like Scotland, the soil is poor, and military considerations such as the protection of Quebec on the seaward side, played a major part in the location of these settlements.

The War of Independence

It is a strange paradox of history, that when the War of Independence broke out a high proportion of the Highland settlers supported the British government. This despite the fact that one reason for their settlement in America was their support of the Jacobite rebellion. The reasons appear to have been partly because they felt gratitude to government for the grants of land received, partly out of their ancient tradition of loyalty to authority. Lowland settlers, more integrated into the life of the States, supported the rebellion, and some took a leading part in the setting up of the Republic. Nevertheless for some years Scots in general were extremely unpopular in the States, although this prejudice did not last.

The 1st Battalion, Royal Highland Emigrants

When fighting began in North America in 1775 the ex-soldiers were recruited again. Lieutenant-Colonel Allan MacLean, late of the 104th Regiment and son of Major Donald MacLean of Torloisk, proposed to Lord North a plan to raise a regiment of Highlanders already settled in North America. Meantime the government had sent an "Additional Instruction" to the governors of New York and North Carolina, dated April 6th 1775, thirteen days before the battle of Lexington, stating that Lt-Col MacLean had emigrated with men and their families and should be allowed to settle together on "one contiguous tract of land". They were to be given specially generous treatment regarding quit rents because they would be required to swear loyalty to King George III and to the laws of the Parliament of Great Britan and "at the hazard of our lives and fortunes oppose all illegal combinations and insurrections whatsoever".[5]

On June 12th General Gage issued an order to Lieutenant-Col MacLean, empowering him to raise a regiment to be called the Royal Highland Emigrants, consisting of two battalions of ten companies each, the whole corps to be clothed, armed, and fitted out in the same manner as His Majesty's Royal Highland Regiment (the Black Watch) and to rendez-vous at Lake Champlain. The first battalion was to be raised from the discharged men of the 42nd (the Black Watch), 77th (Montgomery's Regiment of Highlanders) and 78th (Fraser's Highlanders) as well as recently arrived Highland emigrants. About 300 veterans of the 78th enlisted.[6]

During the summer of 1775 Colonel MacLean visited the settlement of Kingsbury on the Johnson estate (see chapter 4) and enrolled four hundred MacDonells for the new regiment. But the difficulty was to get them to Canada. A small party under Ranald MacDonell escorted the Colonel to Montreal, arriving there in September. All the clan "voted for the British" so that other members of this Catholic Highlander loyalist settlement, which was beleaguered by Americans, made their way to an old outpost of the Jesuit Mission at St Regis on the banks of the St Lawrence. It seems doubtful whether many more of the new recruits followed immediately.

In January 1776 General Schuyler plundered the Johnson estates leaving behind much distress, and took five or six members of the family hostage for the good conduct of Sir John Johnson (son of Sir William) and his followers. They were confined in gaol in Lancaster, Pennsylvania, but when General Schuyler attempted to arrest Sir John in June they were freed from parole and escaped. Leek returned to Mohawk and collected about 50 clansmen and they marched north arriving in Montreal on May 10th.[7] They were followed by some 300 tenants and their families who arrived in Montreal during the winter and spring of 1776-7. Other men went to New York to enlist in Aberchalder's company of the King's Royal Regiment of New York which had been founded by Sir John Johnson.[8] They too were given land on demobilization in 1783.(Fig. 13.2)

Colonel MacLean had written home to Scotland to Murdoch Maclaine, an Edinburgh merchant, asking him for recruits and stores for the new regiment. Maclaine had been named as the man best suited, from his experience with Highland emigrants, to plan the operation and as a reward he was commissioned as Captain in the 2nd battalion of the Royal Highland Emigrants on 14th June 1775. Stores were hastily assembled with the aid of loans from Maclaine's friends and loaded on the *Glasgow Packet* lying at Greenock.[9] Already she was a marked vessel for when she had sailed earlier in the year for Boston, the Americans had been warned to look out for her as she had a large quantity of goods on board, marked for the army, "which they apprehend is for sale contrary to the resolutions of the Congress".[10]

The *Glasgow Packet* sailed with emigrants some time before September 27th for Boston.(Fig 13.3) On board were several kinsmen who pledged themselves for service with the regiment. As they neared the American coast and the risk of attack from privateers increased, Maclaine had his passengers sign a resolution:

We the following subscribers now passengers on board the *Glasgow Packet*, Capt. Porterfield, commander, being fully determined to serve in the Regiment of Royal Highland Emigrants under the command of Lieut. Colonel Allan MacLean Do hereby agree immediately after our landing in America to enter into the said regiment therein to serve in whatever station the said Lieut. Col. MacLean or other officers under his command shall appoint us to, and that upon the terms and conditions mentioned in a letter from the said Lieut. Col. MacLean to Captain Murdoch MacLean, dated at Boston the 14th day of June 1775, which has been communicated to us and wherewith we hold ourselves well contented and further whereas there is cloathing, etc to a considerable value designed for the use of the said regiment on board, and that it is probable our landing may be opposed by the rebell Americans or others and an attempt made to seize the said goods and to make a prize of us and said vessel. Therefore we and each of us respectively oblige ourselves in case of an attack being made upon us by any enemy, to resist and oppose the same to the utmost of our power, and for the purpose of preserving good order we agree and bind ourselves implicitly to obey the said Captain Murdoch Maclaine in every respect in case we should come to an engagement and in every manner of way whatever to behave ourselves as becomes good soldiers under the pain of military discipline. In witness whereof we have subscribed these presents on board the *Glasgow Packet* this 23rd day of October 1775 before these witnesses the said Capt, Porterfield and William Hunter, the mate.

Witness Alexr. Porterfield	Murdoch McLaine
Witness William Hunter	Lauchlan McLean
	Dun. Macdougall
John Stewart	Pat. Grant
X Lachlan McLean (his mark)	Duncan McArthur
Hector McQuarrie	Hector Maclean.[11]

These men were not the only emigrants forced to enlist; Lieutenant-Colonel MacLean had few scruples in seeking recruits. He conceived the idea of stopping emigrant ships and inducing the passengers to volunteer. The scheme was agreed to by General Gage and so Lieutenant Duncan Campbell was sent to New York. Campbell showed his orders to Captain Vandeput of HMS *Asia*, but without orders from a superior naval officer, Vandeput was loathe to impress emigrants. A short time after his interview with Campbell, two emigrant ships arrived in New York. Vandeput had them searched for

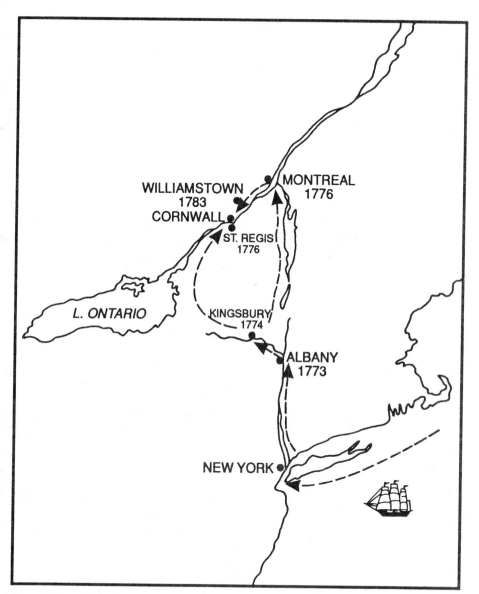

Fig. 13/2   The Glengarry refugees find their way to Canada.

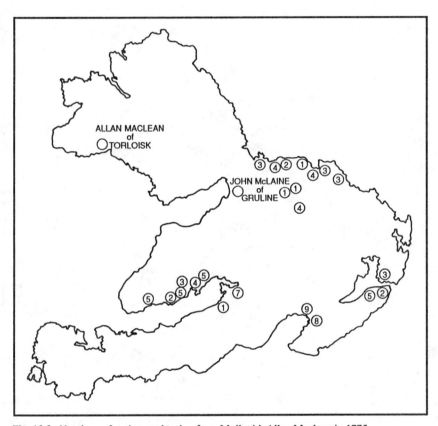

Fig. 13.3   Numbers of emigrants leaving from Mull with Allan Maclean in 1775.

contraband but since their provisions were exhausted he permitted them to dock and land their passengers. Campbell was incensed and wrote to Col. MacLean complaining of the lack of cooperation. MacLean went to General Gage who conferred with Vice Admiral Graves, the flag officer commanding the Navy. The admiral wrote to Vandeput on September 24th, 1775:

> Whereas Gen. Gage has ordered Lieut. Duncan Campbell to New York to raise recruits among the emigrants already arrived and from those expected from Great Britain and Ireland. You are hereby required to give the same Lieut. Duncan Campbell every assistance in your power. You are also required to stop any ship which shall in future arrive, to send such ship with as much despatch as possible to Boston without allowing any of the emigrants to land at New York.[12]

Captain Vanderput was not convinced of the rightness of these orders:

> Whatever may be their pretext for leaving Great Britain it surely can never be right to continue peopling a country in absolute rebellion against us. Most of the men will I believe enlist in the army, and upon consulting with General Howe we are of opinion the rest should be landed at Halifax where a provision is made by the government for their immediate subsistence.[13]

On the arrival of the *Glasgow Packet* in Boston Murdoch Maclaine was given command of a company and made paymaster of the regiment. The boat was immediately boarded by Captain Alexander Campbell of the Royal Highland Emigrants; the men were soon on their way to regimental headquarters at Halifax while the women and children were allowed to continue their journey to Nova Scotia.[14] The *Jupiter*, with 200 people from Appin, Lismore and Glenorchy on board, bound for Newburn, North Carolina, was in the same convoy as the *Glasgow Packet* and forced by bad weather in to Norfolk, Virginia. There General Dunmore, just defeated at the battle of Great Bridge, had the Highlanders put ashore and seized the ship for the accommodation of Tory refugees. He then impressed about 160 (out of the 250) immigrants into his service while the rest were released to continue their journey.[15]

A third ship in the convoy, the *Glasgow*, was also caught. With 255 emigrants, many of them MacDonalds, on board, she had sailed from Fort William on 4th September, on the very day the Lord Advocate halted all emigration from Scotland. The *Glasgow* arrived in New York towards the end of October and the story is taken up some years later from a land grant application in East Branch in Pictou by James Fraser:

> That your memorialists in the year 1775 came and arrived at the harbour of New York from North Britain, paying their respective passages whereby they were much distressed in order to cultivate and improve that ground to assist and suppport their families. But unhappily for them, upon their arrival there, the Revolution breaking out, Memorialists were impressed and taken as captives by his Majesty's Ship of War, *Asia*, being in that harbour till such time as they would voluntarily engage themselves in one body, or otherwise be distributed into other corps. Wherefore memorialists agreed to remain and abide in one body aforesaid in His Majesty's Second Battalion of 84th Regiment until the last reduction thereof as will more fully appear by their respective discharges herewith produced.[16]

Alexander Campbell was given command of the *Glasgow Packet* which had been commandeered as an armed brig. He was ordered to sail to North Carolina to join up with some companies destined for the Royal Highland Emigrants. Caught in the harbour with the American fleet closing in on him, he left the vessel to be burnt and his soldiers taken prisoner.[17]

We have some details of the life of this colourful character. He was the illegitimate son of Duncan Campbell of Glenure, a gentleman with several legitimate and illegitimate children. Alexander appears to have been a man of impulse. We first read of him in a letter to his father in which he apologised for marrying without parental consent. Three years later, dissatisfied with life at home and without money, he announced his intention of going to America. He did not carry out this threat, but instead, from 1767 to 1771, became overseer at North Queensferry quarries, not far from Edinburgh. Next, he tried business in Glasgow, but fell so far into debt that he had to seek the sanctuary of the Abbey lands of Holyroodhouse. Clearly it was time to emigrate, which this time he did, and set up as a provision merchant in the town of Boston. The growing troubles led him to become a loyal volunteer and on April 19th 1774 he joined the Brigade then commanded by General Robert Pigott. The following year he was severely wounded at the battle of Bunkers Hill. When Boston was abandoned Campbell's wife and children escaped in his own 60-ton sloop to Halifax. In November 1778 Campbell planned to return to Scotland with his

> drunken, distracted wife [Mary] and numerous tender family ... to put them upon some scheme of frugality and to put her into Bedlam, there being in the present situation of affairs no possibility of managing her here.

The truth of this statement must be doubted as Mary Campbell was able to set up shop in London after he died some time before April 1783.[18]

In 1779, the Royal Highland Emigrants were recognised by being put on the establishment as the 84th Regiment. This meant that the rewards of service for line regiments would be open to them. Thus in 1783 men of the 1st Battalion, which was nearly 1,500 strong, were granted lands in Lancaster, Charlottenburg, Cornwall, Osnabruck and Williamsburg townships on the banks of the St Lawrence. The Highlanders, along with Hessian veterans and a variety of civilian loyalists, spent the winter in camps at Sorel. With the spring breakup of the ice, they were moved to the St Lawrence by barge. The settlers were provided by the

> Government with everything that their situation rendered necessary ... food and clothes for three years ..., seed to sow on their new clearances ... Each received an axe, a hoe and a spade; a plough and one cow were allocated to two families, a whip and a cross-cut saw to every fourth family ... Pork was then as now the staple article of animal food.[19]

Within three years with incredible hard work they had made the wilderness bloom.

The 2nd Battalion, the Royal Highland Emigrants

The 2nd battalion of the Royal Highland Emigrants was commanded by Major-Commandant John Small. He recruited largely in Nova Scotia, from the South Uist emigrants who had settled in Prince Edward Island under John MacDonald of Glenaladale. The battalion saw little active service during the war, most of their time being spent on garrison duty in Halifax. Although Glenaladale had been so miserably treated because of his Roman Catholicism, he remained loyal to the Crown. His enlistment in the Royal Highland Emigrants however, may not have been purely for patriotic reasons as a correspondent in Prince Edward Island pointed out. Glenaladale

> had no ambition but was brought into it by means of Capt. Alexander McDonald, brother to Mr Tiberiop (Roman Catholic Bishop of the Isles) which he did with a very good intention whatever it may answer expectation. There was indeed a kind of necessity of Glenaladale's following that profession at this juncture in order to arrive at a decent livelihood for it is impossible for any man to live in this part of the world without some employment or other; unless a man should have a yearly income and there is none in this island that has that except three gentlemen.[20]

From the evidence we have of Glenaladale's past actions and character, this seems rather cynical; there is no discredit in his having had mixed patriotic and economic motives. What is clear is that he was a man of high principle who was recognised as such, both before and after the war, by the community he had helped to create.

The Line Regiments

With the outbreak of hostilities in America, the British government had turned its attention to the expansion of the line regiments of the army. Naturally it looked again to the Highlands as a suitable source of military manpower. Highland regiments emerged as the 71st (Fraser's), 73rd (Macleod's), 74th (Argyll Highlanders), 76th (Macdonald's), 77th (Atholl Highlanders), 78th (Seaforths), 81st (Aberdeenshire Regiment) and the 2nd Battalion of the Black Watch. As the war continued Scotland provided a considerable proportion of the British soldiery. The fact that former Jacobites denuded their estates of men to try to preserve and extend a British empire. is but one of the many ironies of this period.

71st Regiment, Fraser's Highlanders

Major-General Simon Fraser suggested that he could raise a regiment of Highlanders of two battalions of 1000 men each. The proposal was put before the King who duly approved the raising of the 71st regiment (Fraser's Highlanders). On November 21st the House of Commons agreed to a resolution of the supply-committee, "that £47,000 be granted to defray the expence of a highland regiment to be raised in Scotland, consisting of two battalions, for the service of the year 1776." Fraser then ordered a captain and two lieutenants to return to Scotland to raise their proportion of recruits. Sir William Erskine was appointed Lieutenant-Colonel of the 1st battalion; his major was Captain Forbes of New who had been the factor on the annexed estate of Cromarty and Lovat.[21]

To encourage recruiting military processions took place in different cities and boroughs. For instance, in the evening of the 8th of January the Duke of Atholl, with Major Macbean of the Royal Artillery and Colonel Brown made a procession through

Perth, with flambeaux, beginning at Marshall's inn, where a hogshead of porter was freely distributed to the populace. Processions and parades of dignitaries were organised in Dundee and other towns. But recruiting was not always easy, as Major Patrick Campbell of the 71st and another of Glenure's son's, found on his arrival in Glasgow:

> I find that I have left the best field for recruiting behind me and I have got but one man since, a barber 5 feet 5 inches. I hope you have been more successful. I have got in all here 8 young boys much about the size of those you saw here. My men in Edinburgh are much stronger and in general taller.
> The 42nd are taking them at 5 feet 3 1/2 inches growing lads. I would not have you part with McKenzie or any other you have except Weir, him I would give Ballangall again upon receiving the leevie money you gave him. Tell Mitchel and Cameron to be particularly careful that the men buy their necessaries out of their leevie money and that they do not sell them again. Let them see them every day after roll call as they do here.

Nor did Campbell have a high regard for the enemy when he reached America:

> We have so infamous a crew to deal with as the inhabitants of this country are, there surely never was collected in any other corner of the earth such a scape gallows race, the genuine progeny of their worthy ancestors from Newgate and the Old Baily.[22]

During the war he pondered:

> Indeed the footing of Highland farmers is such that a man that has no property has only a toleration to stay in his country at his master's will or at best for a term under 20 years and happy is the man that with the utmost of his industry can afford himself a comfortable livelihood for his old age in that part of the world which of all others I would wish to spend my life in, were I on a proper footing in it, but I'm afraid before this war is over I will be very unfit to become a Morven tennant and very imprudent in me it would be to change my way of life upon so slender a footing as the tack of a farm for the term of 10 or 12 years at most could any way avoid it ... all the perquisites etc makes a field officer's situation in this country a very envious one. God knows I think it a line of life far more respectable and I am sure more profitable one than being a Morven drover or tennant or both or either of them.[23]

Patrick Campbell died in 1782 before he had to make this difficult decision about his future.

The Scots Brigade

The Scots Brigade convoy, including the *Glasgow* sailed from Greenock in 1776 with 3000 men, made up of two battalions of the 71st and a batallion of the 42nd regiment (Black Watch).(Fig. 13.4)

John Peebles was born in Irvine (in Ayrshire) in 1739 so that, although probably earning his living when war with France broke out in 1756, he enlisted a year later in the newly raised regiment under Lt Col Archibald Montgomerie. The regiment (Montgomerie's or the 77th) was almost immediately ordered abroad and sailed from Cork on June 30th. The men disembarked at Charleston, South Carolina on September 3rd "a thousand strong with ... only thirteen men on the sick list". Peebles served

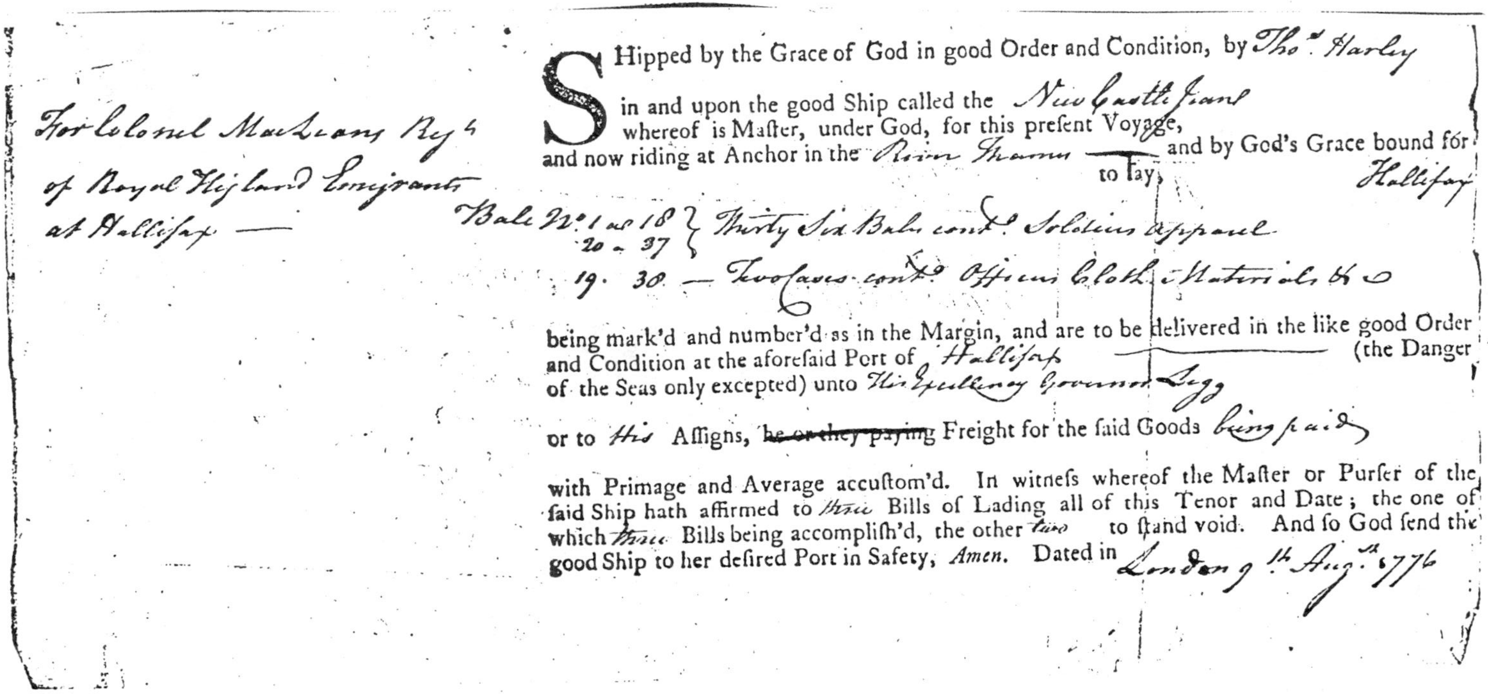

SHipped by the Grace of God in good Order and Condition, by *Tho.ᵒ Harley* in and upon the good Ship called the *New Gaette* ſoul whereof is Maſter, under God, for this preſent Voyage, and by God's Grace bound for and now riding at Anchor in the *River Thames* to ſay, *Hallifax*

being mark'd and number'd as in the Margin, and are to be delivered in the like good Order and Condition at the aforeſaid Port of *Hallifax* (the Danger of the Seas only excepted) unto *His Excellency Governor Legg* or to *his* Aſſigns, he or they paying Freight for the ſaid Goods *beingpaid*

with Primage and Average accuſtom'd. In witneſs whereof the Maſter or Purſer of the ſaid Ship hath affirmed to *three* Bills of Lading, all of this Tenor and Date; the one of which *three* Bills being accompliſh'd, the other *two* to ſtand void. And ſo God ſend the good Ship to her deſired Port in Safety, *Amen*. Dated in *London 9 14 Aug.ᵗ 1776*

For Colonel MacLean Reg.ᵗ of Royal Highland Emigrants at Hallifax

Bale N.ᵒ 1 no 10
20 - 37
19. 30. — *Thirty ſix Bales containg Soldiers cloathing*
Trouſers and 3 Officers Cloth - Matriels &c

Fig. 13/4   A bill of lading for a troopship.

throughout the war as a surgeon's mate, but at the end of hostilities when some regiments were reduced and others, including Montgomerie's, were disbanded, he asked to become an infantryman. He was commissioned as Ensign in the Royal Highland Regiment (the 42nd). His new regiment stayed in America until 1767 when it returned to Ireland and the Isle of Man. Lt Peebles was stationed in the latter place until early 1775 when the regiment was sent to Glasgow. He did not have long in his native country for his regiment was soon ordered to prepare to return to America.

The regiment embarked in the transport *Brilliant* and sailed on April 29th 1776. Peebles served his country for the duration of the war, but when it ended he decided to abandon his military career. He was able to sell his captaincy and return to his native Irvine in the spring of 1782. Peebles married Ann Hamilton who had waited many years for him. He became a surveyor of customs but once again responded to the call to arms when he joined the Irvine Volunteers, which was raised during the invasion scares of the French war. [24]

Lowland regiments also played a significant part in the war. The 2nd battalion of the The Royal Scots was in America between 1757 and 1763, the 3rd Guards and the Royal Scots Fusiliers were there between 1776 and 1783 and 1776 and 1781 respectively, while the Cameronians were stationed in Canada between 1767 and 1783. But as none of these battalions or regiments was disbanded in America or Canada there was little opportunity for the men to take up the grants of land being offered by the government to the men of the Highland regiments.

Few young men chose to join the Royal Navy so customs offficers were required to assist in the impressment of seamen for the service. The Dumfries officers reported in 1779 that they had seized five men but did not know how next to proceed with them. The men were sent before the JPs who bailed them for 15 days. The men duly appeared again and produced certificates from their local minister and gentlemen which convinced the officials that none of them fell under the description of seamen and so were dismissed. The JPs reflected that in fact the men had been wrongly impressed as the officers had no proper press warrants. However, another man had been picked up and when offered the choice of volunteering or being impressed he chose the former and was duly marched off to Kirkcudbright and delivered to the proper authority who issued a certificate for his delivery. The customs officers requested the Board of Customs in Edinburgh to inform them how to act in future and asked that they be reimbursed for the sums they had had to pay out to the various men involved in the affair. [25]

Slaves and Loyalists

Many black slaves and white indentured servants gained their freedom on enlisting in either the American or British armies. When the British evacuated Charleston and Savannah in 1775 over 13,000 Loyalists intended leaving, including nearly 9000 blacks. After the British army had withdrawn from Philadelphia in June 1778, 3000 Loyalists followed and more than 900 left Boston for Halifax after General Howe withdrew. The Loyalists consisted of two broad classes: firstly, English men of property, members of the Anglican Church, the merchants, professional men and the gentry living in such centres of imperialism as New York and Boston; secondly, the Highland Scots grateful to government for their land grants and still, apparently, with an inherent sense of loyalty.

The war was finally ended in 1783. By the Treaty of Paris it was laid down that creditors, both American and Loyalist, were to "meet with no lawful impediment to the recovery of the full value in sterling money of all *bona fide* debts heretofore contracted"; the States were to make restitution of confiscated property and rights; Loyalists were not in future to be prosecuted nor their lands confiscated for their part in the war. In March 1783 the Loyalists petitioned General Guy Carleton as British Commander-in-Chief of New York for provision to be made for disabled soldiers, widows and orphans; for the rank of officer to be permanent in America so that the men could remain on half-pay after disbandment; for grants of land and assistance with settling so that they could enjoy the benefits of British government. Over 4000 claims were made against the British government; although the majority of Loyalists did not
receive money grants, homes, grants of land, and for a short period, rations, were found for them in Canada.

Government in London was reluctant to let large numbers of disbanded soldiers return to the Highlands where life was uneasy as a result of the disruptions of the war and of the agricultural improvements being introduced on some of the estates. A Royal Instruction was therefore issued in 1783 by which lands were allotted to such of the "inhabitants of the colonies and provinces, now in the United States of America" as were "desirous of retaining their allegiance to us and of living in our dominions and for this purpose are disposed to take up and improve lands in our province of Quebec". In May orders were given to lay out townships in what was to become, in 1792, Glengarry County; the following year possibly 1000 Loyalists settled there, amongst them some of the Glengarry people who had originally settled on Sir William Johnson's land in Mohawk Valley, New York. Such was the influx of Loyalists that new provinces had to be founded in Canada - New Brunswick in 1783 and Ontario in 1784. In New Brunswick and Nova Scotia there were already 9000 refugees along the St John River and 8000 at Shelburne while 3000 had gone to Cape Breton Island.[26]

Soldiers were also rewarded for their faithful service by being granted land in communities, either new or already settled, in Canada. In October 1783 Colonel Small, 2nd Battalion Royal Highland Emigrants obtained a grant of land on which to settle his men. Their land was bounded by the Shubenacadie and Nine Mile Rivers and thence from the western shores of Grand Lake to the Kennetcook River in Nova Scotia. Some of the arable land was already settled but most of it was unsuitable for farming and is still forested today. It lacked roads or water routes. A poignant description survives of Douglas, one of these townships. The 1st Battalion disbanded on 10th October and Hector Maclean and thirty men set out to take up their claims in early November. The men soon deserted their lots so that Maclean was left alone to pioneer a farm in the wilderness:

they were positive that these little lots would ruin any who would settle on them. That no benefit could ever be reaped from them, for after expending their labour and provisions all the winter, they would have to begin afresh on their farm lots next year, and that they could not get on these farm lots till so late in the spring that it would be impossible to raise anything to live on the ensuing year. I thought the most eligible plan would be for each individual to build himself a temporary hut, on his town lot immediately, which he would be able to clear and fence in during the winter, and early in spring to put into the ground proper seeds, and I did not doubt each man would raise more than would replace the provisions they would eat, in doing that, which ought not to be much, as we might in a great measure support ourselves by fishing and shooting; and that thus after gaining a footing it would be much easier for us to move to our great lots, than at present to separate widely. The want of mutual assistance, the next to impossibility for those on the distant lots to get their provisions brought thither, and the many other inconveniences that would attend our going on the farm lots previous to our making the connected settlement proposed, must appear plain to every man.

By the following August his morale was low; in his bleak situation, lonely, with little to show for his hard work, he was searching for a vision to carry him through the next difficult months:

Let me now indulge myself with saying something about the fruits of my labour since I parted with you and came to this dreary solitude. A snug house about 30 feet by 22, built of squared logs, clapboard and shingled, the situation delightful as one could wish, only distant from the sea, a clear well settled country. I have sowed a dozen bushels of oats to be reaped for forage, before they are quite ripe, for a horse and two cows, which with some pigs and poultry is all my stock. I have about six or eight acres in all, cleared and sowed and planted with these oats, potatoes, cabbages and turnips. I expect to put in my cellar for the ensuing winter above 200 bushels of potatoes and as many turnips and perhaps 1500 cabbages of my own raising and a few bushels of barley to feed my hens. **N.B.** The house is but a shell of a house and will not be finished or even fit to live in this year. I live in a hut that I have made comfortable enough with two rooms. This remark might as well have been left out, as it disfigures the description of my farm which would have made a pretty landscape, especially had I thrown in my barn, stable and byre. These must not be forgot, and the house may be drawn as if finished completely. The meandering brook that affords me always trout in abundance and runs just at a convenient distance by the west end of my house from S to N, emptying itself into the Kennetcook, which again you know runs from E to W, must be marked, and also the beautiful lawn on the north side of my house, sowed with clover and rye grass down to the river about 20 or 30 roods, an easy, hardly perceptible descent to it. On the south side, 30 or 40 yards from the house, a bank rather high and steeper than a glacis, at the bottom of it a level meadow bounded on the west side by the brook before mentioned. I say nothing of the lofty pine trees, the large spreading beech, the tall straight ashes, more beautiful (if possible) maple and noble oaks. Nature has decked the world with no greater ornamentals. I intend to plant two orchards this fall, one each side of the river. I can get plenty of fruit trees; somebody will reap the benefit of it. Everything must be taken into the landscape.[27]

By this kind of effort, the vast empty spaces of eastern Canada were gradually being settled by discharged soldiers and their families and by groups of people arriving straight from Scotland. In due course many more emigrants arrived, indeed the majority heading across the Atlantic Ocean were now going to Canada rather than to one of the young United States of America.

The soldiers of the Scottish regiments played a major part in the military and political establishment of Canada, but they were also the progenitors of an important part of the national culture. The British army had had a garrison in Halifax, Nova Scotia, since 1749 and when the Royal Canadian Rifles was embodied in 1783 most of the men were Scots. They had taken their native game of shinty from Scotland and during the freezing winters of Canada discovered that ice was the only suitable playing surface. From this the Canadian national game of ice hockey was gradually evolved, becoming more sophisticated as to rules and equipment but still today retaining the native ferocity![28]

Recruitment for the militia

The declaration of war with France in 1793 brought a renewed and increased demand for manpower for the armed services. The press gangs were out and the Highland regiments were actively recruiting. Much of the surplus male Highland population was absorbed, but not without dissent.

The response to recruitment in the 1790s is an index of the changes that had taken place in the relationship between tenants and their landlords during the years since 1775. Although tenure by military service was rarely written into leases, it was not unusual for landlords to consider that if a man of military age did not offer his services then his family was liable to be evicted. For example, many sub-tenants in Lewis were issued with a summons for removing from Francis Humbert MacKenzie's estates in 1796 - 150 from Barvas parish, 133 from Uig, 44 from Lochs and 31 from Stornoway parish. It seems possible that many of these evictions were the result of non-compliance with an instruction to enter military service, although it is not known how many men actually joined the army. No record of an emigration from Lewis that year has been found and the fate of the evicted families is not known.[29]

In order to augment the numbers in the army a Scots militia was established by Act of Parliament in 1797 after an earlier protest by such men as George Dempster, that an English militia had been established but not a Scots one. 6000 men were to be called from Scotland. The schoolmaster or constable in each parish was to make up the list of all those men eligible to serve - men between 19 and 23 years of age inclusive. The long list of exceptions - married men with two or more children, sailors, apprentices, articled clerks, ministers, schoolmasters, professors and officers and men in the regular or volunteer forces - meant that the brunt of the service fell on a very limited section of the population.

Professor Adam Fergusson's response to the Militia Act underlines the general determination to avoid being enlisted; his son told him that:

> there was a full attendance of all the militia men now under ballot, but such is the effect of the law that not one proposed to serve otherwise than by substitute; and the poorest shepherd boy proposes to spend the earnings of a whole life to procure a substitute rather than enlist for an indefinite time for a militia man. James and I are agreed that if substitutes are not to be found he is to serve and he is the only one who will do so quasi willingly but in these times every man must be military whatever else he may be.[30]

So unpopular was the Act that riots broke out in a number of places. Nevertheless recruiting was carried on all over Scotland.

> While almost every person able to bear arms is turning out in one shape or other in the service of the country, I cannot but greatly blame the people of Icolmkill for refusing to allow their sons to go into the militia, a service so mild and at the same time so necessary for the protection of ourselves and our property; and as a mark of my displeasure I desire that ... who were concerned in beating and abusing Hector McPhail, employed to take up the lists of young men for the militia, be removed from their possessions at Whitsunday next, as I will suffer no person to remain upon my property who does not respect and obey the laws, and let it be understood that whoever harbours any of the persons in the island after the time will be served in the same way.[31]

So ordered John, 5th Duke of Argyll. There was a similar response from the

Sutherland estates. Tension between factors acting for a distant landlord and the tenants had been building up for many years as a result of agricultural reforms and many of the populace were uneasy about the future even before the new call to arms.

The 3rd Sutherland Fencible regiment was nevertheless raised and during service in Ireland in 1798 had become prejudiced against General Wemyss who was raising another regiment in Sutherland the following year. Some of the men "had imbibed in the South, particularly at Glasgow and also perhaps in Ireland, Crude and undigested Notions quite inapplicable to a Country like Sutherland". However the people seemed not "to have lost any of the Martial spirit or profound attachment" to the Sutherland family. It was against this background in September 1799 that Colin Mackenzie WS, law agent to the Duchess of Sutherland and who became principal Clerk of Session, surveyed the Assynt estate, with two ends in mind - firstly, to find recruits, secondly, as a preliminary survey for a forthcoming new rental. Only old men, with a few of their sons, had attended a meeting between the factor and tenants. "There was plainly a combination fostered by the hope that if they adhered together any threats would be frustrated. All we got in two days was four recruits". Mackenzie let it be known that action would be taken against any tenant who had been refractory or disobedient, for several who had been quite obstinate at the meeting later offered the young men that were needed.

> I have no doubt, now the Combination is broken, that all the men will be got that are demanded, and am satisfied by all I learnt that the country in its present state will be the better of the drain.

Mackenzie then visited Strathnaver where, again, he found an unsatisfactory response to the recruiting campaign. He wrote to the tacksmen on the Sutherland estates:

> You are no strangers to the wishes which are entertained by the Countess of Sutherland and Earl Gower in respect to the Regiment of Loyal Sutherland Highlanders now raising by General Wemyss, nor to the unexpected and unaccountable delays and difficulties by which the recruiting has hitherto been obstructed in some parts of the Estate of Sutherland. You are also I imagine pretty generally acquainted with the Instructions under which I among others have lately proceeded in forwarding the completion of the Regiment.
>
> I have now in part executed, in part directed such measures as to enable the Countess to judge accurately of the merits and demerits of her own immediate tenants; and now that time has been afforded them for reflection, I am happy in being able to flatter myself that the number of those whose failure in spirit and loyalty must subject them to be removed from the Estate will be found very small.
>
> The object of my present address to you is not to point out or enforce the justice of the Countess's expectations that the tacksmen on her Estate under whom another class of persons possess as sub-tenants, will exert the same means of urging them to perform what is required of them by loyalty and regard to the character of the county, I am fully persuaded that would be quite superfluous, and that you are actuated by the same principle which animates the noble proprietors. But having done so much in the way of ascertaining *correctly* the persons whose situation peculiarly calls on them to enlist in the Sutherland Regiment, I am desirous to make it compleat, and have therefore to request that you will with your earliest convenience transmit to Mr Fraser a list of the names of all persons on your Farm whether subtenants or members of their Families, whose age and size qualify them to be soldiers - distinguishing 1st those whom any peculiar circumstance seem to you to afford them grounds for exemption and to each of these names I beg of you to annex the precise circumstances on which you ground your opinion; 2ndly those who have already enlisted; and 3rdly the remainder; being persons who have hitherto declined to enlist tho' in your own opinion they are called on to come forward in the

service of their country.

As to those in the last class I know I need not enforce the propriety of your making them feel and understand that unless they immediately alter their course they are not to expect any favour or indulgence or be permitted to remain on the Sutherland Estate any more than the Countess's own immediate tenants who are in the same predicament.

You cannot fail to observe that this arrangement will testify to Lady Sutherland and Lord Gower the degree of zeal with which their tacksmen interest themselves in the promotion of their wishes. I am confident you will be far from regretting this. For myself I doubt not it will prove that in that spirit you are unanimous. But should it be otherwise it is but just that the exceptions should be known.

One young man, Donald Sutherland, enlisted but made sure of his future through this letter signed by the agent, the factor and the general:

As you have voluntarily enlisted yourself in the Sutherland Highland Regiment now raising by General Wemyss, we as agent and factor for the Right Honourable Earl Gower and Countess of Sutherland do hereby agree how soon the present lease of the Davybeg of Strathbrora expires to put you, or your father in your name in possession of any of the four possessions on Amat and Dalbreak that you or your father may fix on; that you shall continue thereon for seven years after your entry, at such rent as shall be made thereto by two or four men mutually chosen, or if you prefer, we shall put your father in possession at Whitsunday next, of that half of Crislich presently possessed by the widow of Alexander Clyne, and William his son and to continue thereon for seven years at the present rent after Whitsunday next which you may rely.

His father pursued the claim in 1802, either when Donald was due for release or when the lease fell in.

Prefixed I beg to hand you a copy of a missive granted by you and the other gentlemen whose signatures are adhibited thereto. The father of the young man Donald Sutherland lately applied to me for the purpose of writing you on the subject to which the letter relates. From it you will observe that Sutherland has it in his power to make choice of either of the four possessions on Amat and Dalbrick or the half of the farm of Crislich. The *latter* he seems most partial to and now makes his claim for obtaining possession thereof at Whitsunday next, and therefore gives you this timeous intimation that you may have it in your power to remove the present possessors of Crislich 'ere next term'. Mackenzie passed on this letter 'about our Cursed Recruitin business' to David Campbell the incoming factor.

It is not known whether Donald's application was successful or what became of the widow or William Clyne.

The whole problem of loyalty was discussed further by Mackenzie in conjunction with improving leases:

I take it upon me to say decidedly that it is neither any actual oppression nor any idea or pretence of oppression on which the opposition has proceeded against recruitment ... in addition I must state a relaxation more or less of the Ancient Spirit of Clanship and Vassalage, and this I state with the more confidence that I discovered in Strathnaver, where the intermixture of large farms held by *Tacksmen* tends to weaken those ancient ideas, a great inferiority to the People of Assint (whose farms in general lie distinct from those of the Tacksmen) in point of candour and openness ... As to rewards a certain degree is requisite according to the old fashion which in truth resolves into this that the tenants still hold their lands by a sort of military tenure. A man who furbishes a soldier or has been a Soldier and behaves well enjoys a preferable claim to be accommodated, and this is one of the strongest proofs of the continuance of the old feudal system by which the tribute to the Lord was personal Service in War and the link between the parties and the reward from the Lord was the possession of land which he bestowed.

I beg to suggest that in future the *tenants* (not meaning tacksmen who can improve their farms) should never get a certain hold for any length of time. It may be well to promise that the rents shall not for a certain term (say seven years) be raised, but they should be left, I think, individually dependent for the continuance of their possession on the Landlords sense of their Merits. This seems to me the most effectual way of still fostering the Highland Spirit which in the greater part of the North is nearly extinct. The Highland Spirit must no doubt decline when Civilization and the Spirit of improvement advance, but the object is to preserve the former till the Substitute exists. Indeed in my humble opinion the extinction of the one before the birth of the other would leave a Chasm highly dangerous, the passions of Men especially in a remote Country, requiring either the strong Curb which the Highland Subordination provides, or the cool and regular Superintendance of the law for which only men in a More Civilized State of Society are adapted.[32]

Those who were responsible for managing the Sutherland Estates still felt that if they could not put the clock back they could at least stop it for a time. But while the discussions with Donald Sutherland and his father were taking place and while the hopes of the continuation of the so-called Highland Spirit were being advanced, it was learned that some of the Assynt men were about to emigrate.

In spite of difficulties and opposition to recruiting some thousands joined regiments which served with high distinction abroad, while others served in the Fencible Regiments and saw service within the British Isles. These Highland regiments established in the second half of the 18th century formed a major part of the British Imperial army of the 19th and 20th centuries.

14

"The Want of Bread"

As the war of American Independence was drawing to an end Scotland endured successive disastrous harvests in 1782 and 1783 which left many of the poorer farmers and cottars with no alternative but to abandon their land and seek some other way of life. For many emigration seemed the only option. However in the period from 1783 to 1803 emigrations were rather more organised and began to be subject to both regulation and resistance. The economy was becoming more complex, influenced by the rise of industry and the expansion of the cities. Agrarian changes continued but now many other employment opportunities were becoming available. Politically, the world was changing: the American Revolution was shortly to be followed by the French Revolution. War took on global proportions and government was forced to organise society on a scale never before imagined. In short, it was the beginnings of the modern age.

In 1783 Lord Sheffield declared that emigrants would be miserably disappointed on their arrival in North America, for after all the difficulties were surmounted they would still find that they would have to pay taxes:

The same expense, the same industry that become absolutely necessary to save them from sinking in America, if properly employed in most parts of Europe, would give a good establishment... The absolute necessity of great exertions of industry and toil, added to the want of opportunity of dissipation, in the solitary life of new settlers, and the difficulty and shame of returning home, alone support them there.[1]

While Dr Witherspoon was visiting Great Britain in 1784 his friend Dr Charles Nisbet, minister of Montrose, and supporter of the American cause, wrote to him about the state of Scotland and emigration. Dr Nisbet attempted a detailed diagnosis of the reasons for the surplus population and its wretched condition; not only the new agricultural methods but the declining death rate since the introduction of the potato and of vaccination, the end of clan warfare and better roads. He continued:

The deadness of trade and manufactures and the rise of rents and public burdens has brought the lower ranks to a state of the most abject servitude and poverty. Many would willingly emigrate to America could they find any opportunity of getting a passage. But the avarice of the Glasgow merchants and the terrors thrown out by the Crown lawyers in the *Gazette*, have deterred shipmasters from indenting poor people. It is true the shipmasters have devised a method of evading the law by accepting the bills from poor people instead of money, and making them indent on arrival in America for retiring these bills, but besides that ordinary people have not subtility enough to understand this practice, it turns out to their loss, as the shipmasters make them accept bills for more than double the sum that would have paid their passage, and indent their service for a proportionable time, so that in this manner the poor pay much more than the rich. I think it is incumbent on you as a friend of mankind and of America to say nothing of Great Britain, to encourage poor emigrants and endeavour to procure reasonable terms for them ... A man who is able to pay his passage to America may be reckoned a rich man at present ... The merchants of Aberdeen are sending out two vessels to Nova Scotia, a country unpopular among intending emigrants, who have a sort of notion of freedom, and are not ambitious of enjoying any more of the blessings of His Majesty's Government. The Court and landholders will do everything in their power, except making a positive law to restrain emigrations, which makes it more necessary for the friends of mankind and of America to contrive some method for saving from starvation a great number of poor people in this eastern coast who are not able to transport themselves to Glasgow, tho' they were to get their passage free. There are little hopes that any ships will sail from this coast, at least for a time, for fear of disobliging the Court, and the necessity of the people will not admit of delay. The question is whether they must starve at home, or be conveyed to a country where they may have bread ... I had a letter yesterday from Banff, informing me that great numbers of poor people in that neighbourhood declare themselves willing and ready to indent for America, even tho' they were certain of meeting with very bad usage from the persons who buy their indentures.[2]

An advertisement in the *Gazette* had warned that under law any artificer or manufacturer who illegally exercised his calling in a foreign country, or those who encouraged or enticed these men or the transporting of the trade or the instruments used by them, would be fined £100 with three months' imprisonment; for anyone contracting with the artificer a fine of £500 in the first instance; for putting tools or instruments of trade on board a ship £200; for a captain who knowingly allowed this business to go on on his ship £100; and for the captain of a government vessel or a customs officer a fine of £100 and dismissal from his office. However, when Samuel Slater, one of Richard Arkwright's apprentices, emigrated to North America in 1789 the customs officers carefully searched his baggage without finding any "plans". His skills were in his hands and head, but the authorities continued to search for tools.

Poor harvests

Dr Nisbet was referring to the losses of 1783, "from the failure of the crop in the preceding year and a real want of bread".[3] Heavy rain and flooding in the spring of 1782 resulted in the late sowing of seed; the summer was so cold that the grain barely ripened; early and widespread frosts meant failure of the crops over much of the country. Such grain as could be harvested was in some places not carried in until the turn of the year. One of the consequences of a poor harvest was the poor quality of seed corn for the succeeding year which inevitably produced low yields. The farmer had no easy task in selecting his seed for in 1782 two distinct oat crops had been harvested:

that which had ripened or nearly so and harvested early, or the late harvested which had a poor soft seed. However, it was the latter which proved the more successful the following year.[4]

Although a reasonable crop was garnered in some areas there seems little doubt that the yield of 1782 was only about half the normal. Some oats yielded only mill dust instead of meal; the barley crop was equally meagre. Farmers became more critical of their crops and their methods of working. In Dunoon (Argyllshire) the crops were cut much greener than usual and the yield seemed to be as good in quantity and quality so that the people felt that perhaps they had previously allowed their crops to ripen too much.[5]

The picture again varies across the country when the grass crop and the state of the cattle and other resources are reviewed. In Dumfriesshire the grass grew well and the cattle sold well. In Ballantrae (Ayrshire) there was an abundant growth of grass in 1782 so that the cattle sold well and the farmers were also able to supply corn seed to the eastern counties.

> This gave them an idea of a corn trade, which, together with increasing demand for live cattle since that period and consequent rise in their price, has made a great alteration for the better in the farmers' circumstances, and given a spirit of improvement and demand for farms in a tenfold degree to what it used to be.[6]

In Sutherland there was a great loss of cattle in the spring of 1782 and though many men were brought to the verge of bankruptcy, they recovered within a few years.[7] The seaward parishes were fortunate for the fish were plentiful that year so that others besides the usual fishermen were able to catch cuddies, red codling, flounders and whitebait, also "an extraordinary quantity of fine cockles".[8] The people of Gigha considered themselves better off than people on the mainland because they were able to fall back on their fish and milk. Herrings had been in short supply for three years prior to a bumper season in August 1782 and then, because of the shortage of salt, the herrings were used as manure instead of being salted down for the winter.[9]

The poor harvests and the high prices led to rioting in some places towards the end of 1782 and throughout 1783 - in Kirkcudbright, Perth, Angus and Fife. The rioters were dealt with harshly - they were imprisoned or sent to a plantation. Other problems were highlighted by the minister of the united parishes of Abernethy and Kincardine (Perthshire) who wrote that the more remote areas of his parish had to pay extra transport costs and that they had recently had to support three companies of the disbanded militia going through the county on their way home.[10] The minister of Bathgate (West Lothian) summed up the position as it must have been in many parishes. He suggested that not only the ordinary poor, but the families of many labourers who were before decently supported, would have perished of want without extra assistance in 1782 and 1783. The parishes found it difficult to look after their more numerous poor.[11]

Aid given

Landlords were also severely affected. The income due to them from rents in kind and in money disappeared with the failure of the harvests. They even had to put up with their own form of discomfort - a new tax on servants. This led to the release of manpower and consequent unemployment. Lord Fife knew exactly whom to blame:

> You will see by the papers a horrid list of taxes; we were the more surprised with it yesterday, as Mr Pitt had told us on a former day that if we had any they would be very inconsiderable ones. The tax on Women servants I think a horrid one, and it will fall heavy on the worthy and industrious - the additional tax on Men servants will also be heavy. Mind at the next entry that I am reduced to eleven, for one above that, you will observe, makes a very great difference ... in short this is the effect of the horrid American war.

Furthermore, their social rank threw upon their shoulders resonsibility for their tenants' welfare both morally as well as legally as heritors. Many landlords appear to have acted with compassion; not only did they not collect rent but they also procured supplies of food and seed to distribute to their tenants. Sometimes, however, such onerous conditions were attached to the purchases made by the tenants that their bankruptcy was only delayed. Although Lord Fife remitted some rents and reduced others, it was conditional upon all arrears being paid by February 1st 1784. As many of his tenants were precariously placed even in good times, two successive bad harvests proved disastrous.[12]

Sir James Grant of Grant learnt of the need to import peas and barley for the tenants on his estates of Castle Grant and Strathspey by May 2nd 1783. There was a shortage of cash until the cattle could be sold, so the factor had to give credit both to the best tenants and to those who would not be able to pay

for if I refuse them I do believe they would starve and I imagine you rather that we run risques with such as these than that they should be in danger of perishing.

By September 9th there was little or no demand for either peas or flour as the bere and potato crops were beginning to be harvested.[13]

The kirk sessions and heritors met regularly and were aware of the deteriorating situation; they augmented the poors' fund while being careful "not to be over-indulgent" especially to those not on the poors' list. These gentlemen bought in oats, bere, peas and potatoes from other parts of Scotland, from England, Europe and America; and in many places sold them at prime cost, or at least below the market price, encouraged by banks and trading companies which lent the authorities large sums of money interest free for 12 months. As early as October 1782 magistrates in burghs were setting up funds and/ or buying extra grain and meal for the coming winter and spring. Fortunately the annual fleet of boats with grain from the Baltic arrived early that year.[14]

The government was also worried about the worsening situation throughout Scotland and appointed a select committee which reported early in 1783. A second committee reported a few months later; this one concerned itself only with the north of Scotland. All the leading gentlemen who were consulted told of the desperate state of affairs in their areas, that although they themselves and other landowners had received no rent for one, or in some cases two years, they had had to supply grain for their tenants. One cargo had been delivered to Inverness and had all been sold on the first day, and then over 2000 people had been sent away empty handed. The price of labour had fallen so low that the poor could not pay the high prices for food, as much as 100% more than normal. In response to the reports Parliament passed an Act (23 Geo III, cap 53) to enable the Commissioners of Supply to assess and levy certain sums ... "and to permit the importation of corn in the said counties for a limited time and in ships or vessels belonging to any state in amity with His Majesty, and navigated by foreign seamen," thus temporarily breaching the Navigation Acts of 1651.[15]

Government aid was sent in the form of peas, meal and seed, and distributed in the first instance through the Commissioners of Supply "once for nothing, once for payment". The peas had orginally been bought for the use of the Navy, but with the ending of the American war they were diverted to the north of Scotland. In May 1784 several ships arrived in Shetland with meal but people were so short of money that they could not pay for it so "it will prove small relief to them".[16] A number of poor householders could not be prevailed upon to accept any of the meal allowed by the government until they were assured that it was a present from the king and not furnished from the poors' fund. The only reported complaint about government aid came from Kineff (Kincardineshire): the aid came at least six weeks too late to give the intended relief; moreover it consisted of very bad meal, made of damaged peas and bere ground together. Fortunately the bere meal and potatoes of crop 1783 had already become available.[17]

The distribution of government aid was so novel that even landlords wondered what it was; A.D. Cumming of Altyre wrote to Sir James Grant:

> is it by way of an additional land tax, the land tax for the ensueing year, or what is it, for I have met with nobody hereabouts who can inform me ... I should apprehend such a jolter-head as our sheriff could hardly be trusted with it wholly, without the concurrence of the country gentlemen and as its a sort of land tax, the Commissioners of Supply ought to have some sort of concern in it - but indeed they are not the properest people either - I think those who pay it should be concerned in the distribution ... I think it will be partial and unjust to confine it to the people of any particular region.[18]

Life continued to be very difficult for some years. John Knox was commissioned by the British Fisheries Society to report on the agriculture and fisheries of the west coast of Scotland with a view to possible improvements and future developments. In his vivid description of life in Assynt in 1786, he observed that though fields were no bigger than a common carpet and consisted of patches of soil between rocks, they were cultivated with the spade and produced potatoes and meal to keep the people in supplies until the next seed time. Then they had to look to Mr Donald Ross who had a fish-curing station and wharf. Despite a failing business he attempted to help the local population of about 1000 people by importing oat and barley meal which he sold to the families on credit in money or fish. But they were continually behind with their payments. Knox compared the lot of these people with those on the "fishing shores of Ireland" who were "plentifully supplied, and liberally encouraged, both by the state, and by individuals". No wonder the men were bitter and complained of a rise in rents, "our families were called out to fight our master's battles, and this is our reward".[19]

Other measures

Other measures taken in various localities helped to mitigate the crisis - these included the encouragement of stocking knitting, dyke building and the spinning of linen yarn. But there were still many destitute families who wandered aimlessly through the countryside and into the Lowlands.

However, there were some encouraging innovations in these calamitous years. As a result of the importation of corn different varieties were discovered, especially early ones; bere was sown earlier; more potatoes and turnips were grown. We have seen that a cattle trade developed in the south-west. In Aberdeenshire one laird encouraged tenants to take over vacant farms by offering oxen, oats for feed and a year's rent. Some lairds took the opportunity to accept the payment of their rents in money rather than in services and to start the process of improvement by writing into leases that tenants should lime the ground:

This raised such a spirit of industry among them that they have improved their ground more since that time than they had for double that period before.[20]

However, one minister bemoaned the fact that with the passing of the feudal system there was not the same attachment between lairds and their tenants or vassels.[21] Some useful employment only lasted for a certain period;

The prevailing taste for buildings and improvements among the gentlemen of the parish is a great blessing to artificers and day labourers ... but, as the gentlemens' improvements will soon be completed, many hands who are now employed will be at a loss to provide for themselves and their families unless some manufactures are speedily established.[22]

The disastrous years of 1782-4 became a base line for assessing future years, and marked the end of an age in which the well-being of a large area could be threatened by a single climatic event such as a severe blizzard. Agricultural improvements, industrial diversity, improved trade and communications lessened man's dependence on his local environment.

Discussions

The contradictory position of the landlords can be seen time and again in the reports from this period. On the one hand the lairds wanted modernisation and an increased income; on the other hand they were subject to a deep-seated anxiety that the loss of man power, especially through emigration, would be to the long term detriment of the country. A writer in the *Caledonian Mercury* in 1791 suggested that the weight of taxes on people in Britain was already so great that to increase the burden,

which must be the consequence of a diminution of population would be adding fuel to flame and produce fresh causes for emigration. Taxes must be paid, and the fewer that remain to pay these taxes so much the more oppressive will they be.

The writer regretted that if emigration from the Highlands continued on the present scale manufactures could not be set on foot or improvements carried on; similarly the rise in the sheep population and the consequent greater wool crop meant that the region was now an exporter instead of an importer of wool. A few days later another correspondent castigated the Highland landlords and the state of the fisheries, which suffered from the customs regulations and the obsolete salt laws. He continued:

Ministers know that Highlanders can fight the battles of the state. They seem, however, not to know that a Highlander can be trained to useful labour in times of peace. Nootka Sound and Oczakow have cost Britain millions; Botany Bay costs, it is said, £200 for each colonist; and yet a great part of the united kingdom perishes for want of bread.[23]

Not everyone saw emigration as a threat to the country. In 1793 Mr McNab from Inishinnen in Renfrewshire wrote to Mr Archibald McRa, Kintail, that he would:

rather bring up any of my sons tho' I had a greater number of them than I have to learn farming and send them at a proper age to America where they may have plenty of good lands at a small expense where they and their heirs need not be afraid of being tossed by the avarice of landlords; and if times continue as they are a general bankruptcy of tenants must take place as their landlords will not in time consider their base while they have a penny to pay their present rates ... You'll find it to our advantage to have given over thoughts of stocking with sheep as you lie at such a great distance from market and even we who live near the market scarcely know how to dispose of our lambs and crogg ewes [old ewes].

The price of cattle of all kinds is just now very low and tho' you complain of your price this year I think you very lucky in the price of yours but see you don't trust any dealer and one must be very cautious whom to trust in money matters and likewise learn what banknotes are sufficient and whats not.[24]

Meanwhile a more general discussion on emigration had been taking place as the landlords wrote to each other, to the newspapers and to government officers suggesting reasons for the emigrations and ways to stop them. George Dempster MP, an improving laird in Angus, had urged Henry Dundas in 1784 to seek government help for the fisheries and to listen to what Mr Anderson had discovered about them on his recent tour of the islands. Dempster himself reported that 3000 people had emigrated the previous year, and that a further 150 families from Lochaber had sold up but had been unable to obtain passages. He believed that the introduction of the potato was of great benefit to the poor people who now expected a better standard of living which they thought could be found more easily in a country other than their own over-populated land. In his report to the British Fisheries Society in 1789 Dempster affirmed that:

> every hint for improving the Highlands by finding employment for the inhabitants, is precious at all times, but more particularly so at the present alarming crisis of *Emigration*.

He argued that the Highland proprietors should join forces with the Highland Society and the British Fisheries Society in their mutual efforts in the cultivation of the land, the improvements of the sea coasts and the prosperity of the people. "It is our duty, therefore mutually to communicate such reflections and observations as we believe to be useful to each other".[25]

Two years later the secretary of the Society in Scotland for Propogating Christian Knowledge, in detailing the causes for emigrations, inveighed against absenteee landlords and those who raised rents but:

> furnish neither the *means* nor the instructions as to the *manner* by which the tenants may be enabled to pay them ... indolence is commonly considered as the most predominant feature in the character of the Highlander - nothing can be a greater mistake - no people are more quick-sighted in discerning their own interests, when placed within the sphere of their observation, or more patient and persevering in its pursuit.

In his remarks the following year the secretary was quite bitter about the response he had received from some proprietors to his proposal for the setting up of a school:

> there are proprietors who even in the present times, are not ashamed to avow it as their principle, that knowledge of all kinds, except in the occupations of common life, is not only useless, but pernicious to the vulgar; that it renders them dissatisfied with their condition and ambitious of altering it for the better, either at home or abroad; and hence, say they, *emigration* to America. If proprietors, indeed, wish to render or to continue their people *slaves* perhaps they do well to shut against them every avenue to light and knowledge ... But so far is education from being the cause, or among the causes of emigration, that the want of the means of it is one of the

grievances which many of those who have emigrated have assigned for leaving their own country ... from Moidart, Arisaig, North and South Morar and Knoydart.[26]

A gentleman writing in the *Farmers' Magazine* argued that a proprietor should tell his people of his plans; he should take a census of his people, build a central village for tradesmen and carry on draining and enclosing. Another suggestion was that those proprietors in the east and south of the country needing labourers should arrange with proprietors in the north to take some of their surplus population in an orderly manner.[27] Rev Alexander Irvine, minister of Rannoch parish in Perthshire and who helped in the preparation of the Gaelic Bible for the SSPCK, cited the increase in the population as a necessary cause for emigration, there were just too many people on the land. He claimed that in one west coast parish there were 1900 people in 1790, 500 of these had emigrated to America and 87 had gone into the army or navy, but there were still 1976 persons registered in the 1801 census.[28]

Thomas, 5th Earl of Selkirk was a keen improver and "prompted by a warm interest in the fate of the natives" toured the Highlands in 1792. His continuing interest in the Highlands led him to reflect that emigration was an

unavoidable result of the general state of the country, arising from causes above all control, and in itself of essential consequence to the tranquility and permanent welfare of the kingdom.

He suggested that the indolence of the people under the old system of farming should not be:

ascribed to inherent dispositions, but to the circumstances in which they are placed; to the want of sufficient incitements to industry and to the habits which have naturally grown out of such a situation. This is demonstrated by their laborious exertions when they come into the Low Country, and feel at the same time the spur of necessity and the encouragement of good wages.

Not only that, but those left on the farms could easily do all the necessary work. The Earl claimed that the introduction of sheep farming to the Highlands led to a very unequal struggle between the former possessors of the lands and the graziers. Although some landlords had taken the highest possible rent that a tenant could manage rather than a still higher one from a grazier and in spite of rising prices for cattle the small tenants could still not compete with the grazier from the south of Scotland. The introduction of sheep walks also encouraged the engrossing of farms, thus removing perhaps 30 or 40 families from the particular area. When the farms are thrown together the farmer:

is enabled, merely by diminishing the number of superfluous mouths, to send a part of the produce to market, and from the same land, without any addition to its fertility, to afford a better rent to the landlord.[29]

Selkirk later became perhaps the most important promoter and leader of emigration to Canada. (see Chapter 16)

A correspondent from Baltimore was over-optimistic in his view of Scotland at this time:

It would appear that either the situation of our countrymen is ameliorated of late, or that their eyes are at least opened so far as to see the folly of abandoning their own homes to such a precarious subsistence so many thousands of miles across the Atlantic Ocean ... there is not one in a thousand of these deluded people, who, after twelve months experience do not wish themselves at home again ... They generally resort to the back settlements, all the settlements along the coasts having been taken up.[30]

The Highland Society of Scotland

At the General Meeting of the Highland Society of Scotland on June 29th 1801, Mr Grant of Rothiemurchus and James Grant, writer to the signet, drew the attention of the directors to the problem of emigration and urged the setting up of a committee to consider "the best mode of employment for the middling ranks and labouring classes of people in the Highlands and in certain districts". Their proposal was accepted and the following January the committee presented its report.

It suggested that the rise in population, the engrossment of farms, the introduction of sheep and the deceit of agents, were all leading to a more general emigration, particularly among the better-off tenants, although in the previous few years emigrations had been "partial and local".

The plight of the emigrants was considered in some detail. Tenants in Benbecula had taken two agents to court in Inverness demanding absolution from documents they had signed agreeing to emigrate. Two agents, Roderick MacLellan and Archibald MacLean admitted forging letters encouraging them to go under false pretences. In America, they had said:

they were not troubled with landlords or factors: but that all the people were happy and upon an equal footing and that there were no rents paid there.

Other agents were alleged to have forged many happy letters for the unfortunate illiterate people whom they had hoped to mislead; occasionally a genuine letter arrived home which painted a different picture:

You may tell *Boisdale* about the people that left Uist, that they are crying every day, saying if Boisdale knew their conditions that he would send for them again; but if you hear any of them talking of coming to this place, for God's sake advise them to stay where they are, else they will repent.

Other examples of distress were given, including the case of one boat (probably the *Nancy*) going to North Carolina in 1773 carrying about 450 passengers of whom 25 had no berths until other passengers died. The water for the emigrants was stored in casks made of staves that had previously been used in barrels carrying tobacco or indigo; 23 emigrants had died of dysentry during the twelve week voyage. Two other boats had sailed from Fort William with 565 passengers who had been later joined by a further 135 people; (even under the slave trade regulations these boats should have carried only 355 passengers between them).

The committee therefore recommended a government bill which would regulate the accommodation of passengers according to the size and tonnage of the vessel and would include regulations on the size of berths, the provisions and medical care required by the emigrants. It was argued that the accommodation should equal that on troop ships, that is one and a half to two tons burden per man, and bunks to be two feet broad and four feet high. It also, for the first time, recommended public works in the north to take the form of improved communcations, particularly the building of roads and bridges and the official encouragement of manufactures and the fisheries.

The Society accepted the report on 12th January 1802 and sent it to members of the government and other interested members of Parliament. On 11th June the directors commissioned a second report which was produced within a few weeks. It stated that seven boats with about 2000 people would be leaving from Fort William alone. It was argued that legislation could not be prepared in time for the present season but that the government had shown its concern by its suggestion of help with public works in the Highlands; some proprietors had already agreed to pay their half share towards the building of roads, but others were clearly unable to do so.

A third report was issued on March 25th 1803 stating that emigration "assumes more and more a serious and alarming aspect ... fast approaching to the point of complete depopulation of a large district of the Highlands". Clearly the committee was in a state of panic as it was suggested that 20,000 people could emigrate that year alone. The report suggested that a huge amount of capital - from £10 to £1000 per person was being taken out of the country; and that the loss of population would cause great problems for the army and for the cultivation of the country. The government replied by sending the directors a copy of Thomas Telford's report and confirming that money for public works was coming forward.[31]

Telford' report

In July 1801, Thomas Telford, the son of a Dumfriesshire shepherd, had been instructed by the Treasury to survey the west coast of Scotland in order to select suitable fishing stations; to plan communications between the mainland and the islands; and to consider the possibility of inland navigation between the east and west coasts. In his second survey the following summer, Telford was to consider, also, the problem and causes of emigration. In his report presented in 1803, Telford suggested that about 3000 people had left the Highlands in 1802 and a further 9000 were preparing to go in 1803. He cited six main causes for the emigrations, but the primary cause was the introduction of sheep walks. Not only were fewer men employed but they were mainly brought up from the south, rents from sheep were perhaps three times higher than from cattle, and in this way new sheep farms could be stocked from existing sheep farms, thus keeping prices high. Only when prices stabilised to coincide with demand would farms again be divided and black cattle introduced into the valleys while sheep stayed on the hills; this would be "the most improved state of Highland farming and is consistent with a very considerable population". This happy state of affairs was pertaining on the north side of Loch Tay. Other causes of emigration enumerated by Telford included the lack of communications; the high prices paid for black cattle which gave the intending emigrant his passage money; over-population as on Tiree; and the delusion that America was preferable to the Lowlands or England.

As the evil at present seems to arise chiefly from the conduct of landowners, in changing the economy of their estates, it may be questioned whether government can with justice interfere, or whether any essential benefits are likely to arise from their interference.

Telford argued that if the Highlands were to be regarded as a region of Europe then the Highlands should produce as much food as possible for the least expense in the form of sheep; but that food should be consumed not in the mountains by the unemployed but by those in other areas who were employed. He understood the great injustice of landowners driving away their excess population in favour of sheep but in a few years' time the fact of depopulation, aggravated by the numbers going into the army, would become evident; he therefore urged that it was possibly the "duty of Government to depart a little from the maxims of general policy" and prevent landowners from reducing the population of their estates below a certain level, which anyway would be good for estates in the long run; and cited as examples Breadalbane and the new fishing villages. Telford also urged the immediate commencement of public works, particularly comunications; work would accustom people to labour and give them capital for laying the foundations for future employment.[32]

The House of Commons had presented to it the reports from Telford and from the Highland Society. Members of Parliament were clearly worried, for the Highland Society was an influential body of men, including both Highlanders and Lowlanders. Within three months of receiving Telford's second report a Select Committee of the House of Commons had advised the acceptance of his recommendations with regard to the building of roads, bridges and the Caledonian canal. The Highland lairds themselves were beginning to panic over the imminent loss of so many people from their estates, people who would do the heavy manual labour, for example in kelping, which provided the rental to underwrite further improvements. Also, if the huge number of men really were to emigrate there would be few left behind to form the backbone of the Highland regiments when war broke out with France again. The response of Parliament was dramatic. Large sums of money were voted towards the construction work in the Highlands and the Passenger Act was passed. It was hoped that these two measures would reduce the flow of emigrants.

The Passenger Act

In 1802 a correspondent in the *Scots Magazine* had called for legislation to put a stop to the "destructive depopulation of our island". He argued against those who regarded the prohibition of emigration as an enfringement of the liberties of the subject:

> If this emigration were a mere matter of choice, such reasoning might be plausible; but he who supposes that a Scottish Highlander would, without any cause, leave, in his old age, or with a growing family, those valleys and cottages, where his forefathers have for ages lived and died, is little acquainted with the sentiments of that people.[33]

Other men had been interested in conditions on board ship. A writer from Nova Scotia commented in 1801 that:

> An Act of Parliament restricts shipowners carrying above a certain number of black slaves according to the vessel's tonnage, and obliges them to feed them with wholesome food, water etc but there appears to be no regulation for carrying (what are called in America) white slaves; they are crowded on board in a shameful manner. No wonder that they engender disease and

die in such numbers on the passage.

An earlier correspondent, in 1792 had also likened the emigrant traffic to the slave trade.[34] This contemporary view is hardly sustained by the facts. Slave ships had an appalling record of deaths, while the number of emigrant deaths during the voyages, although substantial, was considerably lower in comparison. However for many the voyages were a terrible experience. At best they were a severe test of stamina, at worst, a six weeks or longer endurance test of indescribable suffering; cramped claustrophobic conditions in airless holds with battened down hatches, water in the holds so that lying down became an impossibility, food turning rotten, stale water and the misery of days of North Atlantic gales in a small sailing vessel continually heeled over.

In the preamble to the Act for regulating the vessels carrying passengers ... (43 Geo III c.56) 1803, it was stated that persons had been seduced into leaving their country under false representation and had suffered hardship on shipboard for want of water and provisions and other necessaries and of proper accommodation. Under the Act one passenger could be carried for every two tons burthen in that part of the ship not laden with goods. Provisions were also to be given out each day by the master- at least 1/2 lb meat, 1 1/2lbs bread, biscuit or oatmeal, 1/2 pint of molasses and one gallon of water per person (adult or child) per day; enough provisions for a 12 week voyage were to be carried. No vessel was to be cleared without a certificate of seaworthiness from either the owner or the master. A muster roll was to be taken at the port of clearance, passengers to be taken on board only at a customs station; if more than 50 passengers were taken then a surgeon with his medicine chest was to accompany the boat. During the voyage the master and surgeon were each to keep a daily journal and to see that bedding was aired and the vessel fumigated with vinegar twice a week. Stiff penalties were introduced for anyone not adhering to the regulations. The Act came into force on July 1st.

By September it was realised that the new law was not sufficiently particular since the customs officers were not required to take note of the emigrants' homes. One officer asked whether water and provisions counted as cargo or space for passengers; his superiors replied that they were not part of the cargo. The Greenock and Port Glasgow officers, at least, from then on supplied this missing information.[35]

The editor of the Highland Society Transactions was able to write in 1807:

> The pause in emigrations which this Act, and the other measures of government for employing the surplus population of the country produced, has been taken advantage of by some judicious proprietors of extensive Highland estates who have devoted such parts of those estates as were most susceptible of improvement, to the use and cultivation of those Highlanders, whom the somewhat rash, perhaps, and sudden adoption of the system of sheep farming, in certain districts, had deprived of their ancient possession. There is every reason to believe, from the success of these experiments, that much may be done to retain and employ the productive industry, which without such encouragement would be lost to this country.[36]

His view proved over-optimistic; a year later (1808) the *Clarendon* sailed from Oban, bound for Charlottetown, Prince Edward Island, with over 200 emigrants. Many of the men gave their reason for emigrating as the "want of employment".[37] While the efforts of landlords and government to provide alternatives to emigration and to regulate it had been temporarily successful they were to prove inadequate in the longer term.

15

"The General Spirit of Industry"

Discussions about agricultural improvements were carried on both in public and in private. At meetings of the local farming societies that were being formed during the second half of the eighteenth century, farmers at all levels of society were encouraged to experiment with new methods, new machinery and new seed. While the prime motive was to increase prosperity, there was much concern about emigration and many remedies were suggested that might encourage the poor people to stay at home.

George Dempster visited the Western Isles in 1784 and threw out many ideas for their development, particularly for Lewis:

> It is no easy matter to suggest any solid means of improving such an island as the Lewis yet it is ridiculous to assert that an island of such extent, bearing corn, grass, potatoes, placed in the centre of the best herring and white fishing, containing 12000 inhabitants, and abounding in excellent lakes, creeks, harbours, cannot be made to produce more than £2500 a year to its sole proprietor ... If I have not grossly misconceived the state of the Highlands its whole valuable inhabitants are meditating a flight across the Atlantic. If an asylum nearer home were opened to them many would prefer it to a distant voyage and a hostile country. They know the Scotch are not welcome to America. It is probable the bulk of them would carry their little all to their own Hebrides could they find there a permanent settlement and juries of their friends and neighbours to decide on their lives and properties.

Dempster suggested the reform of leases; life rent leases to those already resident and freedom from rent for those willing to reclaim land. He demanded the abolition of all services and the proper payment for labour. Dempster was a keen advocate of planned villages and hoped that the environs of Stornoway could be lotted and feued to anyone interested. He recommended that the proprietor of Lewis should reside there for at least six months in the year and take over his farms and fishings; this would lessen the factor's influence. Dempster argued that a sheriff depute and two substitutes should be appointed as there was no seat of justice nearer than Inverness.[1]

A native of Lewis urged the need for more capital and a resolution to persevere in the building up of a fishing industry based on new villages which should include schools. He maintained that the:

> hardy race of people who only want a spirit of industry and commerce to be excited among them to render them usefull members of the state and periodically visited by the vast shoals of fish that issue from the North Seas there is only wanting some proper encouragement from people of influence and substance.[2]

Another plan of improvement was

173

carried on at an expense, exceeding at times the rental of the estate; and yet much expenditure is not lost, if by this means the value of the ground is proportionally increased, and bread is given to the industrious poor. 50 or 60 day labourers, and occasionally a greater number, are employed in planting, hedging, draining, ditching, rooting out whatever might obstruct the plough, making good roads from farm to field, and fencing the young hedges and plantations against injury from cattle. £25 sterling per week, laid out in this manner, have not only fertilized many waste and barren fields, but have also afforded the means of subsistence to not a few families in the neighbourhood.[3]

Another correspondent from the Hebrides hoped that his example would be followed of settling 50 families on 10 to 12 acres of mossy muir to improve the ground. After living rent free for 15 years the families paid him 100 guineas annually and were happy, healthy and independent. This gentleman suggested that the money currently being uselessly spent on buildings could be more usefully spent on small boats, lines, hooks and other necessities for the fishermen, including salt and coal which were both subject to penal taxation. Another gentleman urged that proper leases should be given and rents in kind and services should be commuted to money rents; waste lands should be improved. Secondly, when proprietors built mansions they should give builders and gardeners work and this would encourage the growth of a village with supporting industries nearby. These industries should include forestry, although the forests could not be properly utilised until roads and canals were built. Thirdly, government should consider upgrading the fishing industry and the quickest way to do that would be by removing "the obsolete and obstructive salt laws".[4] The fishermen required salt for preserving fish for export, particularly to the West Indies. Foreign salt was imported duty free but there was an excise duty on home produced salt; both types were lodged in the customs houses until the beginning of the fishing season when security had to be given that the salt would be used only for curing. At the end of the season the drawback of excise duty was calculated by assessing both the remaining stocks of salt and the barrels of herrings produced. There was also a complicated system of bounties (grants), but this was of little value to the Highland fishermen. Customs houses which operated the system were few and far between making the collection of bounties and drawback very difficult. These obstacles were largely removed with the passing of the Fishery Act in 1808. Coal was taxed if carried coastwise until 1793.

"Antiplagarius" suggested three principles that might be laid before improving landlords - that land cannot be improved without industry; that the earth will be productive in proportion to the industry bestowed on it; and that any place might support its inhabitants if they were industrious and that industry prudently directed. It was suggested that anyone wishing to set up a little industry should be encouraged with the necessary help as any artisan would need land and food and this in turn would lead to a demand for a market.[5]

Maclachlan of Maclachlan removed some of the surplus population on his estate of Maldalloch on Loch Fyne to the coast where he set them up with fishing boats and small parcels of land. If the tenant fished hard and successfully he was soon able to repay the outlay on the fishing boat and afford a small rent for his land.[6]

Mr McAlister of Strathaird advertised that he wished to build a fishing villge near Sconser on the east coast of Skye. The editor of the *Edinburgh Advertiser* encouraged this effort to take people out of unemployment as well as suggesting that people could find plenty of work and good wages in the Low countries, in Edinburgh, Glasgow and other places "and live much more comfortably than they can in America".[7]

Sheep farming

Sheep farming had been a part of the southern agricultural economy since monastic times and many Highlanders kept a few ill-bred sheep for their own domestic use- for their milk and their wool. The introduction of modern sheep farming into southern Scotland did not cause as much suffering as in the north because many of the evicted cotters were able to move to nearby towns where alternative employment was available. But the introduction of large numbers of sheep into the Highlands from the 1780s onwards was a drastic change of land use. The Highlander bitterly resented the new "foreign" tenants and shepherds who came from southern Scotland and from England and who were seen to be the immediate cause of evictions. But it was also recognised that:

> some tracks of land, indeed, are fitted only for pasture; but where the ground has been cultivated for ages, and many families maintained decently, with a numerous and hardy offspring, every patriot's heart must bleed to see several ships annually loaded from thence, with human species for foreign shores, and sheep pasturing where men should live.[8]

Sir John Sinclair was a great advocate of sheep farming and hoped to introduce sheep on to his own estate in Caithness without detriment to his tenants. Sir John set up his short-lived British Wool Society in 1791 to improve the quality of wool produced. A deputation from the Society visited the north of Scotland in 1792 and reported that many landowners were preparing to introduce sheep, so there was considerable anxiety about the future among the tenantry. In some places where sheep had already been introduced the local population alleged that the sheep trespassed over disputed boundaries and that their own grazing rights on the hills were being whittled away. This was the situation in Strathrusdale (Easter Ross) after two Cameron brothers from Lochaber took possession of their newly rented farms from Sir Hector Munro of Novar at Whitsunday 1791. Some of the people were evicted and replaced by sheep. Serious friction broke out in June 1792 when the populace determined not to pay any further fines for retrieving their impounded cattle. With help from other parishes about 200 men started to drive the sheep out of a wide area. The landowners retaliated by applying to government officials in Edinburgh for military assistance. They argued that they were "at the feet of the mob and if they should proceed to burn our houses, we are incapable of any resistance". On August 5th soldiers surrounded the drovers and sheep and the "insurrection" was ended. Seven men were tried in Inverness for "advising, exciting and instigation of persons riotously and feloniously to invade, seize upon and drive away the property of ..." Two men were sentenced to seven year's transportation, one was fined £50 sterling and imprisoned for one month, but escaped, and two were banished from Scotland for life.[9]

We have a first hand account of change in the Highlands from James Hogg, the Ettrick Shepherd, when he reported to his friend Sir Walter Scott. Hogg had been surprised in 1792 at the sheep farming in Stirlingshire, Monteith, Breadalbane and Glengarry: "not as I had expected, in its infancy, but managed with as much success and care as the same species of sheep were south of the Tweed". During his second tour in 1803 Hogg noted that:

> There are several low-country gentlemen getting into excellent bargains by their buying land in that country [Wester Ross]; ... and I cannot help having a desperate ill-will at them on that score ... a Highland chieftain is ... unwilling to drive off the people who have so long looked to him as their protector, yet whose system of farming cannot furnish them with the means of paying him one fourth, and in some situations not more than one tenth, of the value of his land ... All things are doubled and tripled in their value, save his lands.

Thomas Gillespie was one of the sucessful southern sheep farmers whom Hogg met. Gillespie leased a farm from Glengarry on very reasonable terms and introduced improved sheep. As every lease fell in he added more to his possessions, so that after twenty years he possessed a tract of land extending over 20 miles "from the banks of Loch Garry to the shores of the Western Ocean". Hogg also visited George Mackenzie of Dundonell's lands and had this to say:

> The glens are so crammed full of stout able-bodied men and women, that the estate under the present system must have enough to do maintaining them. The valleys are impoverished by perpetual cropping, and saving one farm on the north-east quarter ... the extensive mountains are all waste; for the small parcels of diminutive sheep which the natives have, are all herded below nearest the dwellings, and are housed every night. Dundonell asked me what I thought it would bring annually if let off in sheep walks. I said I had only a superficial view of it, but that, exclusive of a reasonable extent near the houses, to be occupied by himself, it would bring not below £2,000. He said his people would never pay him the half of that. He was loath to chase them all away to America, but at present they did not pay him above £700. He hath, however, the pleasure of absolute sway. He is even more so in his domain than Bonaparte is in France. I saw him call two men from their labour a full mile, to carry us through the water. I told him he must not expect to be served thus by shepherds if once he had given them possession.[10]

Dr John Walker, minister in Moffat (Dumfriesshire) and an eminent botanist and geologist, proposed to the Commissioners for the Annexed Estates that he should make a study of the Hebrides. He was assisted financially by the General Assembly of the Church of Scotland and by the S.S.P.C.K. so that he could also report on the state of religion and education in the islands. In his report Dr Walker suggested that before 1764 the depredations of foxes had prevented the keeping of many sheep in the Hebrides and now advocated the grazing of a limited number of sheep to some of the higher ground. Their introduction "certainly ought not to be sudden and universal" because the local population could only use a certain quantity of wool and mutton and it would be difficult to take the animals to market. He did not envisage the building of villages by tradesmen because "every man was his own mechanic so there was no need for these craftsmen".[11]

In 1802 Dr William Porter, of the British Fisheries Society reckoned that the non-residence of proprietors and the consolidation of farms and sheep grazing were originally the prime movers of the emigrations "but now the excitements are various, contradictory and inexplicable" - high rents at home, the promise of better holdings abroad, invitations from those already emigrated or forgeries purporting to be such.

> it is certainly true that proprietors who have no other object than an immediate augmentation of rents find it most convenient to substitute sheep for men, without regard to the moral or

political tendancy of the measure.[12]

In a paper dated March 1803 the anonymous author showed that where sheep had been or were about to be introduced on to estates there had been considerable emigration and in some cases evictions. There was also evidence of substantial increases in the overall rentals. Many of the parishes from Moidart northwards had been turned over to sheep farming; on the estates of Clanranald, the Duke of Gordon and Cameron of Lochiel, of Lovat and Glengarry, of Mackintosh and Lord McLeod. Lord Gower, son and heir of the Duchess of Sutherland, intended building houses on the coast for the "lower orders" while the wadsetters on his Sutherland estate were to remain. In Strathconan, although tenants had been evicted they had been allowed to take over another farm to work in common. On Skye and North Uist Lord MacDonald had consolidated many of his farms and on other estates where long leases had been given for moderately increased rents there had been little emigration. From all this area 4000 people had left since 1801 and 20,000 more were likely to be displaced, including 5000 who would be under arms. The author argued that other causes of emigration included the increasing pressure laid on tenants by absentee landlords or their factors who did not know the country; direct taxation; the enticements of earlier emigrants and of speculators as in Lewis where a tout could receive as much as 10 to 20 shillings for each person he could persuade to emigrate.[13](Fig. 15.1)

Kelping

Kelp had been manufactured from seaweed for local purposes on coastal estates from the end of the 17th century. It was used in the making of soap and glass and for the bleaching of linen. The process was first developed commercially in 1722 in Orkney and had spread throughout the Western Isles by 1762. From this time there was an increasing demand for kelp as an ingredient in industrial chemicals both for peaceful and wartime purposes. The import duty on Spanish barilla and the tax on salt which kept the price of kelp high helped to increase the demand.

Twenty tons of wet seaweed was needed to produce one ton of calcined ashes; the process was very labour intensive during the season when the weed was either raked in or washed in by the sea to the shore where it was dried and then burned. Although the cost of production remained steady at about £2.7s.6d per ton and the price received by the proprietor rose to as much as £20 per ton in 1803 the local labourers received no extra wages. It has been estimated that over 12,000 tons of kelp were being produced annually by the beginning of the 19th century. An influx of population into the kelping areas and an increase in the birth rate meant that some of the farms that had recently been enlarged had to be re-divided in order to accommodate the cottars and crofters, some of whom had to work on the kelp as a condition of their leases. This left them little time to work their holdings.

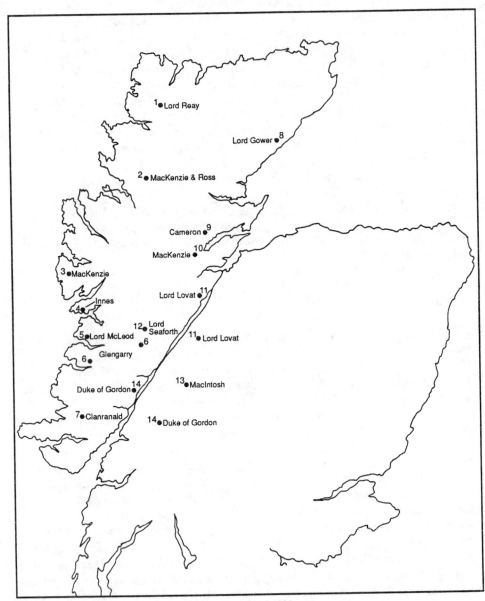

Fig. 15.1 Proprietors of sheep walks in Northern Scotland by 1805.

	Increase head of population 1755-90%	Increase 1755-1811%	Kelp production per 1790-1800 (in tons)
N.Uist	68	102	0.37
S.Uist	56	118	0.32
Harris	29	81	0.18
Barra	39	84	0.12
Lewis	30	58	0.09
Mull	54	81	0.07
Skye	29	31	0.03
Total islands	39	63	-
Mainland (NW)	49	76	-

Table 15.1 The growth of population related to kelp production.

For the first time the money economy was reaching the lower levels of society and tenants and sub-tenants were able to pay their rents from their kelp money. However when the price of kelp collapsed at the end of the Napoleonic Wars the kelpers were left destitute as many of their small farms had been neglected.[14]

Transport systems

The building up of Scotland's transport networks provided work for many displaced farm labourers and helped to solve the problems of the carriage of minerals and manufactured goods. Landowners and industrialists gave large sums of money towards the improvement of roads within their own estates and the many turnpike roads that were constructed during this period. They "were materially interested in promoting a system of improved communications through the districts in which their estates were situated".[15]

The Forth and Clyde Canal had been surveyed by John Smeaton as early as 1762. The Board of Trustees for Fisheries and Manufactures was interested, but the Forfeited Estates Commissioners refused help so a public subscription was opened to which many landowners and industrialists contributed. Work was started in 1768. When the Forfeited Estates Commission was wound up in 1784 some of its assets were passed to the builders of the canal which was opened in 1790 after many interruptions. The Monkland canal was projected in 1769, James Watt surveyed the route and an Act of Parliament obtained in 1770, but the financial crisis of 1772 put a stop to any further work on the project until 1784. After William Stirling and Company became the sole proprietors in 1786 work progressed and the canal was opened in 1790 when it was linked to the Forth and Clyde canal.[16] As a direct result of Thomas Telford's report to Parliament the Caledonian Canal was entirely financed by the government between 1803 and 1820 as a means of affording relief to destitute Highlanders, although in fact more Irishmen than Highlanders seem to have been employed.

A minor source of employment for Highlanders developed as a consequence of the building of the New Town of Edinburgh. The upper classes moved from the High Street to their fine new houses, but they still had to circulate in a town whose roads were disgusting and not fit for elegant feet to tread. The solution was to hire chairmen to carry them through the streets; these chairmen came from Argyllshire, Perthshire and the Islands, whence they had fled from the "principal tenants or wadsetters who live like lairds and the poor subtenants and cottars are almost slaves". Unfortunately we have no earlier data, but a report in 1831 showed that no fewer than 101 men from the vicinity of Blair Castle in Perthshire had migrated to Edinburgh:

Chairmasters/chairmen	44
Porters	16
Coachmasters/coachmen	10
Cowfeeders	8
Servants	3
Writers/schoolmasters	3
Others	17.[17](Fig. 15.2)

Manufacturing

British life from 1789 to 1815 was much affected by the events in France. Revolutionary ideas filtering across the English Channel excited and disturbed many who were already stimulated by the turmoil in America and by the Enlightenment. However, despite interest in the teachings of Tom Paine and the new enthusiasm for joining debating societies and for reading the increased numbers of newspapers available, government, in other words the landlords and the moneyed classes, still kept firm control of society. All moves towards a more democratic political and economic system were vigourously opposed. All attempts to reform local and national government were suppressed in Scotland by the intricate manoevres of Henry Dundas, the "dictator" of Scotland, and of the deeply reactionary judiciary.

There was much popular unrest and support for reform, not only among the "labouring poor". The paradox of Scottish life was that the strong sense of egalitarianism, which Burns expressed in his poetry, existed in a society that had not shaken off the bonds of authority based solely on the ownership of property. The most important organisation for reform was the Friends of the People of Scotland which was inaugurated in October 1792. Colonel William Dalrymple of Fordell, Colonel Norman Macleod of Macleod and Lord Daer (the future Earl of Selkirk) were among its original leaders. However the leading light of the movement was a passionate and reckless young Glasgow advocate, Thomas Muir. Against the advice of his colleagues he delivered an inflammatory speech to a general convention in Edinburgh. This gave the authorities the opportunity to arrest him, and in due course he was convicted of treason and sentenced to 14 years transportation to Botany Bay (transportation to America being no longer regarded as a punishment!). Three other men received similar sentences.[18]

Despite the teaching of Adam Smith and the advances in agriculture and manufactures, mercantilism prevailed. By the passing of the Corn Law of 1790, export bounties were continued on what was intended to be a permanent basis to encourage the export of corn and meal and duties were imposed to restrain their import. The disastrous harvest of

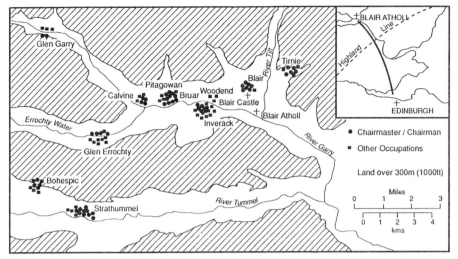

Fig. 15.2 a   The Fermtouns on Blair Atholl estate.

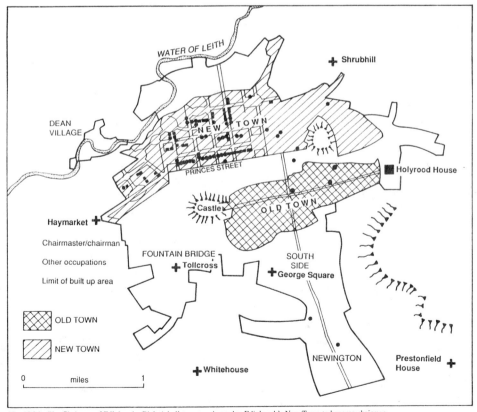

Fig. 15.2 b   The Chairmen of Edinburgh. Blair Atholl tenants migrated to Edinburgh's New Town to become chairmen.
      (sedan-chair carriers).

1792 sent bread prices soaring and social tension increased.

The ignominious end to the American War had already shaken public confidence. The war cost Britain £98 million and added a further £118 millions to the national debt. The loss of monopoly in the colonial markets left merchants unsure how to prosper in a world of wider competition. Despite this, industrialisation developed rapidly. That large scale emigration did not take place was mainly due to this widespread adoption of "manufactury" as the economic salvation of the nation.

In the Borders region population movement did not take place in such spectacular numbers as it did farther north. Nevertheless farm labourers had to remove and many found employment in the growing textile industry. The spinning and weaving of wool was largely a domestic industry and woollen factories were not erected until late in the 18th century. David Loch's encomium could doubtless also describe conditions in other areas of manufacturing and industry:

> The woollen manufacture is peculiarly favourable in promoting matrimony and consequently, population. Children from five years of age may begin to be useful, and are even employed in different branches of it, which are singularly adapted to their infant state.[19]

From 1783 onwards the rapidly growing cotton industry, based on the spinning jenny and suitable water power, made a strong impact on employment prospects and on the country's settlement pattern. For the first time ample urban employment was available to the unskilled cottar leaving the countryside. There was plenty of work for men in the fast growing communications network and burgeoning building industry. Large families were welcomed by mill owners who benefited from the cheap labour of the women and children. One person reckoned that:

> It is the general spirit of industry pervading the whole country, putting employment into every hand, and offering bread as a reward, which is the genuine source of national prosperity. The ingenuity by which machinery to quicken and facilitate labour is formed, as the attending handmaid of industry, by giving more production to her operations, is of great importance.

The inventions that had been introduced first into the spinning and manufacture of linen and the realisation of the importance of water power encouraged the growth of the cotton industry in the 1780s and 90s. From small beginnings at Penicuik and Rothesay in 1778 the Scottish cotton industry grew rapidly, so that by 1838 there were 192 cotton mills in the country. Factories had to be located near ample and reliable sources of water. Surprisingly, suitable sites were not as abundant as many people might think in a country with a high rainfall. When Richard Arkwright came to Scotland in the early 1780s he identified three sites of outstanding opportunity - New Lanark on the River Clyde, Stanley on the River Tay and Persley on the River Don. In time a major textile works was established on each site, yet the size of the developments was limited by the rate of flow and volume of water available.

David Dale, a prosperous Glasgow merchant and philanthropist founded the great New Lanark mills in 1785. From 1800 to 1829 they were managed by his son-in-law, Robert Owen. In 1791, Dale was much concerned by the plight of displaced Highlanders and hoped, with the encouragement of the noblemen and gentlemen of that area, to set up a cotton manufactory in Argyllshire. To that end he sent a man to engage all the available weavers, doubting not that:

in the space of twelve months the number of weavers in Argyll will be increased threefold provided the present weavers can be assisted in getting houses and looms for taking in apprentices to learn their business. I hope that this will be only the beginning of more extensive manufacture in the Highlands to give employment to all the people who chuse to live in their own country and prevent emigrations which are no less hurtful to their country than to the poor people themselves who are deluded by false hopes to leave their native country and subject themselves to toils and hardships that they never knew before.

Dale hoped to go round the Highlands the following summer to look at all the possibilities of setting up more industry.[20] Indeed he was persuaded to join George Dempster and others in another venture, at Spinningdale in Sutherland. 36 jennies and 136 spindles were installed, each employing 100 hands.[21] When Robert Owen visited the place in 1802 he recommended some small improvements but felt that because the local labourers were ignorant and would not work at Glasgow wages, there was little chance of any great extension or of a permanent industry growing up there. The factory was closed after a disastrous fire in 1806.[22] Dempster was also involved in the setting up of the Stanley factory, for which Arkwright trained the workers. Some 80 Highland families went to work in Stanley, until the company was dissolved in 1799.[23]

David Dale assembled his 1800 strong work force at New Lanark "from anywhere and anyhow". They included intending emigrants whose vessel had foundered and evicted crofters from different parts of the Highlands. He also employed 500 children from the Edinburgh orphanages for 13 hours a day with no holidays. He at least did not employ them on Sundays to clean the machinery. As Johnston put it:

Dale's theological convictions kept him from yielding to the temptation of exploiting infant misery on the Lord' day![24]

Contemporary comments suggest however that the conditions at New Lanark were substantially better than either the children or the adults could have found elsewhere.

The development of water power affected all industries during this period. A revitalised agriculture benefited from the introduction of grain threshing mills and from the building of flour and pot-barley mills which supplied the burgeoning urban markets. Water-powered machinery in distilleries began to put whisky production on to a factory basis. The paper industry which saw such a rapid growth in these early years of the Industrial Revolution, was largely powered by water.

The movement to the towns was not condoned by all, and the minister of Dunotter Parish, Kincardineshire was not alone when he declared:

It is to be regretted that the depopulation of the country, by banishing cottagers into towns, has so much prevailed everywhere of late; by which the breed of men is enervated, their morals corrupted, and the strength of the state impaired. It is from the temperate and healthy family of the country labourer or tradesman and not from the loathsome sink of a town, that the race is to be sought, who are to cultivate our fields, or defend our property in the time of danger.[25]

Nevertheless fresh supplies of labour continued to move off the land into the industrial areas, the new urban poor had to learn the painful lesson that continuity of employment was not guaranteed and that when development was affected by trade cycles, it was the labourers who were the first to suffer. Increasingly, emigration became a barometer of such fluctuations.

16

"This Province is Terrible Cold"

Even before the end of the War of American Independence pressures for "improvement" were being increasingly felt in the north of Scotland.

Urquhart

Duncan Grant, factor to Sir James Grant of Grant, had detected the stirrings of "a new spirit of emigration". He wrote to his employer in March 1781 that several families were preparing to emigrate from the Urquhart estate. The factor suggested that, in order to retain the tenants at the expiration of their leases, they should be offered immediate provisions of oatmeal, longer leases and a bounty of grass and flax seeds.[1]

At least the managers on the ground recognised the seriousness of the situation and the matter was picked up in a newspaper report in 1783.

> By accounts from different parts of the country, we learn that a spirit of emigration is spreading fast in the interior parts; from Rothes [Strathspey] there went 30 young lads, besides several whole families, to embark at Greenock; and in the Highlands they are preparing in almost every quarter, to go to America. Indeed, considering the extreme scarcity, even bordering upon want, that prevails in many districts, it is no wonder that emigrations should take place.[2]

Sir James Grant decided to take his Urquhart estate into his own hands on the expiration of the leases at Whitsunday 1784, but his factor again urged him to be cautious as "the spirit of emigration prevails there to a great degree, about 40 young lads have engaged to go in the summer to America and signed an agreement with a MacDonald of Lundie".[3] The "lads" were possibly the ones mentioned in the newspaper report. Certainly the loss of the lads and others was to create labour shortages as Colonel Thornton testified after visiting Strathspey in 1786.

> Went to church where I found a much thinner audience that I ever remembered, and, conversing upon this subject with the Rothiemurcus and other gentlemen of the neighbourhood, they informed me that the spirit of emigration had seized the people of these parts, and that many of the craftsmen and others, whose services I much wanted, had actually left the country. My shoemaker and carpenter were both gone, and with them many more: this fully accounted for the thin congregation.[4]

Glengarry

In 1782 Glen Quoich, part of the Glengarry estate, was turned over to sheep farms. Other farms were expected to be taken over and there were strong incentives for people to move before suffering the indignity of being served with a notice of eviction. The process was speeded up following two poor harvests in 1783 and 1784. Emigrations started again with a vengeance as Bishop MacDonald reported to Rome:

> Our Highland Catholics leave us in great numbers - the hardships they endure oblige them to look for asylum in distant lands. Last year [1784] upwards of 300 people left Glengarry and its neighbourhood, almost all Catholics, and settled in Canada above Montreal, where there are already settled about 800 who had emigrated to America before the commencement of the last war and who are doing exceedingly well. To serve these people and because many of his own clan were of this number, Mr Roderick MacDonell, an excellent minister went to America likewise.[5]

Father Roderick was a son of John of Leek and was following his three brothers who emigrated in 1773. He sailed from London in August 1785. As missionary -in-charge he was able to help Father Alexander Scotus MacDonell who led a further party of between 500 and 600 people to Glengarry, Canada in 1786. They came from the parish of Knoydart, another part of the Glengarry estate, which had also been turned over to sheep. They sailed from Knoydart on the *MacDonald* and reached Quebec on September 7th after 61 days. Among the passengers were Alexander and Roderick MacDonald and two officers of the 71st Regiment - Ensign and Lieutenant MacDonald. The families joined their relations who had settled at St Andrews, north of Cornwall, Glengarry County. It seems that another boat was forced south by bad weather down the American coast to New York, where the emigrants disembarked and they did not arrive at their destination until the following year. In 1788 a further 60 passengers sailed in the *Neptune* for Glengarry.

1792 was another year of crisis for the Highlands, marked by the poor harvest which sent the price of bread rocketing. In addition, several more of the Highland estates started to introduce large scale sheep farming. (Fig. 16.1) Pressure to emigrate again began to build up. Another Glengarry emigration in 1792 was led by Alexander Macdonell of Greenfield and Alexander McMillan, to Glengarry, Canada. Some 40 families, perhaps 200 people, reached Quebec in September after a voyage of nine weeks in the *Unity*. Another group of MacDonells from Glengarry boarded a ship bound for America in 1792, but it was wrecked. The people managed to reach the shore and straggled back to Glasgow where they were found work by their priest, Alexander MacDonell, who had come from Lochaber. In 1793 Captain Alexander McLeod chartered a vessel to take 40 families, about 150 people, mostly McLeods and MacGillivrays from Glenelg, Glenmoriston, Strathglass and Knoydart, to Glengarry, Canada. They sailed on June 15th but had to return to Scotland after the boat was disabled in a storm. Their relief vessel was damaged after only four days' sailing and when the journey was finally resumed again the emigrants only reached Prince Edward Island before winter set in so that they had to stay there several months before going on to Quebec, arriving there on June 3rd 1794; then they travelled overland to their final destination of Lochiel, Glengarry County.[6]

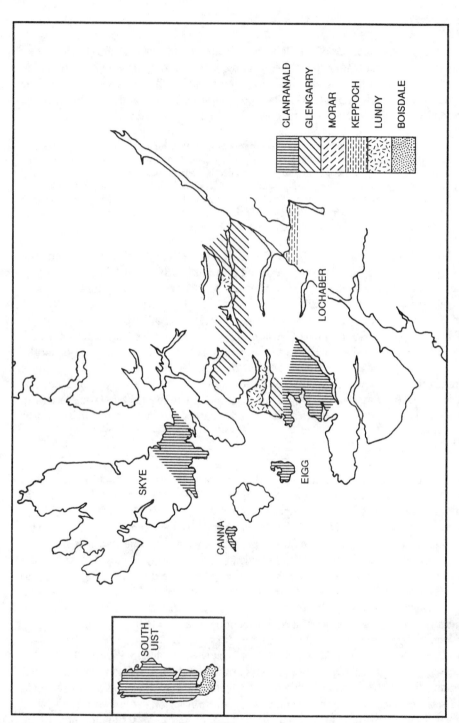

Fig. 16/1 Some of the Lands held by members of the Macdonald Clan in the 18th century

CLANRANALD
GLENGARRY
MORAR
KEPPOCH
LUNDY
BOISDALE

SKYE

CANNA

EIGG

LOCHABER

SOUTH
UIST

These emigrations had so depleted the population of the McDonell estates that the few remaining sub-tenants were mostly old and poor, however they still looked to their chief for what they regarded as his traditional responsibility and support. After war broke out the pace of encroachment of the holdings by sheep walks slowed and those few small tenants who remained were secured in their farms, so chose not to emigrate; some who were already dispossessed were offered farms if they sent recruits to the army. Some men did join their young chief Alexander MacDonell who was given command of a company in the Grant Fencibles. When Alexander attained his majority the following year his priest, Father Alexander, was able to persuade the government that they should re-form as the Glengarry Fencibles, the only Roman Catholic Fencibles.[7] Fencibles were regular troops, both cavalry and infantry, raised for home service for the duration of the war. Local militias, in contrast, were raised to serve only in their own counties except during a revolution or invasion. All this time Father Macdonell had been carrying out his duties as a priest in Glasgow although there was considerable anti-Catholic feeling there and it was in fact illegal to say Mass. Many of his flock who, after shipwreck, had found some employment in Glasgow were dismissed when war was declared. He persuaded them also to join the Fencibles. Unlike other Fencible regiments the Glengarrys were prepared to serve outwith Scotland and were thus sent to Guernsey and then to Ireland where they spent three years, with Macdonell as their chaplain.[8]

The Glengarry Fencibles were disbanded in Ayr in 1801 and Alexander MacDonell, who eventually became Bishop of Upper Canada, appealed to the Secretary of State for the Colonies for assistance to emigrate. The Secretary, Lord Hobart, was impressed by his plea and wrote to Lt-General Hunter, Lt-Governor of Upper Canada, in March 1803:

A body of Highlanders, mostly MacDonells and partly disbanded soldiers of the Glengarry Fencible Regiment, with their families and immediate connections, are upon the point of quitting their present place of abode, with the design of following into Upper Canada some of their relatives who have already established themselves in that province.

The merit and services of the Regiment in which a proportion of these people have served, give them strong claims to any mark of favour and consideration which can consistently be extended to them; and with the encouragement usually afforded in the Province they would no doubt prove as valuable settlers as their connexions now residing in the District of Glengarry, of whose industry and general good conduct very favourable representations have been received here.

Government has been apprised of the situation and disposition of the families before described by Mr MacDonell one of the ministers of their church and formerly chaplain to the Glengarry Regiment, who possesses considerable influence with the whole body.

He has undertaken, in the event of their absolute determination to carry into execution their plan of departure, to embark with them and direct their course in Canada.

In case of their arrival within your Government, I am commanded by His Majesty to authorize you to grant, in the usual manner, a tract of the unappropriated Crown lands in any part of the Province where they wish to fix, in the proportion of 1200 acres to Mr MacDonell and 200 acres to every family he may introduce into the Colony.[9]

During the short time of peace many of the discharged Fencible men returned to their homes on the Glengarry estate hoping that their chief would reward their service by giving them land. They were disappointed, for MacDonell increased the speed of "improvement". Many sub-tenants were removed and, as in many other parts of the Highlands, only southerners were able pay the increased rents, so many families decided to leave. The ship *Neptune* sailed in late June 1802 from Loch Nevis on a nine weeks' voyage. On board were 550 passengers of whom 400 paid full fare; a number of the emigrants stated on arrival at Quebec that the vessel carried "upwards of 600 persons, men, women and children". This was yet another party from Clanranald's estate - from Knoydart, North Morar, Glenelg, Kintail and Lochalsh and was probably under the leadership of Norman Morrison, Duncan McDonald and Murdoch McLennan.[10]

More families from Lochaber and Glengarry went to join relatives in Glengarry County. The customs officer at Fort William recorded that in May, Archibald and Alan MacMillan were "to carry 400 or upwards of this country people to the province of Canada". The two cousins, Archibald MacMillan of Murlaggan, a tacksman on Cameron of Lochiel's estate and Allan MacMillan of Glenpean chartered the brigs *Friends* and *Helen* and the ship *Jane* to carry 463 passengers, including children. The *Jane* and *Helen* arrived in Quebec on September 5th and the *Friends* ten days later. Some of the people went to Glengarry County, others went to Suffolk (later renamed Lochaber) and Templeton near Ottawa to lots of 200 acres each.[11]

A nineteenth century historian stated that 1100 of the discharged soldiers and their dependents, mainly from Glengarry but including some from Glenelg and Kintail, sailed to Canada in 1804 on a voyage that lasted four months. Later authors argue that very few of the soldiers actually left Scotland, although Father MacDonell certainly did leave in 1804 after a dispute with his chief.[12] Lord Selkirk noted that about 160 emigrants who had arrived in Glengarry County in 1802 had still not been settled fifteen months later.[13] Whatever the initial hardships of these and the earlier settlers there is no doubt that the Macdonells from Glengarry soon became prominent in their new society. Between 1791 and 1840 all but two of the members elected from Glengarry to the State Assembly were connected by blood or marriage with those who first went to America on the *Pearl* in 1775.[14]

Skye

As the Macdonells went to settle near their relations in Glengarry so the Skye folk went to North Carolina to be near their families. The local gentlemen and tacksmen had tried to stem the tide of emigration by employing their men in building roads, but conditions were such that their efforts were unsuccessful. The men had to walk eight or more miles to reach their day's work amd most had to sleep in the open. Furthermore, according to John Knox, "their labours could not be expected to produce effectual roads and much less effectual bridges without the aid of the military and proper tools".[15] The *Fame* of Greenock sailed from Greenock on July 7th 1788 to pick up 250 passengers from Skye to go to Wilmington, North Carolina. Another group of 200 people left Skye for America on one of the seven boats that sailed from Bracadale in 1790.[16]

John Stewart of Prince Edward Island understood why the emigrants chose to go to the older settled colonies rather than the newly won lands in Canada. He claimed that

it is the terror of encountering with the supposed difficulties of clearing woodland that induced so many people from Great Britain and Ireland, to prefer the American states to our own colonies in America, expecting from the more advanced state of improvement and settlement in the former that they will be able to get into lands already cleared and cultivated: but for such lands they will pay very high, and will often find them worn out, and not worth the occupying;

so perfectly is this understood among them that it is generally accounted more profitable for a young farmer settling in life to go upon new, than to remain upon old cultivated lands, and this change they are frequently enabled to make to great advantage, by the avidity of Europeans for old cultivated in preference to forest lands.[17]

Still more people left Skye in 1791, but their plans met with disaster. About 480 people were crammed into the *Fortune* in which the accommodation was appalling; the bunks were only 18 inches broad and there was only 24 inches of height between the three tiered bunks running fore and aft, a little more in the two tiers amidships. Inadequate supplies of victuals and only two cooking pots of 24 pints each were provided. The boat was dismasted when only twelve days out from land and limped back to port; some passengers had died, the others were rescued by David Dale.[18] The editor of the *Edinburgh Evening Courant* of October 15th used this incident to introduce some general thoughts about emigration:

The appearance of the passengers is pitiable, being chiefly poor people who had small farms but cannot now live longer in their native land, the country in the Highlands is being set by some landholders in large grass farms; this has left the poor without employment, and at the same time meal has risen. Another vessel sailed last summer from the Highlands for Carolina, two to Nova Scotia and one to Canada; in all 1500 people were encouraged to emigrate by agents for settling lands; they were a sober industrious people and all paid their passage.
The same measures are expected to be used so as equal numbers may be procured in 1792. A spirit of emigration prevails all over the mainland of Inverness and throughout the islands, from dire necessity.
As more hands are required for the manufacturers, trade and labour, in the low country than can be procured, now or never is the time for such to exert themselves, for if they do not the stock of hands will be diminished; such who go over will draw over their friends in shoals. If a society were formed, and either by advertising or agents were to give some encouragement, a great number may be got. Some of the emigrants here would have settled in this part if such measures had been used.
It is worthy the attention of the gentlemen of Scotland, were they to follow the example of the patriotic Mr Dempster, in encouraging them, the emigrations might be checked as much as might be useful; and it is worthy the attention of the nation at large.

But as far as the survivors of the *Fortune* were concerned, according to the *Caledonian Mercury*

Information was no sooner brought to that public spirited Citizen and Honorable Magistrate, David Dale Esq, than his benevolent heart suggested what his unbounded activity immediately executed.

He offered to employ every man, woman and child, to clothe and educate the children *gratis*, to give them their school books *gratis* as he already did with the other children of his work force. Many of the emigrants were already indented to the ship's master but over 100 persons accepted the offer and set off for New Lanark either on foot or in wagons provided by Dale. Moved by this experience, Dale was determined to reduce the number of emigrations. He sent men to the North and to the Islands to encourage intending emigrants to turn to the Lowlands instead, particularly Glasgow, Paisley and the neighbouring villages. The many gravestones in New Lanark with Caithness names bear witness to his success in at least one area. Colonel Dalrymple of Fordell also offered employment in his iron works on his estate at Hamilton.[19]

Other groups of people emigrated to the United States during the inter-war years. In 1784 the *Jean* arrived in Newbury Port, Maine, after a voyage of ten weeks and two days, with many passengers aboard. Another vessel was not so fortunate, for the *Almy* of Greenock, bound for New York, was forced back by a storm; it is not known what ultimately happened to the 300 passengers who were on board.[20] The Americans were not entirely happy with the continuing emigrations from Scotland. After a brig from Glasgow arrived with more than 50 families aboard, mainly husbandmen and merchants heading for Vermont, an American commented

> It must make every generous mind expand at the thought, that America is now become the asylum for the oppressed and indigent of every nation.[21]

While the people from Skye were suffering shipwreck and rescue in 1791 another 600 people were embarking in two vessels in the West Highlands to go to North Carolina. The *Caledonian Mercury* had already commented on the need for relief in the Highlands:

> If manufactures could be established in the Highlands it would be a great benefit to the country by stopping these emigrations which proceed only from the increasing number of the people since the peace and want of employment.[22]

There was little emigration to America during the war with France, but as soon as peace was declared the movement started again. The *Draper* sailed from Greenock for New York on June 6th 1802 with 63 people, most of the men were farmers and had come from Inverness, Aberdeen, Perth, Peebles, Roxburgh and Ayrshire.[23] The *Scots Magazine* for August 1802 stated that three vessels with emigrants had already left Fort William for America; but

> there are no less than twelve ships engaged for the West Highlands which must carry off 1400 or 1500 of those deluded people. Before they had been three hours at sea, some of the poor creatures next morning came and asked one of the sailors if the land they saw was America, which shows what an idea they have of the voyage.

Western Highands and the Small Isles

In the *Statistical Accounts* we learn from ministers in Argyllshire that 140 people had left the parishes of Ardchatten and Muckairn, more were going between 1790 and 1792 and more were expected to go. Emigrations were frequent and numerous from Kilninver and Kilmelfort at the time, that is, from the areas to the north and south of Oban and 36 people went from the island of Coll. No fewer than 176 people left from another small island, Eigg, between 1788 and 1790. When the people of Eigg

> heard from their friends and relatives settled in the upper parts of this Province [Quebec] that upon removing to this Country they would be able to obtain portions of the waste lands of the Crown contiguous to them they were glad to embark for Canada.

Yet fewer people than were expected went in 1790 because the pressgangs arrived and the men were afraid to move out of their houses, even to go on board an emigrant ship. During the summer of 1791 "a considerable proportion of the inhabitants" of Colonsay crossed the Atlantic. Another group of 96 people who had been evicted from Clanranald's lands in Arisaig and Eigg in favour of sheep walks sailed from Drimnin on the coast of Morvern on July 12th 1790. The *Jane* and *Lucy* carried 186 and 142 passengers respectively, for Prince Edward Island.(Fig. 16.2) The *British Queen* sailed in the same convoy with another 90 people from Arisaig on board. The party had been organised by Miles MacDonell, a son of Spanish John, who had gone over in 1773. The boat arrived late in the year and as many of the families were nearly destitute they needed assistance during the winter before being able to move to their new homes, possibly to Johnstown above Montreal where some of their relations had settled four years earlier.[24] A letter written by Rory Steel, a former servant, to Colin MacDonald of Boisdale, gives his impressions of his new country. Steel emigrated from Uist with a party to Prince Edward Island in 1791.

> We had a fine passage of six weeks and three days but some of them were very sick with fevers the reason was that they were too much confined in the vessel. This province is terrible cold ... If you please Sir to inform the people if any gentleman intends to cross the Atlantic Ocean let him be their guide and governor of the people of Uist. You may tell them from me if you please which you know Sir to stay at home for their constitution will not answer to the climate here ... If you see the poor people and situation that left you I'm afraid they'll perish both with cold and hunger - those that came here from lowlands of Scotland they are well off but the Uist is too high and they cannot do but a living, we came here we thought ourselves to make money but we came to freeze instead of making money suppose I work here four years it is impossble for me to make £4 cash.[25]

A contingent of 200 destitute people from Barra "had been inveigled" to Prince Edward Island. They probably sailed on the *Argyle* in 1793. Other emigrant ships were fitting out; the *Eliza* and *Minnie* at Port Glasgow and two unnamed boats at Saltcoats. These boats may have been those chartered to carry about 700 people, of whom some 200 were said to come from North Uist, to Prince Edward Island.[26]

To Nova Scotia

Despite the hardships suffered by earlier emigrants to Pictou, they were followed by numerous families in later years, including soldiers discharged at the end of the war. Some of the men and their families who had served with the 2nd battalion of the Royal Highland Emigrants were given grants of land in the region of Pictou. A number of these men had been recruited from amongst the Loyalists, others were said to have been impressed as they were sailing from Scotland as emigrants rather than as soldiers. The latter

> were not only in poverty but many were in debt for their passage, and they were now told that by enlisting they would have their debts paid, have plenty of food as well as full pay and would receive for each head of family 200 acres of land and 50 more for each child as soon as the present unnatural rebellion is suppressed.

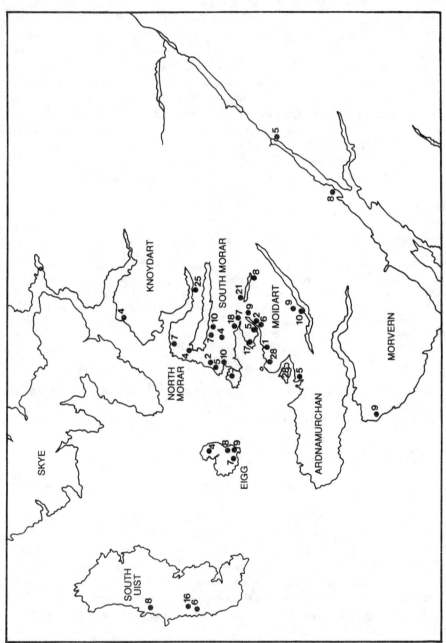

Fig. 16/2   The homes and numbers of emigrants who sailed on the Jane and the Lucy in 1790.

Eight families from Beauly arrived in Halifax, Nova Scotia, in 1784.[27] A party from South Uist was taken to Prince Edward Island in 1790 by their priest (later Bishop) Angus McEachern, whose relations had gone with Glenaladale's party in 1772. These people eventually went on to Pictou. The people of Pictou (by now a district of some 700 inhabitants) were dismayed when the *Dunkeld* arrived, accompanied by yet another emigrant ship so that in the course of the year 1300 persons had landed from four vessels from Port Glasgow, Greenock and Fort William. These people who were mostly Roman Catholics were indigent and some had had to indent, others had had to part with most of their possessions to the agents in order to pay for their passage. They had been duped into believing that they would get land *gratis* on arrival.[28] The families had to ask for government help but since they were refused, the governor (John Parr) dug into his own pocket. They eventually settled at Arisaig and Antigonish Harbour.

One group of people from Barra and Kirkconnel parish had gone to Glasgow to look for a ship to take them across the seas but were met by David Dale who persuaded them to go instead to New Lanark and engage in his new textile factory. A further emigration of 379 people from Barra went to increase the Roman Catholic community at Antigonish and another 800 went with their priests Augustine and Alexander MacDonell to Arisaig.[29] In 1793 66 families settled at Pictou on the Philadelphia Grant after members of the Pagan family had bought out Dr Witherspoon's shares.

The flow of emigrants stopped for a few years until 1799 when some Camerons of Lochiel went to the Canadian Lochiel.[30] During the few years when Britain was not at war with France, Robert Brown, factor on Uist to Clanranald, warned of the general unrest in the islands and on the mainland

> in these times a cautious mode of proceeding is necessary in regard to our small tenants, the more especially as a pretty general emigration is about to take place from our Mainland estate and some of the neighbouring Countreys.[31]

One emigration was sparked off by Elizabeth, widow of William Chisholm of Chisholm, who cleared Strathglass in 1801. 799 people emigrated, mainly the victims of these evictions, but also some from the Aird and Glen Urquhart. The arrangements were made by George Dunoon, an agent from Pictou who had left his native Scotland a few years earlier. Dunoon, who was determined to carry as many people as possible, tangled with the customs officers over how to count half-passengers (those under 16 years old). The people sailed from Inverness on June 1st in the *Dove* of Aberdeen with 219 emigrants and the *Sarah* of Liverpool with 350 people. Customs officers recorded that on these two ships 24 of the men were tenants, 62 farmers and 95 labourers; most of the 175 spinsters were the wives of these men. The people came from many of the surrounding parishes, including

Over 150 from Kilmorack parish,	96 from Urquhart,
49 from Strathglass,	51 from Kiltarlity,
38 from Arisaig,	24 from Moidart.

The *Dove* had an uneventful voyage, but the *Sarah* was boarded by men from a British man-of-war who attempted to pressgang 25 men before Dunoon was able to dissuade the commander from taking them. Then illness broke out and 47 passengers died before the ship reached Pictou after 13 weeks at sea. (Fig 16.3) Dunoon also dispatched another boat, the *Hope* of Lossie from Isle Martin in Loch Broom with 100 "full passengers" from Strathglass bound for Pictou. The *Andrew* of Dundee reportedly took 130 people from the same anchorage to Maryland.[32]

Bumsted has listed some 1200 people as going to Nova Scotia in 1802, but details are inadequate to form an accurate picture of the movements. We know that a group of 128 people went to Pictou that year and the ship *Eagle* left from Greenock with 21 passengers. But we do not know where the 845 Presbyterians who arrived in Pictou off other boats were from. One of the few records of timber ships from Canada being backloaded with emigrants shows that the *Jean, Helen* and *Northern Friends* sailed for Quebec in June from Greenock and called in at Fort William. The *Northern Friends* landed 340 passengers at Sydney harbour, Cape Breton Island in August. This was the first direct sailing from Scotland to the colony.[33]

The beginnings of control

After war with France was declared in 1793, the pace of emigration slackened. When the wave of enthusiasm for the Revolution had expended itself, many who had been considering emigration, enlisted in both line regiments and the Fencibles. However as soon as there was a short break in hostilities with France between 1801 and 1803 there was a surge in the flow of emigrants. Within a few weeks of the signing of the Treaty of Amiens in March 1802, vessels were again leaving the west coast of Scotland for North America. Eighty-nine vessels left Greenock alone to cross the Atlantic in this period, but no record has been found of how many passengers these ships carried.

Destination	1801	1802	1803
New York	21	12	15
Philadelphia	2	1	1
Wilmington	-	1	-
Charlestown	8	5	3
Virginia	3	1	3
Georgia	1	-	-
Baltimore	-	1	-
Boston	1	-	1
Halifax	-	-	1
Pictou	1	-	2
Quebec	2	1	2
	39	22	28

Table 16.1. Destinations of vessels carrying passengers (not necessarily with emigrants) from Greenock, 1801-1803.

Attempts to restrict emigration by regulation had begun in 1773. Customs officers were then instructed to send returns of the numbers of passengers who went through

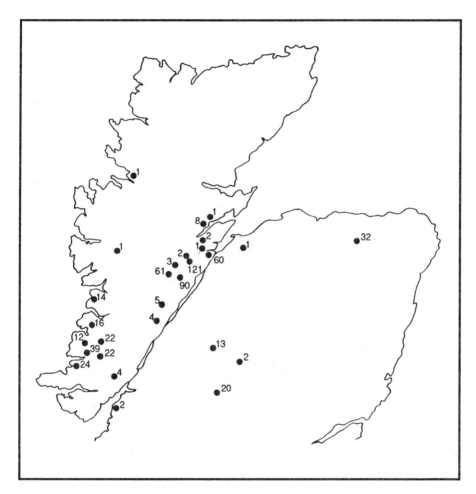

Fig. 16.3 The homes of the emigrants who sailed on the *Dove* and the *Sarah* in 1801.

their port. The letter books have survived for the relevant period only for Greenock. In them there is a regular entry every week or fortnight that a list of passengers had been sent to head office in Edinburgh. From 1801 the lists were sent to the clerk to the Privy Council in London. Only the names of ships carrying passengers were entered in the letter books. Very few of the lists have survived.[34]

Public opinion in favour of further regulation increased. At the end of April 1801 the Collector of Customs at Inverness, Edward Fraser, reported to Edinburgh that there was a vessel taking on board 300 persons at Fort William and that other agents were advertising for passengers. An opponent of emigration, he had hoped to persuade authority to prevent the sailings, but the Board of Customs merely instructed him to make further enquiries "into the true cause of the Spirit of Emigration which has entered into so many people, and into the general character and disposition of those people".[35]

A leading legal figure in Inverness, Mr James Grant, advised that the passengers could expect reasonable accomodation but if vessels were so overcrowded as to endanger human life "by filth, bad air or confinement" then passengers should have their passage money refunded. Others have suggested that it was not Grant, but Robert Brown, factor on Uist, who had made this comment and proposed the regulation of the liberty of the subject in his own interest.

Charles Hope, Sheriff of Orkney, MP for Dumfries and Lord Advocate, was prominent among those who attempted to stem the flow of emigrants: "knowing well not only the hardships which these poor people often suffer on their passage, but also the miserable disappointment which they generally meet with after their arrival"; learning of further large scale emigrations, he requested the Board of Customs to instruct their officers to list passengers and to stop vessels sailing which might be taking away artisans or seafaring men and to check on the provisions for the emigrants. Some of the Greenock merchants refused to cooperate in providing this information,[36] but those attempting to halt emigration were slowly getting the upper hand, at least for a time. Control of emigration in the name of safety and the welfare of the emigrants became government policy. "The lairds were thus not evil villains seeking to end emigration, but paternal humanitarians protecting their people from abuses".[37] The call for action came at a favourable time for reform, when the first factory legislation was being debated and demands for the regulation or abolition of the slave trade were being made. In July 1803 the Passenger Act became law.

However groups of people had been preparing for their journey before the passing of the Act and some were able to leave after the restrictions came into force. Lord Reay's Fencibles had been raised in Assynt and many of the men, who were now discharged, may have been among the 500 people who sailed from Ullapool on August 1st on the *Favourite* of Kirkcaldy for Pictou. After a voyage of five weeks and three days the passengers and baggage were landed safely at Pictou, although mysteriously the vessel then sank at its moorings.[38] It was reported that six ships had left Greenock during August and September, all with passengers from Perthshire. The *Recovery* and the *Pitt* took 20 and 12 passengers respectively to New York and 12 families, 70 persons, went on the *Commerce* from Port Glasgow to Pictou; on one of these boats fever broke out and 53 people died, so that the rest were quarantined when they reached Pictou and thus suffered further hardships.[39]

Lord Selkirk

Advertisements such as this one on October 20th 1802 had appeared in the newspapers, encouraging young men to go abroad.

Encouragement to Plowmen to go to America

A few young men who will go to America as plowmen to cultivate an estate in Upper Canada, the property of a Scots nobleman and a gentleman of the greatest respectability, will learn the terms to be given by applying for Mr Mure at the house of Archd Marqice in Taymouth on Wednesday first. The terms will be very beneficial and well worth attention. Those persons that intend to apply must bring certificates of their abilities and good character.[40]

It is possible that the Earl of Selkirk was the Scots nobleman and gentleman mentioned in the advertisement for he regarded emigration as unavoidable and challenged the government to encourage would-be emigrants to go to the uninhabited lands in British colonies which were at the disposal of the Crown. He received a favourable response from the government though he was not to get a grant of land in Prince Edward Island until he could find settlers. He therefore urged Dr William Porter in Lochbay, a British Fisheries Society village, to persuade the people "who had already taken passage for the United States to volunteer with him for Canada". There were no volunteers in Skye "but it seems that the Roman Catholics in Uist have sent him a deputation and that he has an agent at this time in the Long Island". Dr Porter had estimated in 1802 that some 9700 people had gone to Carolina, Canada and Nova Scotia since the peace and

I can assure you all the islands from the Butt of Lewis to Barra Head are in a ferment, every measure has been taken by the tacksmen to avert the spirit of emigration but it appears to have too deep a root ... The people themselves know not where they are going, America is not now what it was when best known to Highlanders, I mean before the civil war of 1774, they found it then a paradise where they had nought to do but pluck and eat; now they shall find it as the land of Egypt in the days of the Plagues of Pharoah.[41]

Between the passing of the Passenger Act and its coming into force on July 1st 1803, some tenants had not renewed their leases while others had even sold their properties; they were therefore ready to leave immediately. Thus 800 people from Skye, Ross, Uist and Argyll who had originally determined to go to Carolina, eventually agreed to go to the Earl's lands in Prince Edward Island. They were so unsure that the Earl would keep his promises that they insisted on his going with them - he sailed in the *Dykes*, one of the three boats taking the emigrants. The *Polly* took 280 full passengers or nearly 400 persons from Skye; the berths on the *Polly*"were fully confined though the abundance of hatches gave a good opportunity of air, yet it had proved very close in the hot weather, the berths were dirty enough". The *Polly* and the *Dykes* arrived on August 12th and the *Oughton* on the 27th. The settlers from the *Oughton*"appear to be very poor compared with the *Polly's* and would be unable to maintain themselves during the coming year".[42] Aeneas Macaulay was chosen by the Earl to be his factor and surgeon to the party. He had been chaplain to the 1st West India Regiment and then returned to Glasgow University where he gained his M.D. He eventually became Speaker of the Provincial House.[43]

The Earl had acquired the island lots 10, 31, 57, 58, 60, 62, half of 12, one-third of 53 and one-third of 59. He was able to help the emigrants to choose their new land, and although some were indecisive, they eventually settled on lot 53 at the east end of the island. Most of the families from Skye and Ross were able to buy land and Lord Selkirk gave 10 acres to each of six or seven of the poorest families. Lord Selkirk had very decided views on new settlements and their effects on the newcomer so the lots were laid out to enable several families to live near one another to give help and encouragement and to work together.

> The progress of each, insulated by itself, might have appeared poor and insignificant; but when united, when the forests were seen recediing on every side, all were animated by the encouraging prospect of advancement ... He has a new set of ideas to acquire: the knowledge which all his previous experience has accumulated, can seldom be applied; his ignorance as to the circumstances of his new situation meets him on every occasion. The disadvantages to which he is thereby subjected are such, that emigrants who are taken at once from Europe to such a situation, and abandoned to their own exertions without aid or guidance, can scarcely fail to involve themselves in inextricable difficulties. To settlers of this description, success can be insured only by well calculated arrangements, and an unremitted attention in directing their efforts.

He argued that settlers ought not to have leased lands, at least not near areas where land could be bought at a reasonable price.

> At any rate, the people who begin a new settlement, ought to have every stimulus to exertion which the most permanent tenure can afford. But the opposite extreme also has its dangers; the profusion with which gratuitious grants of Crown lands have been given in some situations, has been scarcely less pernicious. It has taught the settlers to despise what they procured with so little difficulty; and, by diminishing their estimation of the spot on which they were fixed, and their attachment to it, has tended to enfeeble their exertions for its improvement.[44]

Later, Lord Selkirk admitted that the people he took to Prince Edward Island had not

> totally escaped all difficulties and discouragement, but the arrangements for their accommodation have had so much success that few perhaps, in their situation, have suffered less or have seen their difficulties so soon at an end.[45]

Other would-be emigrants were not so fortunate in their efforts to cross the Atlantic and groups of them were stranded in Scottish ports by the enforcement of the new Passenger Act. When the Canadian Fencible Regiment was raised in August it was hoped to resolve this problem and also strengthen Britain's defence of Canada. Recruiting was not limited to these groups but was soon extended to others residing at home. Men flocked to the colours when land and free passages to Canada for wives and children were promised. The regiment was over subscribed by 683 private soldiers who were accompanied by 432 wives and 1069 children. Charles Hope complained that "it is in vain for any other officer to offer his paltry bounty, in competition with the paradise of America". Hope voiced the fears of the Highland landlords who condemned the raising of such a regiment because it was rekindling the fever of emigration that was just beginning to die down in the Highlands under the impact of the Passenger Act.

However, deception and mishandling of the regiment by the recruiting agents, its officers and the government provoked a mutiny in August 1804. The order to march from Glasgow to the Isle of Wight was taken as a betrayal of the promise that the regiment was to serve in Canada for the soldiers believed that once in the Isle of Wight they would be sold to the East India Company. The mutineers were lightly punished but it was decided that the regiment should be disbanded at the end of 1804. Some of the men were taken into other regiments but the fate of the other would-be emigrants is unknown.[46]

Throughout the period there is much contradictory evidence. On the one hand of men of integrity trying to help the families living on their estates. On the other hand of many rogues who were only interested in "making a fast buck" and were contemptuous of their fellow men and women. Unused to handling such a difficult situation those in office, whether customs officers, other government officials or Members of Parliament, found it difficult to regulate the movement of people in an humane and orderly manner. The enforcement of the Passenger Act certainly, as was hoped, reduced the pace of emigration and improved conditions on those emigrant ships which continued to sail, but the hazards of the Atlantic passage were not eliminated. It is recorded that between 1847 and 1853 at least 49 emigrant ships were lost at sea.

Epilogue

The number of people who actually left Scotland for America in the eighteenth century cannot now be determined. In 1931 H.F.Barker used the United States Government census of 1790 to estimate the numbers of the various national stocks making up the population at that time. He listed surnames, state by state, and allocated them under national headings, the figure for Scots being 263,330. The calculations dealt only with the United States which still excluded Florida. The method is obviously rather crude but gives a rough idea of the make up of the American population at the end of the 18th century.(Appendices 1. & 2.).

There are no records of the population of Scotland in the 17th century but if the estimate of the Scots Parliament of 1,048,000 in 1707 is accepted, it seems that numbers increased steadily through the 18th century. The total population of Scotland in 1790 is said to have been about 1.5 million, when that of England can be taken as 8.5 million. Barker gives the English population of the USA as 2.2 million. Thus the estimate of Scots of 8.3% of the total does not seem unreasonable.[1] Of course large scale settlement from England had begun early in the 17th century and there were said to be 25,000 in New England alone by 1640.

Settler families had a high net reproductive rate, about 3%, which means a doubling of population every 23/24 years. However even after that has been allowed for, it does not seem possible to relate the figure of 263,330 with the estimates of emigrants from Scotland made by a range of authorities. The reasons for the wide gap cannot be known but probably include:

1). Barker's estimates may overstate the number of Scots, for example by including some Scotch Irish, though he states explicitly that the two categories were separated, and the estimates for the Irish look equally reasonable.

2). A larger number of Scots than has been suggested had settled in the seventeenth and early eighteenth centuries.

3). A significant number of emigrant ships sailed unrecorded.

4). Some port records only recorded cabin passengers while emigrants were not listed, or masters declared lower numbers than they actually carried, for example they excluded children.

5). Emigrants travelled to North America through English or Irish ports or via the continent.

While the documentary sources do not give complete figures of the numbers of emigrants, they do throw some light on the causes of emigration, where the emigrants came from and in some cases the success or failure of their enterprise. From an analysis of the emigrant boats in the period from 1760 to 1803 we can form a picture of the flow and pattern of the movements that occurred. It can be shown that the underlying reasons for emigration were present throughout our period, but that years of particular stress caused more emigrations. Our research suggests that in the period 1760 to 1775 earlier estimates of 29,000 enigrants are over-stated and a figure of around 19,000 is the highest that can be substantiated from the actual records. This figure would be increased significantly if the number of soldiers and their families who settled after the Seven Years' War could be known. The number of emigrants for the second phase (1783-1803) is also difficult to establish. Donaldson has suggested a figure of 20,000, but again a considerable number of men went to serve in the army and navy and settled, mainly in Canada.[2] The best estimate we have reached is about 14,000.

It has been extraordinarily difficult to match the figures in any two reports of emigrations as, for example, there was no fixed definition of the term 'passenger'. Sometimes only full fare cabin passengers were listed. Where steerage passengers were included in the total, sometimes children under eight years who were charged half-fare and sometimes babies who were not charged were included in the total number. The family might also embrace a number of servants who were not listed.

Whatever the actual numbers may have been, the emigrations produced violent public reactions in Scotland, probably because in most cases people moved as a group from a particular area, which was often sparsely populated so that the effect of their removal was dramatic.

The first estimate, in 1707, of the Scottish population was 1,048,000. The first attempt at a national census was undertaken by Rev Alexander Webster in 1754-5 who calculated the total as 1,265,000. This census gives a rough indication of where the people lived at that time: 51% of the total population in Northern Scotland, which included Perthshire, 37% in Central Scotland, 11% in Southern Scotland, giving densities of 31, 110 and 36 persons per square mile in the three regions.[3] There were several reasons for the increase in numbers in the first half of the 18th century. There were fewer wars; there was a slight improvement in the climate which is likely to have made a significant difference to the harvest, both because of heavier crops and a better chance that it would ripen and be safely harvested. Again, improvements had begun to take effect in a few areas of the country - improved seed led to heavier yields; also new crops, particularly the potato, were being introduced and with other vegetables were beginning to provide a healthier diet. People no longer accepted that living on the edge of starvation was inevitable, although dearth and famine continued to afflict many areas in years of poor harvests.

The famines that were recorded in the 16th and 17th centuries and which were sometimes associated with outbreaks of bubonic plague were not always nation-wide, but the effect in local areas was often disastrous. In the worst years communities were forced to eat their seed corn in a desperate attempt to survive for a few more months. Communications were so bad and there was so little food to spare that it was difficult to take relief to stricken areas.

In some instances poor tenants, unable to pay their rents, which were still being paid in kind, were turned off their holdings and forced to beg. As early as 1424 the Statute of Perth had ordained that the heritors and kirk session of each parish should be responsible for licensing their beggars so that they could beg only within their own parishes. One way of dealing with the able-bodied beggars was to ship them off to the new colonies.[4] In addition, so many poor Irish came into Scotland in 1642 that special provisions had to be made for them. At times Government tried to ease the situation by permitting more grain to be imported. After 1653 there was a series of good harvests which led to lower grain prices. Other factors helped to ease the situation too - for example there was no further outbreak of plague; burghs which held the monopoly for trading grew in number, thus making it easier to market farm produce. The slow improvements were rudely set back during the period 1692-99 when the nation suffered such a series of famines that it was called the Seven Ill Years.

Webster's census of 1,265,000 was followed by Sir John Sinclair's estimate in about 1795; this he calculated from the Statistical Account which had been assembled during the previous five years. These and the first government census of 1801 of 1,608,000 are the only ones available for our period. The 1755 and 1795 figures cannot be considered to be very accurate and by 1801 there had been some boundary changes which causes some difficulties of comparison.

Scotland had been an exporter of people for many years; substantial numbers left to earn a living, to trade, or for military service in various continental armies. Yet if Sinclair's figure is to be accepted then the population increased by 217,000 in the first half of the century and by 343,000 in the second. The general improvement in health and the increasing numbers as a result of employment in the kelping parishes were beginning to show up in the figures. The population of the Highlands has been estimated as 230,000 in 1747 and 325,000 in 1795.[5] It increased sharply over the following seventy years before starting the decline to the present day. The three sets of figures for 1755, 1795 and 1801 show a dramatic overall increase in the population, a 21% increase between 1775 and 1795 and a further 22% increase between 1795 and 1801, from 1,263,800 persons to 1,546,715 to 1,608,420.

The table in Appendix 5. gives a breakdown on a county basis of the three censuses. A number of conclusions can be reached from the changes in population. The dramatic move to the industrial areas had begun; the weaving and textile areas showed marked increases but the biggest increases were in Lanarkshire and Renfrewshire. Six counties- Clackmannan, East Lothian, Moray, Peebles, Roxburgh and Banff lost population in the overall period. The decrease was doubtless accounted for by migration to the towns as a result of the reorganisation of the farms and the pull of new industries. There were no significant emigrations from any of these counties and the population was able to stabilise through natural growth after the initial loss. Despite emigration and migration to Lowland areas most Highland counties showed a significant increase in population. The waves of panic which seized the Highland landowners that they would be left without labour is hardly borne out by these figures, although as has already been pointed out, the effect on particular areas may have been severe. For example, a whole parish in Knoydart of about 600 people was said to have been led by their priest to Glengarry, Canada in 1785.

The growth of basic and manufacturing industries went hand in hand with the expansion of the urban population, which was increasingly concentrated round Glasgow and in the Clyde valley, but extended to Renfrew, Dumbarton and Stirling. Increases in some Ayrshire parishes were associated with coalfields and cotton manufacturing. In the east, Edinburgh, Dunfermline and Kirkcaldy continued to grow, with smaller concentrations of people in the outlying textile towns. It is reasonable to suppose that all these growing towns drew people from those nearby parishes which show a declining population.

North of the Highland line there is considerable variation at parish level and it is not always easy to understand the reasons. Most of the emigrations took place from the western coastal districts, yet where large scale kelping took place, the overall population increased. Each of the islands except Islay shows an increase of more than 1000 people, Mull gained 3000, Tiree 1000, Skye 4500, Harris 1000 and N. & S. Uist and Benbecula 3400. Islay was not a kelping island and lost 1300 people. Although certain parishes in Argyllshire lost 12,000 between 1755 and 1801 the county as a whole gained 15,000 in the period, a gain of 23%. Similarly, Inverness town and some of the parishes close by lost population to the tune of 5000 while the increase for the county was over 14,000. A similar analysis may be made for Ross and Cromarty- east coast parishes declined while those in the west gained- especially Lochalsh, Lochbroom and Applecross, which each gained 1000+ and Lewis which gained 2700.

Even allowing for the degradation of land by over-grazing and inappropriate land management over the past 200 years, the Highlands were over-populated in the 18th century, and with a rise in numbers averaging 7400 per annum the pressures on what were already subsistence levels were considerable. This study has concentrated on the economic reasons for the dramatic social changes of the period. It is perhaps necessary to realise that those changes were common to many European societies and began the movement to a largely urban society, where instead of more than 90% of employment being on the land, today only a few per cent of the labour force remains. But, in addition, the Highlands had its particular crisis; the rapid collapse of a social system, the ambiguous values which had sustained it and, tragically, the rich culture which had nourished it. The responses of its erstwhile paternalistic chiefs varied from the abstract application of their new understanding of market economics to attempts to sustain the ancient paternalism; from enlightened endeavours to find alternative employment for displaced tenants to, in a few instances, the planning and leading of emigrations. The seeds of the notorious brutalities on the Sutherland estates in 1819-20 were, as is shown, sown years earlier by factors who preceeded the egregious Patrick Sellar. Equally disgraceful policies were pursued by other lairds and factors, particularly Boisdale and Glengarry. But the actions of others varied from those who were concerned but showed little ability to act, those who acted responsibly and those who were overwhelmed by economic pressures such as Lord MacDonald.

Although outwith our period, the story of Lord MacDonald's estate in Skye can be taken as typical of the predicament of landlords in many parts of the Highlands and Islands during the 200 years covered by this book. Lord MacDonald knew he was facing financial disaster yet he found it difficult to increase his income either by raising rents or improving his lands without losing his tenants by emigration. In 1799 he had ordered John Blackadder to survey his estate of Kilmuir in Skye and to

consider every possible mode of improvement and ... report your opinion how far the estate would be improved by enclosing and draining and what kind of fences and drains ought to be adopted.[6]

The report made clear that traditional farming should be abandoned if revenues were to be substantially increased. However, Blackadder warned MacDonald that very few tacks should be let out for sheep farming as "the islander who is turned out of his possession will emigrate unless another way of gaining his bread is pointed out to him". By 1812 the new lots for crofts had been laid out, runrig had almost disappeared and the shielings had been turned over to sheep farming. Potato blight followed by famine in the winters of 1837 and 1838 meant that the crofters were reduced to dire poverty. Nevertheless the population continued to grow and with the sub-division of the crofts, 421 families in Kilmuir were living in only 190 divisions of land by 1847. In the light of these conditions Lord MacDonald started to encourage emigration, especially after his factor pointed out the financial advantages of clearing crofts and adding them to large tacks for sheep farming. The price of wool had risen considerably because of the demand of the mills in the south. The factor also noted the condition of the people and Lord MacDonald reluctantly admitted that "on these overcrowded areas the people ... could no more prosper than trees that have been too closely planted". The evictions that followed were accompanied with the promise that once the emigrants reached Canada their rent arrears would be forgiven. The estate continued to amass debts which reached £218,000 in 1847 and Lord MacDonald had then to sell his lands.[7]

The revolt of the tacksmen, from being the strong allies of chiefs to being their bitterest enemies, is remarkable and it is unfortunate that so few details exist of the personal conflicts that must have arisen. As for the sub-tenants, the cottars and their families, we know even less. They were forced to make decisions with what little information they had obtained from either the tacksman who up to then had been their grasping landlord, or, from the even more distrusted factor of the laird. Worse still were the promoters of emigration schemes, the merchants or their agents from the ports, who proved to be conscienceless and without scruples, and willing to sacrifice safety standards for profit.

During the second half of the 18th century the landscape of Lowland Scotland and the way of life of the rural community were changed fundamentally. Industrialisation, with the consequent rapid growth of the towns, was well under way. The intellectual explosion in Edinburgh and Glasgow was producing great ripples across the country's life from industrial chemistry to engineering, from improved health and nutrition to the standardisation of weights and measures[8]. Most of all, while the country was still in the grip of mercantilism the teaching of Adam Smith was being debated and slowly absorbed. In all this excitement the plight of a few destitute Highlanders did receive some scant attention as potentially lost units in the labour market, or as cannon fodder for the French wars. But, as has been seen, while some individuals on either side of the Atlantic saw the human misery in their midst, only a few tried to do something constructive about it.

The first proposals for public works to provide alternative employment and the first serious attempts to regulate conditions on board ship were only made in the early years of the nineteenth century. The implementation of the Passenger Act in 1803 played an important part in reducing the flow of emigrants by significantly increasing costs. The low standards that were common, often made the Atlantic passage a hazardous affair.

We know that many did not survive the rigours of a voyage which at best took six to eight weeks although some took much longer. The laconic way in which the deaths, particularly of children, are recorded tells us something of the hardships the emigrants endured.

The attempt of Scottish magnates to transfer the feudal system to North America was a deserved failure- the ideas of the Enlightenment had taken root too firmly. Geography played its part- for the nearest American lands to Scotland- Newfoundland and Nova Scotia- were then bleak inhospitable areas where the business of survival of the well-equipped was hard and for the feckless and the resourceless, impossible. The early years of settlement even for free men were desperately hard while the predicament of the many indentured men and women can barely be imagined. Yet many did survive and in time prospered and played their part in the building up of their new country, both the United States and Canada. Many unfortunate men and women who had indented themselves to pay their passage found themselves virtual slaves for many years. Although some movements were well planned and organised by landowners or the displaced tacksmen, there was a good deal of mismanagement, futile optimism, inadequate capital resources, and not a little skulduggery. The smaller number of emigrations from the southern half of the country, where resources were greater and no language difficulties existed were on the whole better organised and had a high rate of success.

In addition to the large scale movements of people many individuals crossed the Atlantic to live and work in North America, either permanently or for some years. In particular, Scotsmen played a highly significant part in education- Jefferson, Madison and Monroe all paid tribute to their Scots teachers. The Rev James Blair was President of William and Mary College in Virginia for 58 years and introduced other Scots. There and in other colleges the curriculum was influenced by the models of the Scottish Universities, especially in the emphasis on moral philosophy and the encouragement of the sciences. The Rev John Witherspoon built Princeton into a great university and was one of the two native Scotsmen and the only clergyman to sign the Declaration of Independence. Even then he retained his Scots patriotism, protesting at a clause in the original draft which suggested that "Scotch and foreign mercenaries" were used to put down the rebellion, saying that he would not have the Scottish nation insulted. So "Scotch and" was deleted. The other Scots signatory, James Wilson, was jointly responsible, with Madison, for drafting the Federal Constitution of 1787. Wilson, Witherspoon and the many Scots teachers and clergymen, both Presbyterian and Episcopal, were deeply influenced by the philosophers of the Scottish Enlightenment, by Hutcheson, Reid and Kames. A further educational link between Scotland and the Colonies was through the Edinburgh Medical School and in due course Edinburgh graduates set up the first American schools in Philadelphia and New York.

Lowland merchants were early involved in commercial affairs and in the years up to the war came to dominate the tobacco trade. In 1774 one firm operated six ships between Chesapeake and Glasgow and maintained 21 agencies and stores in Maryland and Virginia.[9]

Scots were prominent in every walk of life in Canada, from the fur trade, fishing, and lumbering to politics and banking. Roman Catholic and Presbyterian clergy were active both in planning emigration and developing the young Dominion.

After 1803 emigration was virtually halted until the hungry years after Waterloo. The economic collapse of the country, destitution and the large scale evictions of the 19th century in favour of sheep set the tide of emigration flowing again and are outwith the scope of this book. During the following 130 years hundreds of thousands of Scots were to follow in the wake of the early pioneering emigrants. Dr Johnson, who met some of them on his Highland tour in 1773,   talked of the "epidemical fury of emigration", but to suggest that emigration was an infectious and irrational response seems wide of the mark, it may rather be seen as the last desperate remedy taken by sufferers of an incurable disease.

Glossary

Barque: a sailing vessel having the foremast square-rigged and the main and mizzen masts fore and aft rigged

Bear, bere: four-rowed barley

Brig: a vessel having two masts square rigged with her main mast fore and aft rigged with a gaff and boom

Brigantine: a vessel having the foremast square rigged and the main mast fore and aft rigged

Burden: a measurement of the capacity or volume of a ship expressed in units of 100 cubic feet- one unit being termed a ton measurement

Conventicle: a secret meeting for worship by the Covenanters

Customs and carriage: works and services due to the laird or chief by his tenants as part of the rent

Displenish: to sell the furnishings and implements of a house or farm

Engrossing: the enlarging of a farm by removing the holders of the surrounding, usually smaller, holdings

Entail: to settle an estate on a number of persons in succession so that it cannot be dealt with by any other possessor as absolute owner

Execute diligence: to serve a warrant to enforce the attendance of a witness or the production of a document

Factor: a farm or estate manager

Fee simple: an estate limited to a man and his heirs and assigns with or without conditions

Grasssum: money paid on entry to a farm

Heritor: landed proprietor liable to pay public burdens in his parish

Jointure: the legal provision of an estate for a widow

Leevie money: bounty paid to recruits

Lispund: an old Orkney measure of weight (20-30lbs)

Meal: oatmeal

Multure: a payment to the miller for grinding corn at the lord's mill; a prohibition from using any other mill

Patent: a piece of land conferred by letters patent

Police: the civil administration of a town or city

Precinct: an area of land in Ulster assigned for settling by colonists

Provender: provisions

Quit rent: payment in lieu of services to the landlord

Rack-rent: an extortionate rent

Schooner a vessel having two masts fore and aft rigged

Scots pint: equivalent to two English pints or one litre

Sett of an estate: the introduction at one time of new leases on all the farms of an estate

Ship: a large vessel having a bowsprit and three masts

Snow: a vessel having a main and foremast and a small topsail mast close behind the mainmast

Sorner: beggar

Spinster: a man or woman who spins

Tierce: a widow's portion, the third part of her husband's property

Victuals: provisions

Wadset: mortgage

Several authors have researched the numbers of persons who have left Scotland in different periods:

Graham		1768-75		20,245
		1763-8		c.5,000
		1768-75		5,000+ to N.Carolina
Somerville				6,598 to N.Carolina
M I Adam	who used			
	Knox	1763-73		20,000
	Garnett	1773-5		30,000
	Sc Mag	1763-75		10,000
	Ministers	1772-3		3,169
	PRO	1773-4		6,000+
Somerville		1773-4		7,494
Bailyn		1760-75		40,000
Simmons		1763-75		25,000
Somerville		1768-75		19,017
			+PRO	c.200
			arrived	17,302
		1783-90		2,504
			arrived	1,094
Bethune		1771-90		2,000 from Skye
SSPCK		1772-92		6,400 from Inverness and Ross

From the United States census of 1790
Brock estimated that there were 260,322 Scots or 8.3% of the total white population
Brander   189,000 Scots
Simmons   c.700 Highlanders before 1763

Appendix 1. Estimates of emigrant numbers

State	Whites	%	English	%	Irish	%	Scots
Maine	96107	60	57660	11.7	11350	4.5	4320
New Hampshire	141112	61	86060	7.5	10580	6.2	8750
Vermont	85072	76	64650	5.1	4340	5.1	4340
Massachussetts	373187	82	306010	3.9	15550	4.4	16420
Rhode Island	64670	71	45920	2.8	1810	5.8	3750
Connecticut	232236	67	155600	2.9	6740	2.2	5110
New York	314366	57	179190	8.1	25460	7.0	25010
New Jersey	169954	58	98570	9.5	16150	7.7	13090
Pennsylvania	423373	40	169350	14.5	61390	8.6	36410
Delaware	46310	60	27790	11.7	5420	8.0	3700
Maryland	208649	72	150230	12.3	25670	7.6	15860
Kentucky & Tenessee	93046	78	69780	12.2	11350	10.0	9300
Virginia	442227	84	371380	11.7	51730	10.2	45100
N.Carolina	289181	98	283400	11.1	32100	14.8	42800
S.Carolina	140178	75	105130	13.8	19340	15.1	21170
Georgia	52886	70	37020	15.3	8090	15.5	8200
Estimated numbers	3172444	70	2207760	9.7	307070	8.3	263330

Appendix 2. The composition of the national stocks as a percentage of the white population of the United States, taken from the National Census of 1790 by Barker.

	1629	1650	1651	1684	1685	1686	1696
Political prisoners		1250	1827			?	
Civil prisoners				390	100+		112
Others	60						

	1715	1735	1738	1739	1740	1745	1753	1756	1760	1764	1765	1767
Political prisoners	1000					610						
Others		345	100	650	323		70	250	300	17	47	350
Boys					500							

Appendix 3. Numbers of early emigrants.

Origin	1768	1769	1770	1771	1772	1773	1774	1775	1783	1784	1785	1786
Argyll			800				160	300				
Kintyre		144	200				128	618				
Arran						101						
Islay		300	500				62	500				
Jura	450											
Skye			300	300	960	800	372					
Barra												
Uists				30	100							
Eigg, Coll												
Lewis					750	840	163					
Lochaber				270	110	425		255				
Knoydart												600
Glenmoriston					70		150					
Wester Ross				80		85	59					
Strathglass												
Glengarry						350				300		
Sutherland					700		127					
Caithness						380						
Orkney							55	53				
Shetland							25	24				
Inverness		80					212			80		
Strathspey						490	172	252	30	40		
E. Scotland						53		88				
Perthshire			60					572				
Clydeside				32			212	175				
Galloway							1033	254				
Unknown ?			200		240	290	756	300		300		

Destination

	1768	1769	1770	1771	1772	1773	1774	1775	1783	1784	1785	1786
Quebec										300		600
Nova Scotia						253	59			80		
Pr.Ed.Island ?			260	30	210		67	94				
C.Breton Island												
Massachussetts			200	14								
New York						1275	1768	540		300		
Philadelpia					200		186	532				
N. Carolina	450	444	1600	300	1400	800	586	1018				
S. Carolina							17					
Virginia						101						
Maryland				80			55					
Georgia							54	303				
Unknown		80		288	1120	1735	700	1087	30	40		

Appendix 4. The homes & destinations of emigrants to N. America

Origin	1787	1788	1789	1790	1791	1792	1793	1800	1801	1802	1803
Argyll				140							
Kintyre											
Arran											
Islay											
Jura											
Skye		250		200	480						800
Barra						200					1179
Uists										200	
Eigg, Coll			176	328		36					
Lewis											
Lochaber										600	
Knoydart											
Glenmoriston							150				
Wester Ross									230		
Strathglass									1268		480
Glengarry						320				463	1100
Sutherland											
Caithness											
Orkney											
Shetland											
Inverness											
Strathspey											
E. Scotland											
Perthshire											
Clydeside											
Galloway											
Unknown ?		60			1940		528			1052	915

Destination	1787	1788	1789	1790	1791	1792	1793	1800	1801	1802	1803
Quebec		60				320	150			1063	1100
Nova Scotia				1300			528		1368	128	2594
Pr.Ed.Island ?							200			700	800
C.Breton Island										340	
Massachussetts											
New York					60					63	
Philadelpia					290						
N. Carolina	250		328	770							
S. Carolina											
Maryland									130		
Georgia											
Unknown			176	340		36				21	

County	Webster 1755	Sinclair 1795	Census 1801	% increase
Aberdeen	116168	122921	121065	4
Angus	68883	91001	99053	44
Argyll	66286	76101	81277	23
Ayr	59009	75030	84207	43
Banff	38478	38487	37216	-3
Berwick	23987	30875	30206	26
Bute	7125	11072	11791	65
Caithness	22215	24802	22609	-
Clackmannon	9003	8749	10858	21
Dumfries	39788	52329	54597	37
Dumbarton	13857	18408	20710	49
East Lothian	29709	28966	29986	1
Fife	81570	87250	93743	15
Inverness	59563	73979	72672	22
Kincardine	23057	26799	26349	14
Kinross	4889	5302	66725	38
Kirkcudbright	21205	26959	29211	38
Lanark	81726	123254	147692	81
Midlothian	90412	122655	122597	36
Moray	30604	26080	27760	-9
Nairn	5694	6054	8322	46
Orkney	23381	43239	24445	5
Peebles	8908	8107	8735	-2
Perth	120116	133274	125583	5
Renfrew	26645	62858	78501	195
Ross & Cromarty	48084	55430	56318	17
Roxburgh	34704	32020	33721	-3
Selkirk	4021	4314	5388	34
Shetland	15210	20223	22379	47
Stirling	37014	46662	50825	37
Sutherland	20774	22961	23117	11
West Lothian	16829	17570	17844	8
Wigton	16466	20983	22918	39
Total	1265380	1546715	1608420	27
Aberdeen	15600		27400	76
Dundee	12400	15700	26800	116
Edinburgh	57000		81600	43
Glasgow	31700	66578	83700	164
Inverness	9700		8700	-10

Appendix 5. The population of the Counties and cities of Scotland and the percentage increase or decrease between 1795 and 1801.

BOAT	MASTER	LEFT	FROM	HOME	NO	ARR	DESTINATION
1764							
Douglas	R.Manderston	May	Greenock		17	July	Boston
1766							
Jenny	A.Orr	Sept	Greenock		11	Oct	Boston
Lovely Betsy	Wm. Hayman	June	Greenock		6	Oct	Boston
Stirling Castle	J. Colquhoun	Mar	Greenock		6	Apr	Boston
1767							
Pearl	W. Buchan	Aug	Pt. Glasgow		50		S. Carolina
?					40	Nov	
1768							
Bell	A. Iver	June	Greenock	Jura	300		N. Carolina
Peggy	R. Speir	May	Greenock	Paisley	7	Aug	Philadelphia
?	Apr		Fraser's Highlanders	Jura	200+		N. Carolina
?							Pr. Ed. Island
1769							
Helen	J. Mattie	July	C'town		144	Sept	N. Carolina
Mally	J. Speir	July	Greenock	Islay		Sept	N. Carolina
?						Sept	N. Carolina
?						Sept	N. Carolina

Appendix 6.   The boats that are known to have sailed to North America carrying emigrants.

1770

Ship	Master	Month	Port	Origin	Number	Month	Destination
Annabella	D. Stewart	July	C'town	Argyll	?100	Sept	Pr. Ed. Island
Edinburgh	J. McMichael	Aug	C'town	?Islay	120		N. Carolina
Falmouth	J. McWhae	Apr	Greenock	Perthshire	60	June	Pr. Ed. Island
Hector	W. Miller	Aug	Pt. Glasgow		200		Maryland
Hector	W. Miller	Aug	Pt. Glasgow				Maryland
Nancy	N. Chivers		L. Tarbert	?Islay	302		?
Neptune	J. Ewing	Feb	Pt. Glasgow	?Kintyre	360		Virginia
?				Perthshire	?300	May	Pr. Ed. Island
?				Arran	100		New York
			linen workers		c 100		N. Carolina

1771

Ship	Master	Month	Port	Origin	Number	Month	Destination
Argyll	J. McMichael	July	S. Uist		30		Pr. Ed. Island
Edinburgh			C'town	S. Uist	100		Pr. Ed Island
Friendship			Greenock		14		Boston
Nancy	N. Chivers			Skye	300		N. Carolina
?				L. Broom	270		?
?			linen workers		c 100		N. Carolina

1772

Ship	Master	Month	Port	Origin	Number	Month	Destination
Adventure	A. Smith	July	K'caldy	Sutherland	350		N. Carolina
Alexander	J. Kirkwood	Mar	S. Uist	S. Uist	210	June	Pr. Ed. Island
Britannia	Scott	Aug	Clyde		some		?

Ship	Captain	Month	Port	Origin	Number	Date	Destination
Magdalene or St. Andrew							
Pearl	R. Tucker	Aug	Greenock	Strathnaver	100		Philadelphia
?		July	Greenock	Skye	300		N. Carolina
?			L. Broom	Skye	400		N. Carolina
				Lewis	700		?

1773

Ship	Captain	Month	Port	Origin	Number	Date	Destination
Batchelor	A. Ramage	July	Leith	Caithness	264		went into Shetland
Britannia	Ayr	Mar	Dublin	Ross	70	May	New York
Brunswick	T. McLarty	Aug	Greenock	Dumfries	70	Dec	Virginia
Buchanan	J. Moody	Apr	Greenock	Caithness	90	May	New York
Concord	A. Ramage	Aug	Leith	Caithness	240		?
David & Ann	A. Ritchie	Aug	Ft. George	Strathspey	250	1774	New York
Donald	Th. Ramsay	Jan	6 Highlanders broke ship				Virginia
Favourite	Th. Fisher	May	Whitehaven	Skye	140		New York
Hector	J. Spiers	June	Greenock	L. Broom	200	Aug	N. Carolina
Margaret	Speir	July	Greenock				N. Carolina
Matty	T. Cochrane	Mar	Greenock	Paisley	?	May	Philadelphia
Nancy	G. Smith		Dornoch	Caithness	240	Dec	New York
Nestor	J. Harrison	Sept		Skye	280		Georgia
Pearl	Rd. Tucker	Aug	Ft. William	Glengarry	308	Oct	New York
?		July		Lewis	840		?
?				Skye	244		N. Carolina
?				Skye	120		N. Carolina
?			Greenock	Arran	102		N. Carolina
?				Lochaber	425		?

1774

Ship	Captain	Month	Port	Region	No.	Note	Destination
Adventure	W. Loudon	May	Dumfries	Galloway	65		New York
Balliol		July	C'town		some		N. Carolina
Brave Corsican		Mar	Greenock		some		N. Carolina
Carolina Packet	J. Dean	Oct	Greenock	Islay, Mull	62	1775	N. Carolina
Cato	M. McNeil	Aug	Greenock	Skye	372	Dec	N. Carolina
Commerce	J. Deniston	Feb	Greenock	Paisley	270+		New York
Countess	D. Ferguson	Oct	Greenock	Dumfries	17		S. Carolina
Diana	R. Easson	Sept	Greenock	Kintyre	36		N. Carolina
Favourite	D. Ruthven	May	Wigtown	Wigtown	75		New York
Friendship	Th. Fisher	May	Stornoway	Stornoway	106		Philadelphia
Gale	Th. Jann	May	Stranraer	Galloway	230		New York
George	H. Jefferson	Aug	Leith		some		S. Carolina
George	A. Clunie	May	Greenock	Strathspey	172	July	New York
Golden Rule	A. Boag	June	K'kudbright	Wigtown	250		New York
Jamaica Packet	Ch. Cragg	Oct	K'caldy	Shetland	25?	1775	N. Carolina
Jenny	Th. Smith	June	K'kudbright		250		New York
John & Jane	J. Welsh	Apr	Aberdeen		59		Pictou
Lovely Nelly	B. Baxter			K'kudbright	67	?Aug	Pictou
Magdelene	J. Wallace	Aug	Greenock		24		Philadelphia
Marlborough	G. Preswick	Sept	Kirkwall	Orkney	55		Georgia
Matty	Th. Cochrane	May	Greenock	Glas, Stirl	53	July	New York
Moore	McLarty	Aug	Mull	Glenmoriston	150		New York
Nelly & Ann	R. Crosbie	Apr	Wigtown		60		New York
Peace & Plenty	C. McKenzie	Nov	Stornoway	L. Broom	59		New York
Peggy	Wm Hastie	Mar	Greenock		some		Phil/New York
Sally	J. Bruce	Sept	Greenock		53	Philadelphia	

Name	Captain	Month	Port		Number		Destination
Sharp	N. Rodger	June	Greenock		160	Sept	New York
Ulysses	J. Wilson	Aug	Greenock	Kintyre	92	Oct	N. Carolina
?		June	Greenock				?
?			Greenock		700		?
?			Pt. Glasgow				?
2 more boats went north to pick up emigrants							

1775

Name	Captain	Month	Port		Number		Destination
Albion	Hogg	June	Whitehaven		some		New York
Christy	A. Lee	Jan	Pr. Glasgow	Greenock	9		Georgia
Christy	H. Kellie	May	Greenock		46		NY, Georgia
Clemintina	P. Brown	July	Stornoway	Inverness	211		Philadelphia
Commerce	J. Mattie	June	Greenock	Breadalbane	116		New York
Diana	Elphinstone	May	Greenock				New York
Favourite	Fisher	June	Whitehaven		some		New York
Friendship	Th. Jann	May	Leith	E. Scotland	88	July	Philadelphia
Friendship	J. Smith	Mar	Pt. Glasgow	Ayr	8		Quebec
George	Deans	Aug	Gigha	Kintyre	150	Oct	N. Carolina
Georgia	Th. Bolton	July	Greenock		24		Georgia
Glasgow		Sept	Ft. William		250	Nov	NY, Georgia
Glasgow Packet	A. Porterfeild	Apr	Greenock		30		Salem
Happy Union	Coates	Nov	Leith		recruits		Boston
Jackie	J. Morris	June	Stranraer	Wigtown	81		NY, N. Carolina
Jamaica Packet	Th. Smith	June	Kirkcaldy	Leith, Shet	20		N. Carolina
John & Elizabeth					52	?Aug	Pt. Ed. Island
Jupiter	S. Brown	Sept	Oban	Appin	136	?Nov	N. Carolina
Lilly	Th. Cochrane	Apr	Greenock	Breadalbane	188		New York

Ship	Captain	Month	Port	Region	Number	Date	Destination
Lord Dunluce	R. Shutter	Aug	C'town		some		N. Carolina
Lovely Nelly	Wm Sheridan	May	Dumfries	Galloway	130?		Pr. Ed. Island
Marlborough	Th Walker	Sept	Orkney	Ork, Cai	53		Georgia
Monimia	Ed Morrison	May	Greenock	Stirl, Per	230?	July	Philadelphia
Neptune	Morris	May	Greenock		87	Aug	NY, Virginia
Ulysses	J. Wilson	May	Greenock	Argyll, Gla	13		N. Carolina
?		Aug	Gigha	Kintyre	350		N. Carolina

1775-1783 The war of American Independence

1784

Ship	Captain	Month	Port	Region	Number	Date	Destination
Jean	Ritchie			Greenock	50 families		Newbury
Almy	Hastie		Greenock		300		New York
?				Glengarry	300		Glengarry
?				Beauly	?50		Halifax

1786

Ship	Captain	Month	Port	Region	Number	Date	Destination
Macdonald	Stevenson	July	Knoydart	Glengarry	5-600	Sept	Quebec

1788

Ship	Captain	Month	Port	Region	Number	Date	Destination
Fame	Leithc	July	Greenock	Skye	250		N. Carolina
Joanna	McShane				?		Philadelphia
Jeannie	Martin		Greenock		60		Halifax
Neptune					60		Quebec

1790

Ship	Master	Origin	Number	Date	Date	Destination
British Queen	Deniston	Arisaig, Eigg	30-90			?
Jane			186			Pr. Ed. Island
Lucy			142			Pr. Ed. Island
?		Ardchattan	140			?
		Skye				
		Skye	200			?

6 boats from Bracadale

1791

Ship	Master	Origin	Number	Date	Date	Destination
Brunswick	Milne	Greenock	20	Apr		N. Carolina
Dunkeld						Pictou
Fortune	McLeod	Greenock	50	Aug		N. Carolina
Fortune		Skye	480			?
Gen Washington	Miller	Greenock	50	Aug		N. Carolina
Mally	Maxwell	Greenock	30 or 174	June		Quebec
Mally		Greenock	290			Philadelphia
Mary Ann	Young	Greenock	50	July		N. Carolina
Queen	Morison	Greenock	40 or 240	June		Quebec
?		Pt. Glasgow			Dec	Pictou
?		Greenock)1300			Dec	Pictou
?		Greenock)			Dec	Pictou
?		Ft. William)			Dec	Pictou
?		Glengarry				Glengarry

1792

Ship	Master	Origin	Number	Date	Date	Destination
Unity		Glengarry	200	July	Sept	Quebec

1793

?Argyle	June		Barra	200		Pr. Ed. Island
?			Glenmoriston	150		Pr. Ed. Island

1798-1801 no emigration

1798-1801 French Revolution

1801

Dove	Crone	June	Inverness	Strathglass	219		Pictou
Sarah	Smith	June	Inverness	Strathglass	350	Aug	Pictou

1802

Draper	Taylor	June	Greenock	Inv, Pbls	63		New York
Eagle			Greenock		21		?
Friends				Lochaber)		Sept	Quebec
Helen				Lochaber)	473	Sept	Quebec
Jane				Lochaber)		Sept	Quebec
?				Lochaber)	128		Pictou
George					49		New York
Jean		June	Greenock	Ft. William			Quebec
Neptune	Boyd	June	L. Nevis	Strathglass	550		Quebec
Northern Friends				Greenock	340	Aug	C. Br. Island

1803

		Port	Origin	No.	Month	Destination
Commerce		Pt. Glasgow		86		Pictou
Dykes	Ballantyne		Skye	200	Aug	Pr. Ed. Island
Favourite		Ullapool		500		Pictou
Oughton			Skye	200	Aug	Pr. Ed. Island
Polly			Strathglass	480		Pictou
4 boats		Greenock		700		Philadelphia

1804

			Origin	No.		Destination
			?Glengarry	1100		Glengarry

Notes

Introduction

1. Meinig, 1986, 6,7
2. Somerville, 1815, vol 2, 155-6
3. Kyd, 1952, 9
4. Smout, 1969, 514
5. Plumb, 1963, 124
6. Mitgang, 1986
7. Creswell, 1925, 205
8. Dunn, 1953, 27
9. EA January 24th 1774

Chapter 1

1. Donaldson, 1971, 253-4
2. Somerville, 1815, vol 2
3. MacKenzie, 1919, 60-2; Anon, 1899
4. MacGregor, 1954, 149,168; Argyll, 1887, 218
5. McKerral, 1948, 23, 24-37, 55
6. Perceval-Maxwell, 1973, 10-126 *passim*; Insh, 1922; Lomas, 1904, 178
7. Register of Privy Seal of Scotland 2nd series, vi, 198
8. Beckett, 1972, 26-46
9. Insh, 1922, 31-78, *passim*
10. Perceval-Maxwell, 27, 31
11. Insh, 1922, 93-112 *passim*
12. Johnston, 1974, 65
13. Insh, 1922, 175-8; Pryde, 1930, 14; Smith, 1947, 150-5
14. Landsman, 1983, 135
15. Smith, 1947, 150
16. SRO GD 24/1/826, Abercairney muniments; *Historical Manuscripts Commission* X, app137
17. Insh, 1947

Chapter 2

1. Bean, 1970, 6; Smith, 1947, 153,155; Whyte, 1972 lists the names of 265 transported convicts; Donaldson, 1966, 39
2. Exhibition at Saugus Iron Works National Historical Monument
3. Smout, 1963, 240
4. Chalmers, 1858, 353
5. Seton and Arnot, 1928, 24
6. Insh, 1922, 167, 163
7. Burton, 1853, 211
8. Graham, 1956, 43-5
9. SRO GD 1/53/73 Irvine Robertson papers; Smith, 1947, 153
10. Seton and Arnot, 1928, *passim*; Smith, 1947, 201
11. Insh, 1922, 27-30
12. Gouldesborough, 1961, 56-62
13. Insh, 1922, 115
14. Shaw 1/87 The Shawfield papers in the Mitchell Library, Glasgow Corporation Public Libraries
15. Grant, 1959, 404-7
16. EEC March 11th 1775
17. VG, February 25th 1768
18. SRO GD 214/726/1 Professor Hannay's papers; Smith 1947, 116
19. Keith, 1972, 317-9
20. CHOP, no.637, 673
21. CM, August 3rd 1774; Smith, 1947, 201
22. EA, November 9th 1770; EEC, January 2nd 1771

Chapter 3

1. Johnston, 1974, 183
2. Adams, 1979, xii-xlii
3. Somerville, 1984
4. Cameron, 1976
5. Adam, 1920, 73-89; Adam, 1922, 75
6. Adams, 1978,68
7. SRO GD 9/166/2
8. Geddes, 1945, 19-22
9. OSA vol 11, 159
10. OSA vol 5, 570-2; Lobban, 1969
11. Daiches, 1950, 99
12. Forbes, 1860, 39-40
13. Heron, 1793, Vol II, 334-5
14. Kerr, 1918, 83
15. *The Precipitation ...*, 1778, 23
16. Kerr, 1918, 87
17. SM, vol 35, 1773, 668
18. *The Precipitation ...*, 21

19. Hamilton, 1955, 415, 405
20. Sheridan, 1960, 162-73
21. Devine, 1984, 58, 69
22. Campbell, 1961, *passim*; Cadell, 1913, 155-192
23. Report from the Committee appointed to enquire into the Present State of the Linen Trade in Great Britain and Ireland, in *House of Commons Report* III, 1773, 113, 112
24. SCA, Bishop Hay to John Geddes, January 15th and February 12th 1773

Chapter 4

1. NLS HP 3 78.1020; Meyer, 1961, 86
2. NLS 9854 ff.221-3 Mackintosh Genealogical Extracts from C.Cooper Lovell, *The Golden Isle of Georgia*, Boston; Coulter, 1966, 30-1; Brock, 1982, 77-8
3. APC, vol IV, 1745-66, 818-9
4. Pryde, 1935, 147-50
5. Kelly, 1933, 34
6. Pryde, 1935, 153
7. Brock, 1982, 81; Budge, 1960, 125-7
8. Mowat, 1943, 71
9. NLS RBm 103, Menzies, Archibald, *Proposals for Peopling His Majesty's Southern Colonies on the Continent of America*, Scotland 1763
10. Mowat, 1943, 71
11. SRO GD 219/317 Murray of Murraythwaite muniments
12. Mowat, 1943, 58-61
13. Hamilton and Corey, (hereafter Johnson Papers), vol XII, 1957, 250
14. SRO GD 25/9/27/1(1),(2) Ailsa Muniments
15. SRO GD 248/49/2(22) Seafield Muniments
16. SRO GD 345/916/4 Grant of Monymusk muniments; SM, vol 29, 1767, 385; SRO GD 345/1235*
17. Hamilton, 1976, 301
18. Black, 1921, 23; Pryde 1935, 154
19. Adam, 1964, 448-9
20. Johnson Papers, vol IV, 824
21. *ibid*, vol XII, 250
22. *ibid*, vol V, 767
23. *ibid*, vol VI, 191, 330, 337
24. *ibid*, vol XII, 894
25. *ibid*, vol VIII, 195
26. SRO GD 248/349/3/9
27. Johnson, 1925, 107-8
28. Boswell, 1786, 118
29. SCA Bishop Hay to Mr James Grant, November 17th 1769
30. Scott, 1934-5, 22-32
31. SRO E 504/15; Whyte 1972; Graham 1956, 81; SM, vol 35, 1773, 499
32. SCA Bishop Hay to Mr Gordon, January 23rd 1774

33. SRO GD 1/787/37/1 Kinloch of Gourdie and Mercer of Aldie papers; Scott 1934-5, 29
34. Johnson Papers, vol XII, 1041
35. Kelly, 1933, 35
36. SCA Bishop Hay to Mr Gordon, January 23rd 1774
37. Johnson Papers, vol VII, 1026; vol XII 1023
38. VG, May 20th, June 7th 1773; Graham, 1956, 83
39. Johnson Papers, vol XII, 1111
40. SM, vol 36, 1774, 446

Chapter 5

1. Stewart, 1806, 149-154; Harvey, 1935, 47
2. Stewart, 1806, 160-1
3. SRO RH 4/56
4. NLS ms 2671 f.73
5. Smith, 1982, 64-6
6. SRO GD 293/2/79/(18) Blackwood and Smith WS Peebles
7. SRO GD 293/2/79/31
8. SRO E 504/15; Diary of William Drummond 1977
9. SRO RH 4/56; Harvey, 1931-2, 450; Stanhope, 1984, 12
10. SRO GD 293/2/79/(5)
11. SRO GD 293/2/18/28; 293/2/18/8
12. DCB, vol IV, 550
13. SRO GD 293/2/18/29
14. DCB, vol IV, 352
15. NLS ms 1399 f.68,70-72 Lauriston Castle collection, Delvine papers
16. SRO GD 293/2/72-77; APC, vol V 1766-1783, 382
17. SRO E 504/15; SM, vol 30, 1768, 446; MacKay, D. 1980, xx
18. SRO E 504/8; PRO SP 54/45 State Papers Scotland series II; SM, vol 33, 1771, 379; Berry, 1960, 3, 7-15; Harvey, 1931-2, 450; Sinclair, 1943, 4, 214
19. GJ, July 18th 1771
20. SRO GD 44/27/11 Gordon muniments; GJ, August 29th 1771; CHOP 1773-5, no.331
21. Cameron, 1976
22. SRO GD 293/2/78/65-6, 32-4
23. SRO GD 293/2/78/59,52
24. Harvey, 1955, 9-40
25. Harvey, 1931-2, 455
26. McLeod, 1931-2, 323
27. Harvey, 1931-2, 459, 450;
28. Stewart, 1806, 205-220

Chapter 6

1.   Johnson, 1983,5-31 *passim*
2.   SCA Bishop Hay to John Geddes, November 11th 1770
3.   SCA Bishop Hugh McDonald to Mr James Grant, June 7th 1770
4.   SCA Bishop Hay to Mr John Geddes, October 12th 1770 and June 24th 1771
5.   SCA Bishop John MacDonald to Bishop Hay, October 29th 1771
6.   SCA Bishop Hay to Mr Grant, May 22nd 1771
7.   Blundell, 1917, 32-8
8.   SCA Mr Peter Grant to Bishop Hay, March 27th 1772
9.   SCA Bishop Hay to Mr John Geddes, April 20th 1772
10.   SCA Bishop John MacDonald to Bishop Hay, September 22nd 1772
11.   SCA Glenaladale to Bishop Hay, 1772
12.   SCA Bishop James Grant to Bishop Hay, October 30th 1770
13.   SCA Bishop Hay to Mr James Grant, November 17th 1769; Harvey, 1931-2,
14.   SCA Bishop Hay to Mr John Geddes, October 12th 1770
15.   SCA Bishop Hay to Mr Charles Cruikshank, March 30th 1772
16.   SCA Glenaladale to Bishop Hay, November 8th 1771
17.   MacKay, 1965, 19
18.   SCA Glenaladale to Bishop Hay, December 21st 1771
19.   VG, February 28th 1772
20.   SCA Bishop Hay to Mr Charles Cruikshank, February 21st 1772
21.   SCA Bishop John MacDonald to Bishop Hay, October 29th 1771
22.   SCA Bishop John MacDonald to Mr John Grant, April 3rd 1772
23.   SCA Glenaladale to Bishop Hay, December 18th 1771
24.   SCA Mr Peter Grant to Bishop Hay, April 30th 1771
25.   SCA Mr Charles Cruikshank to Bishop Hay, February 28th 1772;
      Glenaladale to Bishop Hay November 11th 1771
26.   SCA Glenaladale to Donald MacDonald 1772; Mr Charles Cruikshank to
      Bishop Hay, March 26th 1772
27.   SRO GD 128/30/3/17 Fraser of Mackintosh colletion; SCA Mr Charles
      Cruikshank to Bishop Hay, February 28th 1772
28.   SCA Glenaladale to Bishop Hay, July 23rd 1772, April 16th 1773
29.   SCA same to same, October 16th 1773
30.   McLeod, 1931-2, 317; Bumsted, 1979, 15-20
31.   SCA Glenaladale to Bishop Hay November 11th 1771
32.   SCA Bishop Hay to Mr John Geddes, September 25th 1774
33.   SCA William Harrison to Bishop Hay, August 11th 1772
34.   M'Robert, 1776, 317
35.   DCB, vol V, 1801-20, 553-7
36.   MacKay, D. 1980, 126
37.   SRO E 504/15; Collins, vol I 1969, 150-1; Princeton University
      Library, Department of Rare Books and Special Collections
38.   MacKay, D. 1980, 49, 84
39.   MacKay, D. 1980, 76; EA, October 2nd, 9th, 16th, 27th 1772; SM, vol
      34, 1772, 483-4
40.   *The Works of John Witherspoon D.D.*, vol III, 1805, 293-303

41. MacKay, D. 85; SRO RD 220 f.1006
42. PRO SP 54/45
43. SRO E 504/15; *The Dumfries Weekly Magazine*, vol III, 1773, 413; MacKenzie, 1914, 264-70; Patterson, 1879, 450
44. Mackay, D. 1980, 141-6
45. M'Robert, 1776, 17-21
46. Sherwood, 1975, 72

Chapter 7

1.   SCA John Paterson to Charles Cruikshank, February 18th 1772; EEC, June 10th 1772; Youngson, 1974, 192
2.   EA, June 9th 1772; CHOP, 1773-5 no 585; Adam, 1960, xxvi-xxxiii
3.   Adam, 1960, xxiii-xxxvi
4.   EEC, June 1st and 13th 1772
5.   SCA Bishop Hay to Mr John Geddes, June 12th 1772
6.   Adam, 1960, 14
7.   GJ, July 20th 1772
8.   SRO E 504/20
9.   Adam, 1960, xxv, n.78
10. EA, June 2nd and July 3rd 1772
11. Adam, 1960, xxv, n.77
12. GJ, September 16th 1773; EA, September 28th and November 1st 1773; SM, vol 36, 1774, 221; Dexter, 1901, vol 1, 428
13. Adam, 1960, xxi n.103
14. EA November 1st 1773
15. SRO GD 44/27/11
16. PRO T 1/500 Treasury Board papers
17. PRO SP 54/45
18. SM, vol 35, 1773, 557
19. SRO GD 44/27/11
20. Fraser-MacIntosh, 1877, 418-26
21. SRO GD 248/349/3/83
22. SRO GD 44/27/11
23. SRO GD 248/508/4/21
24. Dexter, 1901, vol I, 425
25. SRO E 504/15; SM, vol 36, 221, 446; Cameron, 1976
26. SRO GD 248/508/4/43
27. SRO GD 248/244/4; 248/462/1/34
28. SRO GD 44/27/11
29. EA, June 6th 1775
30. Cameron, 1976
31. SRO GD 248/508/4/71
32. SRO GD 174/1303
33. Haldane, 1952, 31; Haldane, 1973, 7
34. Gilpin, 1789, 169-71
35. Cameron, 1976

36. SRO E 504/28; SM, vol 30 1768,446; EA June 3rd 1768; Budge, 1960,125-6
37. Brock, 1982, 81; SRO E 504/29; Graham, 1956, 100
38. SRO E 504/8; SRO E 504/15; PRO SP 54/45; SM, vol 31 1769, 602
39. EA, August 24th 1770; SM, vol 32, 1770, 457
40. Paton, 1895-6, vol III, 259
41. SRO E 504/8; PRO SP 54/45; GJ, Janaury 20th 1770; EA August 10th 1770
42. Meyer, 1961, 84
43. EA, February 26th 1771; GJ, March 28th 1771; SM, vol 33, 1771, 500
44. SRO E 504/8; PRO SP 54/45; EA, July 17th 1772
45. Meyer, 1961, 84
46. EA, August 8th 1772
47. SRO E 504/15; VG, December 23rd 1773; Graham, 1956, 85
48. PRO SP 54/45; EA, February 8th 1774
49. SRO E 504/15; Meyer, 1961, 86; Newsome, 1934, 129
50. Scotus Americanus, 1773
51. GJ, April 23rd 1772; EA, May 5th 1772
52. SRO E 504/15; GJ, August 20th 1774; Cameron, 1976; Meyer, 1961, 86
53. SRO E 504/18; SRO GD 170/1063/24/1 Campbell of Barcaldine papers;
     EEC, June 2nd 1774; GJ, June 16th 1774
54. EA, May 26th and September 29th 1775
55. Cameron, 1976; SM, vol 37, 1775, 690; *Annual Register of 1775 (1776)*,
     160
56. EA, September 8th 1775

Chapter 8

1. Johnson, 1925, 119
2. NLS 3431 Lee Papers f.177
3. Paton, 1895-6, vol 3, 259; Mackay, 1980, 62, 65
4. NRAS The Dunvegan Castle muniments, Section 4, correspondence no 113,
    Alexander McLeod of Glendale to Sir Norman McLeod, February 18th 1771
5. Macleod, 1939, 9
6. NRAS no 221, Sir Alexander McLeod to Norman McLeod of McLeod
    June 16th
    1771
7. NRAS no 114, Alexander McLeod of Glendale to Sir Norman McLeod,
    March
    11th 1771
8. SCA Bishop Hay to Mr Grant, October 11th 1771
9. SM, vol 33, 1771, 500; EA, February 26th and September 20th 1771;
    GJ, February 26th 1771; PRO SP 54/45; EA, May 15th 1772; Brock,
    1982, 82
10. APC, vol V AD 1766-1783, 346
11. NRAS no 92, Norman McLeod to Sir Norman McLeod, August 16th 1771
12. NRAS no 92, Memoir of his own life written by General McLeod (b.1745)
13. EA, April 13th, July 17th and 21st, August 10th 1772
14. NLS ms 1306 f.72 Lauriston Castle Collection, Delvine Papers;

MacKinnon 1938, 85
15.   NLS ms 1306 ff.67-8
16.   NLS HP 3 78.1020; McKerral, n.d.; Meyer, 1961, 86
17.   Boswell, 1786, 241
18.   Morison, 1972, 293
19.   SRO E 504/15; EEC, July 2nd 1774; Boswell, 1786, 162; Donaldson, 1966, 62; Meyer, 1961, 86, 62; Brock, 1982, 82
20.   Nicolson, 1930, 295; Johnson, 1968, 220
21.   Boswell, 1786, 266
22.   GJ, October 29th to November 5th 1772; Cameron 1976
23.   *The Dumfries Weekly Magazine*, vol 2, 1773, 192; GJ July 21st 1772; Meyer, 1961, 62
24.   EEC July 1773; MacDonald, 1978, 160
25.   Cameron, 1976
26.   Miller, 1976, 100
27.   Clouston 1937, 39-43
28.   Steuart, 1913, 42
29.   *Aberdeen Journal*, November 1st 1773
30.   SM, vol 36, 1774, 559; vol 37, 1775, 690; Cameron 1976
31.   Bruce, 1909, 101
32.   Diary of John Harrower, 67, 77; Haws, 1980, 64
33.   Cameron, 1976

Chapter 9

1.   EA, October 22nd and 24th, 1773
2.   SRO E 504/22; SRO GD 1/787/37/; EA, June 10th 1774
3.   James Hog Papers; SM vol 36, 1774, 345-6; vol 34, 1772, 578
4.   James Hog papers; SM, vol 36, 1774, 221
5.   Goudie, 1889, 40
6.   SRO RH 4/81/16; James Hog papers
7.   James Hog papers
8.   James Hog papers
9.   Morison, 1811, 9181
10.   EA, May 10th, 17th, June 21st, July 19th 1774
11.   James Hog papers
12.   Newsome, 1934, 130-8
13.   James Hog papers; Bailyn, 1986, 521-533
14.   SM, vol 36, 1774, 263-4, 157-8
15.   CM, May 30th 1774
16.   SM, vol 36, 1774, 158
17.   Dexter, 1901, 428
18.   EA, June 7th, 1774
19.   Goudie, 1889, 40; Bruce, 1909, 102
20.   EEC, May 16th to June 6th 1774
21.   VG, July 1774
22.   Andrews, 1939, *passim*

23. SRO E 504/20; Cameron,1976
24. Andrews, 1939

Chapter 10

1. Johnson, 1968, 88
2. A Minister of the Gospel, 1770
3. Haws, 1980, 70-73,89
4. Ross, 1896, 16
5. Graham, 1956, 25
6. SRO E504/18; EA, August 7th 1767
7. EA, September 6th 1771; Graham, 1956, 25
8. Devine, 1984, 38
9. Graham, 1956, 92
10. CHOP, 1773-5, no.324
11. Wylie, 1884, 313-327
12. *A Plan agreed upon ...* 1772
13. Journal of the Managers of the Scotch American Company of Farmers 1926-28, 181-203
14. Thomson, 1774
15. Journal of James Whitelaw, 133
16. Dexter, 1901, 447
17. Journal of James Whitelaw, 146-51
18. SM, vol 36, 1774, 221; EA, April 22nd and June 10th 1774
19. Journal of Colonel Alexander Harvey, 201-262
20. EA, November 25th 1774
21. Journal of Colonel Alexander Harvey, 201-262; Whyte, 1972
22. SRO E 504/8; EA, March 24th 1775 and August 22nd 1775; SM vol 37, 690; Cameron, 1976
23. *The Dumfries Weekly Magazine*, vol 1, 1772, 135
24. OSA vol 11, 1794, 16
25. *The Dumfries Weekly Magazine*, vol 3, 1773, 31
26. SRO E 504/37; Graham, 1956, 102; VG, August 13th 1773; SM vol 37, 1775, 340
27. SRO E 504/15; Cameron, 1976
28. Graham, 1956, 29
29. PRO T 1/500
30. SRO E 504/34; EA May 5th and July 8th 1775; Cameron, 1976
31. EA 26th May & 29th August 1775
32. SRO E 504/34; Cameron, 1976
33. SRO E 504/8
34. SRO E 504/37;21;34; GJ May 31st 1774; Cameron, 1976
35. M'Robert, 1776, i, xi
36. SCA Bishop Hay to L'Abb'e Grant, March 8th 1773; EA March 24th 1775
37. SRO E 504/1; PRO CO 217, vol 50
38. Robertson, 1799, 484-507
39. SM, vol 34, 1772, 692; vol 35, 1773, *passim*

40.   *House of Commons Report* III 1773, 101-133
41.   EA, May 12th 1775
42.   SRO GD 50/230 Scottish Emigration...

Chapter 11

1.   Lettsom, 1783, 383-416 *passim*
2.   *A Candid Enquiry ...*
3.   Mackay, D. 1980, 58
4.   SM, vol 33, 1771, 325
5.   EA, August 16th 1772
6.   SM, vol 34, 1772, 698
7.   GJ, April 23rd 1772
8.   GJ, September 16th 1773
9.   A Highlander ... 1774
10.   SRO GD 248/349/3/20
11.   CM, February 19th 1774
12.   EA, September 14th 1784
13.   PRO T 17/20, p.445; PRO T 1/500; SRO CE 1/13, Scottish Board of Customs minute book; PRO T 17/20, p.478
14.   SRO CE 60/1/7
15.   PRO T 1/500
16.   CHOP, 1773-5, no.585; see also Blacker, 1963
17.   CHOP, no.609, 610
18.   CHOP, no.633
19.   Burke, 1955, 108-9
20.   SRO GD 248/244/4
21.   SRO E 504/9
22.   EA, April 6th 1774
23.   GJ, March 17th 1774
24.   EA, May 12th 1775
25.   EA, August 4th 1775
26.   EA, July 25th 1775
27.   EA, October 20th 1775

Chapter 12

1.   SRO GD 170/1065/1
2.   EA, May 5th 1775; SM, vol 37, 1775, 340; EEC, August 30th 1775
3.   SM vol 37, 1775, 340
4.   CHOP, no.1091
5.   CHOP, no.1130
6.   SRO JP 6/2/2, p.33-4, Records of the Justices of the Peace of the County of Dumbarton
7.   EA, September 8th 1775
8.   Fay, 1956, 11-14
9.   EA, September 29th 1775

10.   EA, October 20th 1775
11.   North Riding Office, Northallerton, Yorks, Zetland papers,
       ZNK (1/2 no.222)
12.   SRO JP 1/2/1
13.   NLS ms 8258, ff.34-6, Andrew Steuart papers

Chapter 13

1.   Stanley, 1976, 140
2.   Lenman, 1981, 66
3.   McKay, M. 1980,
4.   Kyd, 1952
5.   Pryde, 1935, 156
6.   Adam, 1965, 448-9
7.   Scott, 1934-5, 31
8.   Kelly, 1933-4, 37
9.   SRO GD 174/34; EA, August 22nd 1775
10.   SM, vol 37, 1775, 690
11.   SRO GD 174/2093
12.   CHOP, no.1245
13.   CHOP, no.1348; *Historical Manuscripts Commission*, 1906, 11, 181
14.   SM, vol 37, 1775, 690; Morgan, 1966
15.   Graham, 1956, 170
16.   Logan, 1976
17.   SRO GD 174/34
18.   SRO GD 170/2705/4; 1595; 1176; 1545; 1385/5
19.   Gibbon, 1911, 66
20.   SCA Mr James MacDonald to Bishop Hay, November 4th 1776
21.   Adams, 1979, 274; *Historical Manuscripts Commission*, 1,24;
       SM, vol 37, 1775, 690
22.   SRO GD 170/1176/9 &/10/1
23.   SRO GD 170/1176/12
24.   Adams, unpublished paper
25.   SRO CE 51/1/14
26.   Lucas, 1909, 211-225
27.   SRO GD 174/34 Mclaine of Lochbuie papers
28.   *The Scotsman*, November 17th 1990
29.   Macdonald, 1978, 160
30.   Edinburgh University Library, ms Dc 4.41.58
31.   Cregeen, 1964, 195
32.   Adam, 1972, 6-10,24,25

Chapter 14

1.   EA, September 2nd 1783
2.   Whitfield, 1954, 281-6
3.   OSA vol 6, 432n

4.   OSA vol 4, 396
5.   OSA vol 2, 392
6.   OSA vol 1, 112-3
7.   OSA vol 21, 230
8.   OSA vol 4, 299
9.   OSA vol 8, 65n
10.   SRO GD 248/358/4
11.   OSA vol 1, 353
12.   Tayler, 1925, 174; *Historical Manuscripts Commission*, 1909, iv, 397-8
13.   SRO GD 248/358/4,5
14.   OSA vol 9, 348n
15.   Documents relative to the Distress and Famine in Scotland ...
      Parliamentary Papers Accounts and Papers, vol XXXVII, 1846
16.   Goudie, 1889, 72
17.   OSA vol 6, 210
18.   SRO GD 248/358/3/98
19.   Knox, 1787, 246-7
20.   OSA vol 13, 157n
21.   OSA vol 2, 545
22.   OSA vol 1, 288
23.   CM, October 20th and 24th 1791
24.   NLS Acc 6945
25.   NLS ms 6602 Dundas muniments; Dempster, 1789, 5,15
26.   SRO GD 95/11/8, Society in Scotland for Propagating Christian
      Knowledge Reports, 92n, 95n, 44-5
27.   A Rural Economist ... in FM vol IV, 1803, 253-62
28.   Edinburgh University Library, D.S.h.8.15/4 Rev A Irvine, An Enquiry
      into the Causes of Emigration from the Highlands...1803
29.   Selkirk, 1805, 2, 80-1, 30, 35
30.   SRO GD 248/702/5
31.   Sederunt Book of Highland Society of Scotland, vol 3, 441-657, passim
32.   Telford, 1803
33.   SM, vol 64, 1802, 705
34.   EEC, October 31st 1801; EA January 10th 1792
35.   NLS ms 1053 f.104; SRO CE 60/1/31
36.   *Prize Essays and Transactions of the Highland Society of Scotland*,
      vol III, 1807, xxi
37.   Stanhope, 1984, 286

Chapter 15

1.   Aberdeen University Library ms 2787/4/2/9, James Anderson papers
2.   NLS Adv ms 20.5.5. *Observations on the Improvement of Highland Estates
      on the North West Coast of Scotland*, London 1782
3.   OSA vol 6, 96-7
4.   EA, January 10th 1792
5.   Antiplagarius, in FM 1803, 43

6.   Selkirk, 1805, 101
7.   EA, April 15th 1803
8.   OSA vol 11, 626-7
9.   Richards, 1982, 255-8, 271; Selkirk, 1805, 122
10.   Hogg, 1981, 14, 102-3
11.   Walker, 1808, 149-52
12.   SRO GD 9/166/23, British Fisheries Society muniments
13.   NLS Adv ms 35.6.18
14.   Rymer, 1974b, 142-152; Rymer, 1974a, 127-32; Gray, 1957, 258
15.   *Parliamentary Papers*, vol XXXVIII, 1860, no.1596, p.XIV
16.   Campbell, 1965, 89
17.   University of Aberdeen Library, Blair Atholl Papers
18.   Ferguson, 1948, 252-8
19.   Loch 1778, vol 1, 114
20.   SRO GD 174/1460/1,3
21.   Henderson, 1812, 117
22.   Owen, 1920, 104
23.   Edinburgh University Library, Laing Papers III, 379 f.217
24.   Johnston, 1974, 302
25.   OSA vol 11, 229

Chapter 16

1.   SRO GD 248/3410/10
2.   *The Aberdeen Journal*, April 21st 1783
3.   SRO GD 248/229/3
4.   Youngson, 1974, 214
5.   MacDonald, 1933, no.3, 269
6.   Gibbon, 1911, 69-70; MacGillivray and Ross, 1979, 8-10; McLean, 1982, 174-180, 206-7
7.   Adam, 1964, 479; McLean, 1982, 222-3
8.   Boss 1952, 385-90
9.   MacDonell, 1893, 147-8
10.   MacGillivray and Ross, 1979, 12; McLean, 1982, 229-30
11.   Sederunt Book of Highland Society of Scotland, vol 3, 534; MacGillivray and Ross, 1979, 13; MacMillan, 1971, 177, 236-9;
12.   MacDonell, 1893, 149; MacGillivray and Ross, 1979, 14; McLean, 1982, 248-9
13.   White, 1958, 199
14.   Reid, 1976, 98
15.   Knox, 1787, 246-9
16.   SRO E 504/15/48; Nicholson, 1930, 295
17.   Stewart, 1806, 142-3
18.   Sederunt Book of Highland Society of Scotland, vol 3, 478
19.   CM, October 20th 1791
20.   EA, October 22nd and September 21st 1784

21.   EA, November 15th 1785
22.   CM, August 4th 1791
23.   SRO RH 2/4/87/63
24.   OSA vol 4, 178; vol 10, 324; vol 17, 495; vol 12, 329; McLean, 1982, 199; Cowan, 1961, 20
25.   NLS Adv ms 73.2.13f.27 Royal Highland & Agricultural Society in Scotland papers
26.   Sederunt Book of Highland Society of Scotland, vol 3, 534; Jones and Fraser, 1984, 36-41
27.   Gibbon, 1911, 44; Mackay, D. 1980, 167
28.   EA, December 20th 1791; CM, December 22nd 1791; MacKay, D. 1980, 182
29.   OSA vol 13, 1794, 332n; OSA vol 10, 444n; Donaldson, 1966, 68;
30.   Gibbon, 1911, 70
31.   Bumsted, 1982, 88
32.   SRO RH 2/4/87/66-73; Mackenzie, 1946, 187-8; Bumsted, 1982, 72, 91
33.   Hornsby, 1985
34.   SRO CE60/1/16,30,31
35.   Bumsted, 1982, 88
36.   SRO RH 2/4/87/53,54
37.   Bumsted, 1982, 89
38.   Gibbon, 1911, 45,72; MacKay, D. 1980, 197
39.   NLS ms 1053, f.106-7; MacKay, D. 1980, 197
40.   SRO GD 112/61/1, Breadalbane muniments
41.   SRO GD 9/166/23,2
42.   White, 1958, 12
43.   MacQueen, 1929, 124
44.   Martin, 1916, 177n; White, 1958, 12; Selkirk, 1805, 178,187
45.   Shortt and Doughty, 1913, 357
46.   Prebble, 1975, 435-89 *passim*

Epilogue

1.   Barker, 1972, 126
2.   Donaldson, 1966, 66
3.   Kyd 1952, xviii
4.   Ferguson, 1948, 166-171
5.   Sinclair, 1826, 148-9
6.   SRO RH 2/8/24, John Blackadder, Report on Estate in Skye
7.   Smith, 1865, 181
8.   Somerville, 1989
9.   Morison, 1972, 239

References

Aberdeen Journal & North British Magazine

Adam, Frank, *The Clans, Septs and Regiments of the Scottish Highlands*, revised by Sir Thomas Innes of Learney, Edinburgh 1964

Adam, M.I. The Highland Emigration of 1770, in *Scottish Historical Review*, XVI, 1919

Adam, M.I. The causes of Highland Emigrations of 1783 to 1803, in *Scottish Historical Review*, XVII, 1920,

Adam, M.I. Eighteenth Century Highland Landlords and the Poverty Problem, in *Scottish Historical Review*, XIX, 1922

Adam, R.J. *John Home's Survey of Assynt*, Scottish History Society 1960

Adam, R.J. *Papers on Sutherland Estate Management 1802-1816*, vol 2, Scottish History Society 1972

Adams, I.H. (ed), *Papers on Peter May, Land Surveyor, 1749-1793*, Scottish History Society 1979

Adams, I.H. *The Making of Urban Scotland*, Croom Helm 1978

Adams, I.H. John Peebles, an unpublished paper

Andrews, W.A. and Andrews, C.M. (eds) *Journal of a Lady of Quality 1774-76*, Yale University Press 1939

Anon, *Stornoway and its Charter*, Inverness 1899.

Antiplagarius, On Emigration and the means of preventing it, in *Farmers' Magazine*, vol IV, 1803

Annual Register of 1775 (1776)

Argyll, Duke of, *Scotland as it was and is*, Edinburgh 1887

Bailyn, Bernard, *The Peopling of British North America, an Introduction*, New York 1986

Barker,H.F. Report of a committee on linguistic & national stocks in the population of the United States, Annex A: National Stocks in the Population of the United States as indicated by surnames in the census of 1790, in *American Historical Association: Annual Report, Proceedings* vol 1 1931, Washington 1932

Bean, Birnie, The Life and Family of John Bean of Exeter, Seattle 1970

Beckett, J.C. *Confrontations - Studies in Irish History*, London 1972

Berry, E.M.E. Seeking the Emigrant Scot, in *Scottish Genealogist*, VII, 1960

Black, G.F. *Scotland's Mark on America*, New York 1921

Blacker, I.R. (ed), *Prescott's Histories: The Rise & Decline of the Spanish Empire*, London, 1963

Blundell, Odo, *The Catholic Highlands of Scotland*, Edinburgh 1917

Boss, W. *The Stormont, Dundas & Glengarry Highlanders 1783-1950*, Ontario, 1952

Boswell, James, *The Journal of a Tour to the Hebrides with Samuel Johnson LID*, London 1786

Brander, Michael, *The Emigrant Scots*, London 1982

Brock, Wm. R. *Scotus Americanus*, Edinburgh University Press 1982

Bruce, R. Stuart, Some old time Shetland Wrecks VIII, in *Orkney and Shetland Miscellany of the Viking Club*, II, 1909

Budge, Donald, *Jura, an Island of Argyll*, Glasgow, 1960

Bumsted, J.M. John MacDonald and the Island, in *The Island Magazine* Vol VI, 1979

Bumsted, J.M. Sir James Montgomery and Prince Edward Island, in *Acadiensis*, VII, 1978

Bumsted, J.M. *The People's Clearance*, Edinburgh University Press 1982

Burke, Edmund, *Letters and Speeches on the American Affairs*, Dent 1955

Burton, J.H. *History of Scotland* vol 11, London 1853

Cadell, H.M. *The Story of the Forth*, Glasgow 1913

Cameron, V.C. *Emigrants from Scotland to America 1774-1775*, Baltimore 1976

A Candid Enquiry into the causes of the late and intended migrations from Scotland, in a letter to J.R. Esq, Lanarkshire, Glasgow ?1771

Campbell, R.H. *Carron Company*, Edinburgh 1961

Campbell, R.H. *Scotland since 1707*, Oxford 1965

Chalmers, Robert, *Domestic Annals of Scotland* vol II, Edinburgh 1858

Clouston, J.Storer, Orkney & the Hudson's Bay Company, in *The Beaver, A Magazine of the North*, Outfit 267, number 4, March 1937

Collins, Varnum L. *President Witherspoon*, New York, vol I, 1969

Coulter, E.M. *Georgia, a Short History*, Chapel Hill 1966

Cowan, Helen I. *British Emigration to North America*, University of Toronto Press 1961

Cregeen, E.R. (ed), *Argyll Instructions 1771-1805*, Scottish History Society 1964

Creswell, Nicholas, *The Journal of Nicholas Creswell, 1774-1777*, London 1925

Daiches, David, *Robert Burns*, Spurbooks 1950

Dempster, George, *A Discourse containing a Summary of the Proceedings of the Directors of the Society for extending the Fisheries and Improving the Sea Coasts of Great Britain since the 25th March 1788 and some thoughts on the Present Emigrations from the Highlands*, London 1789

Devine, T.M. *A Scottish Firm in Virginia 1767-1777*, Scottish History Society 1984

Dexter, F.B. (ed) *The Literary Diary of Ezra Stiles*, New York 1901

Diary of John Harrower 1773-1776, in *American Historical Review*, VI, 1900

Diary of William Drummond in *Island Magazine*, Vol II, 1977

Documents relative to the Distress and Famine in Scotland in the year 1783, in consequence of the late harvest and loss of the potato crop, in *Parliamentary Papers Accounts and Papers*, vol XXXVII, 1846

Donaldson, Gordon, *The Scots Overseas*, London 1966

Donaldson, Gordon, *The Edinburgh History of Scotland*, vol III *James V - James VII*, Edinburgh 1971

Dumfries Weekly Magazine

Dunn, Charles W. *Highland Settler: a Portrait of the Scottish Gael in Nova Scotia*, University of Toronto Press 1953

Fay, C.R. *Adam Smith and the Scotland of his Day*, Cambridge University Press, 1956

Ferguson, Thomas, *The Dawn of Scottish Social Welfare*, London 1948

Forbes, Sir William, *Memoirs of a Banking House*, London and Edinburgh 1860

Fraser-MacIntosh, Ch. The Depopulation of Aberarder in Badenoch, in *The Celtic Magazine*, vol II, 1877

Geddes, Arthur, The Foundations of Grantown-on-Spey, in *Scottish Geographical Magazine*, 1945

Gibbon, J. Murray, *Scots in Canada*, London 1911

Gilpin, William, *Observations, Relative chiefly to Picturesque Beauty, made in the Year 1776, on Several Parts of Great Britain: particularly the Highlands of Scotland*, vol 1, London 1789

Goudie, Gilbert (ed) *The Diary of the Reverend John Mill ... Shetland 1740-1803*, Scottish History Society 1889

Gouldesborough, P. An attempted Voyage to New York in 1669, in *Scottish Historical Review* 1961

Graham, I.C.C. *Colonists from Scotland: Emigration to North America 1707-1783*, New York 1956

Grant, I.F. *The Macleods. the History of a Clan 1200-1956*, London 1959

Gray, Malcolm, *The Highland Economy 1750-1850*, Oliver & Boyd 1957

Haldane, A.R.B. *The Drove Roads of Scotland*, Edinburgh University Press 1952

Haldane, A.R.B. *New Ways through the Glens*, David and Charles 1973

Hamilton, Henry, The Failure of the Ayr Bank 1772, in *Economic History Review*, 2nd series 8, 1955

Hamilton, Milton W. and Corey, Albert B. (eds) *Sir William Johnson Papers*, University of State of New York, XII vols, 1957

Hamilton, Milton W. *Sir William Johnson, Colonial American, 1715-1763*, New York 1976

Harvey, D.C. Early Settlements & Social Conditions in Prince Edward Island, in *Dalhousie Review*, XI, 1931-2

Harvey, D.C. (ed) *Holland's Description of Cape Breton Island and other Documents*, Halifax, N.S. 1935

Harvey, D.C. *Journeys to the Island of St John or Prince Edward Island 1775-1932*, Toronto 1955

Haws, Charles H. *Scots in the Old Dominion 1685-1800*, Edinburgh 1980

Henderson, Cpt John, *General View of the Agriculture of the County of Sutherland*, 1812

Heron, Robert, *Observations made in a Journey through the Western Counties of Scotland 1792*, Perth 1793, vol II

A Highlander, *The Present Conduct of the Chieftains and Proprietors of lands in the Highlands of Scotland*, 2nd ed, 1774

Historical Manuscripts Commission, Royal Institution 1906

Hogg, James, *Highland Tours*, Byway Books 1981

House of Commons Report III, Report from the Committee appointed to enquire into the Present State of the Linen Trade in Great Britain and Ireland, 1773

Hornsby, Stephen, An Historical Geography of Cape Breton Island in the Nineteenth Century, unpublished thesis, University of British Columbia 1985

Insh, G.P. *Scottish Colonial Schemes 1620-1686*, Glasgow 1922

Insh, G.P. *The Darien Scheme*, The Historical Association 1947

James Hog papers in the Southern Historical Collection, University of North Carolina Library, Chapel Hill

Johnson, Christine, *Developments in the Roman Catholic Church in Scotland 1789-1829*, Edinburgh 1983

Johnson, Samuel, *Selected letters of*, Oxford University Press 1925

Johnson, Samuel, *A Journey to the Western Isles of Scotland 1773*, Scolar Press 1968

Johnston, Thomas, *The History of the Working Classes in Scotland*, EP Publishing 1974

Jones, Orlo and Fraser, Douglas, Those Illusive Immigrants, in *The Island Magazine*, no. 16, 1984

Journal of Colonel Alexander Harvey of Scotland and Barnet, Vermont, in *Proceedings of the Vermont Historical Society*, 1921-3

Journal of James Whitelaw, Surveyor-General of Vermont, in *Proceedings of the Vermont Historical Society*, 1905-6

Journal of the Managers of the Scotch American Company of Farmers, in *Proceedings of the Vermont Historical Society*, 1926-28

Keith, Alexander, *A Thousand Years of Aberdeen*, Aberdeen University Press 1972

Kelly, Rev, Edward, The Reverend John McKenna, Loyalist Chaplain, in *Canadian Catholic Historical Association Report*, 1933-4

Kerr, A.W. *History of Banking in Scotland*, London 1918

Knox, John, *A Tour through the Highlands of Scotland and the Hebride*

Islands in 1786, London 1787

Kyd, J.G., *Scottish Population Statistics*, Scottish History Society 1952

Landsman, Ned C. *Scotland and its First American Colony 1683-1765*, Princeton University Press, 1983

Lenman, Bruce, *Integration, Enlightenment and Industrialisation in Scotland 1746-1832*, Arnold 1981

Lettsom, J.C. (ed) *The Works of John Fothergill M.D.*Vol II, London 1783

Lobban,R.D. The Migration of Highlanders into Lowland Scotland (c.1750-1890) with particular reference to Greenock, (unpublished PhD thesis Edinburgh University) 1969

Loch, David, *Essays in Trade, Commerce, Manufactures & Fisheries of Scotland*, 3 Volumes, Edinburgh 1778-9

Logan, G Murray, *Scottish Highlanders and the American Revolution*, McCurdy Printing Co., Halifax, N.S. 1976

Lomas S.C. (ed) *Letters and Speeches of Oliver Cromwell*, vol III, New York 1904

Lucas, Sir C.P. *A History of Canada 1763-1812*, Oxford 1909

Macdonald, Donald, *Lewis: a history of the island*, Edinburgh 1978

MacDonald, Ewen J. Father Roderick MacDonell, Missionary at St. Regis and the Glengarry Catholics, in *The Catholic Historical Review*, XIX, 1933, no.3

MacDonell, J.A. *Sketches Illustrating the Early Settlement and History of Glengarry in Canada*, Montreal 1893

MacGillivray, Royce and Ross, Ewan, *A History of Glengarry*, Ontario 1979

MacGregor, Edith, *The Story of Fort William*, Inverness 1954

MacKay, Donald, *Scotland Farewell*, Edinburgh 1980

Mackay, Iain R. Glenaladale's Settlement, Prince Edward Island, in *Scottish Gaelic Studies*, vol X, 1965

McKay, Margaret M, *The Rev Dr John Walker's Report on the Hebrides of 1764 and 1771*, Edinburgh 1980

MacKenzie, Alexander, *History of the Highland Clearances*, Stirling 1914

MacKenzie, W.C. *The Book of the Lews*, Paisley 1919

McKerral, Andrew, Early Emigration from Kintyre to America, n.d.

McKerral, Andrew, *Kintyre in the Seventeenth Century*, Edinburgh 1948

MacKinnon, Don (ed), MacDonald, Allan R. *The Truth about Flora MacDonald*, Inverness 1938

McLean, Marianne L. In the new land a new Glengarry, unpublished PhD thesis, University of Edinburgh 1982

McLeod, Amy, The Glenaladale Pioneers, in *Dalhousie Review*, XI, 1931-2

Macleod, R.C. *The Book of Dunvegan, vol II 1700-1920*, Spalding Club 1939

MacMillan, Somerled, *Bygone Lochaber*, Glasgow 1971

MacQueen, Malcolm A. *Skye Pioneers and "the Island"*, Winnipeg 1929

M'Robert, Patrick, *A Tour through Part of the North Provinces of America*, Edinburgh 1776

Martin, Chester, *Lord Selkirk's Work in Canada*, Oxford Historical and
  Literary Studies, vol 7, Oxford 1916
Meinig, D.W. *The Shaping of America- A Geographical Perspective on 500
  Years of History, Atlantic America 1492-1800*, Yale University Press 1986
Meyer, Duane, *The Highland Scots of North Carolina, 1732-1776*, Chapel Hill
  1961
Miller, Ronald, *Orkney*, Batsford 1976
A Minister of the Gospel, *Seasonable Advice to the Landholders and Farmers
  in Scotland - a Sermon*, Edinburgh 1770
Mitgang, Herbert, Review of *Bound Over: Indentured Servitude and American
  Conscience*, by John van der Zee, New York 1986
Morison, S.E. *The Oxford History of the American People*, vol 1, *Prehistory
  to 1789*, Mentor 1972
Morison, W.M. *The Decisions of the Court of Session*, vol XI, Edinburgh
  1811
Morgan, W.J. *Naval Documents of the American Revolution*, Washington 1966
Mowat, Charles L. *East Florida as a British Province 1763-1784*, University
  of California Press 1943

Newsome, A.R. Records of Emigrants from England and Scotland to North
  Carolina 1774-1775, in *North Carolina Historical Review*, XI, 1934
Nicolson, Alexander, *History of Skye*, Glasgow 1930

Owen, Robert, *The Life of Robert Owen by Himself*, London 1920

Parliamentary Papers, vol xxxviii, 1860
Paton, H. (ed) *The Lyon in Mourning by R. Forbes, bishop ... 1746-1775*,
  Scottish History Society 1895-6
Patterson, George, *A History of the County of Pictou, Nova Scotia*, Montreal
  1879
Perceval-Maxwell, M. *The Scottish Migration to Ulster in the Reign of James I*,
  London 1973
*A Plan agreed upon by a great many farmers and others in the shires of
  Dumbarton, Clydesdale and Renfrew etc for erecting a company of
  farmers, and others who shall become joiners thereto; for purchasing
  and improving of land within H.M. dominions in North America, in such
  manner as is or shall be, comfortable to the Laws and Priveleges of
  H.M. subjects of Great Britain*, Paisley 1772
Plumb, J.H. *England in the Eighteenth Century*, Penguin History of England,
  vol 7, 1963
Prebble, John, *Mutiny: Highland Regiments in Revolt, 1743-1804*, London
  1975
The Precipitation and Fall of Messrs Douglas Heron and Company, Edinburgh
  1778
Prize Essays and Transactions of the Highland Society of Scotland, vol III,
  1807

Pryde, George S. The Scots in East New Jersey, in *Proceedings of the New Jersey Historical Society*, XV, 1930

Pryde, George S. Scottish Colonization in the Province of New York, in *New York State Historical Association Proceedings*, XXXIII, 1935

Register of the Privy Seal of Scotland

Reid, W. Stanford, *The Scottish Tradition in Canada*, Minister of Supply & Services, Canada 1976

Richards, Eric, *A History of the Highland Clearances*, London 1982

Robertson, James, *General View of the Agriculture in the County of Perth*, Perth 1799

Ross, Peter, *The Scot in America*, New York 1896

A Rural Economist, Cursory Reflections on the means of preventing emigration, in *Farmers' Magazine*, vol IV, 1803

Rymer, L. The Kelp Industry in North Knapdale, in *Scottish Studies*, 18, 1974a

Rymer, L. The Scottish Kelp Industry, in *Scottish Geographical Magazine*, 90.3.1974b

The Scotsman

Scott, W.L. The MacDonells of Leek, Collachie and Aberchalder, in *Canadian Catholic Historical Association Report*, 1934-5

Scotus Americanus, *Informations Concerning the Province of North Carolina*, Glasgow 1773

Sederunt Book of Highland Society of Scotland, vol III

Selkirk, Earl of, *Observations on the Present State of the Highlands of Scotland with a view of the Possible Causes and Probable Consequences of Emigration*, London 1805

Seton, Sir Bruce Gordon and Arnot, Jean Gordon, *The Prisoners of the '45*, Scottish History Society 1928

Sheridan, Richard B. The British Credit Crisis of 1772 and the American Colonies, in *Journal of Economic History*, vol XX, June 1960, no.2

Sherwood, Roland H. *Pictou Pioneers*, Lancelot Press, Hartsport, N.S. 1975

Shortt, Adam and Doughty, Arthur G. *Canada and its Provinces*, vol XIII, Toronto 1913

Simmons, R.C. *The American Colonies from Settlement to Independence*, Longman 1976

Sinclair, D.M. Highland Emigration to Nova Scotia, in *Dalhousie Review*, XXIII, 1943

Sinclair, Sir John, *Analysis of the Statistical Account of Scotland*, Edinburgh 1826

Smith, A. *A Summer in Skye*, London 1865

Smith, A.E. *Colonists in Bondage: White Servitude and Convict Labour in America 1606-1776*, Institute of Early American Hisotry and Culture, Virginia 1947

Smith, A.M. *Jacobite Estates of the Forty-five*, Edinburgh 1982

Smout, T.C. *A History of the Scottish People 1560-1830*, London 1969

Smout, T.C. *Scottish Trade on the Eve of the Union*, Edinburgh 1963

Somerville, James, 11th Lord, *Memorie of the The Somervilles*, 2 vols, Edinburgh 1815

Somerville, Meredyth (ed), *The Diary of James & Alexander Noble, 1762-1827*, Biggar Museum Trust 1984

Somerville, Meredyth, *The Standardization of Weights & Measures in Scotland*, Occasional Paper no 11, Department of Geography, University of Edinburgh 1989

Stanhope Women's Institute History Committee, *Stanhope: Sands of Time*, Charlottetown 1984

Stanley, George M. The Scottish Military Tradition, in W. Stanford Reid (ed), *A History of Canada's Peoples. The Scottish Tradition in Canada*, McClelland & Stewart, Toronto 1976

Steuart, A.F. Orkney News from the Letterbag of Mr Charles Steuart, in Old Lore Miscellany of Orkney, Shetland and Caithness and Sutherland, in *The Viking Society for Northern Research*, vol VI, 1913

Stewart, John, *An Account of Prince Edward Island in the Gulph of St Lawrence, North America*, London 1806

Tayler, A. and H. *Lord Fife and his Factor*, London 1925

Telford, Thomas, *A Survey and Report of the Coasts and Central Highlands of Scotland*, 1803

Thomson, Alexander, *News from Glasgow*, Glasgow 1774

Walker, John, *An Economical History of the Hebrides and Highlands of Scotland*, vol 2, 1808

White, P.C.T. (ed) *Lord Selkirk's Diary 1803-4, A Journal of his Travels in British North America and the North eastern United States*, The Champlain Society, Toronto 1958

Whitfield, J. Bell, Scottish Emigration to America. A Letter of Dr Charles Nisbet to Dr John Witherspoon, 1784, in *William and Mary Quarterly*, 3rd series, vol XI, no.2, 1954

Whyte Donald (ed) *A Dictionary of Scottish Emigrants to the United States*, Baltimore 1972

The Works of John Witherspoon D.D., vol III, *Essays and Sermons*, Edinburgh 1805

Wylie, T.W.J. Franklin County One Hundred Years Ago, in *Pennsylvania Magazine of History & Biography*, VIII, 1884

Youngson, A.J. *Beyond the Highland Line*, London 1974

Index